Practising reflexivity in health and welfare

Making knowledge

Carolyn Taylor and Susan White

Open University Press

Open University Press
McGraw-Hill Education
McGraw-Hill House
Shoppenhangers Road
Maidenhead
Berkshire
SL6 2QL

email: enquiries@openup.co.uk
world wide web: www.openup.co.uk

and

Two Penn Plaza
New York, NY 10121-2289, USA

First Published 2000
Reprinted 2009

Copyright © Carolyn Taylor and Susan White 2000

A catalogue record of this book is available from the British Library

ISBN-10   0 335 20518 6 (pb)   0 335 20519 4 (hb)
ISBN-13   978 0 335 20518 9 (pb)   978 0 335 20519 6 (hb)

Library of Congress Cataloging-in-Publication Data
Taylor, Carolyn, 1950–
    Practising reflexivity in health and welfare: making knowledge / Carolyn Taylor and Susan White.
        p. cm.
    Includes bibliographical references and index.
    ISBN 0-335-20519-4 – ISBN 0-335-20518-6 (pbk.)
    1. Medicine–Decision making.   2. Evidence-based medicine.
3. Medicine–Philosophy.   I. White, Susan, 1961 – II. Title.
R723.5 .T39 2000
362.1–dc21

00-036733

Typeset by Graphicraft Limited, Hong Kong
Printed in Great Britain by Bell & Bain Ltd., Glasgow

Contents

For Patrick, Tom and Joe

Acknowledgements

Many people have helped us to make the knowledge in this book. First, we should like to thank our families and friends, particularly Patrick, Tom, Joe, Jenny, Alex, Cath and Katie, for living with the enterprise throughout 1999. Second, we are grateful to our students, particularly, Rachel Leigh, Viv Farey and Eleanor Hirst for testing out this version. Third, thanks are also due to Mary Varley for comments from a practitioner perspective on Part I, and to John Stancombe for reading and commenting on the whole manuscript. Any errors are obviously our own. John has also given permission for us to use previously unpublished data extracts from his own ongoing research. Finally, we are grateful to Nigel Parton, Ian Shaw, Neil Thompson and an anonymous referee for comments on the original proposal. White's data extracts are drawn from research supported by ERSC studentship number 0042 and research grant number R000222892.

Preface

This is a book about making knowledge. It examines how professionals in various health and welfare settings make sense of and process cases. In the contemporary policy climate, with its emphasis on performance indicators, clinical audit and evidence-based practice, practitioners across the range of health and welfare agencies have become accustomed to evaluating and justifying how they make use of knowledge. We shall argue that these methods of ensuring quality have their place, but that they leave the messy business of categorization or 'diagnosis' unexplored. This process of screening and assessment is simply taken as read, or is assumed to follow unproblematically from eligibility criteria, or from procedural or clinical guidelines.

Alongside these policy developments, however, practitioners and academics have sought to try to reflect on decision making in different ways. This has notably been through the development of ideas about reflective practice, or in social work, about anti-oppressive ways of working. Again, these have been important developments, but both have their problems. For example, practitioners may know they *should* be 'reflective' or 'reflexive' (our use of these words is explained in due course) in their decision making, but they often have few ideas about how they may accomplish this, or even what it means. Similarly, there is a tendency for anti-oppressive practice to become a rather empty exercise in which practitioners assert their knowledge about various forms of 'oppression' or 'disadvantage', or simply gloss people into categories as 'oppressors' and 'oppressed' without understanding or interrogating how 'oppression' is brought about by practitioners in their encounters.

We are arguing, then, for a refocusing of ideas about reflexive practice. Instead of providing introspective accounts of inner thoughts and feelings, or 'structural' analyses of oppression, we want to emphasize the active processes of meaning making. We are certainly not suggesting that the other domains do not matter, but they are not the business of this book. Here, we want to show how words and language have powerful consequences. Of course, the words may be driven by some internal emotion, such as anger or fear, or they may be oppressive in their effects, but it is with the performative aspects of the language – the work it does – that we are concerned here. Our intention is not to delete individuality or social 'structures', but to explore a further dimension, and one which we consider to be crucially important for practice.

The concepts and ideas we have used in this book were first brought together as part of the development of an MA module, 'Critical thinking and reflexive decision making in health and welfare practice', which was specifically designed to bridge what we perceived to be a gap in current professional education. We both have academic backgrounds in sociology and we have drawn upon literatures originating within that discipline, which have been added to and developed by the 'discursive psychology' movement. We have said that we wish to focus on the powerful effects of language, and these literatures provide a means to explore conversations (talk) and written documents (text) of various kinds: for example, they provide concepts and ideas to assist our understanding of the ways in which speakers or authors seek to establish the plausibility and believability of their assertions. This kind of analysis is of fundamental importance to health and welfare practitioners, who routinely have to make complex judgements about whom to believe in what are often messy and contested situations.

Some of the ideas we present may be new to you and we have endeavoured to write in an intelligible way and to illustrate what we are saying with examples from everyday life or professional practice. However, there is a danger that, in the act of translation from one discipline to another, or from academic research to professional practice, ideas become transformed and oversimplified. This oversimplification limits their utility as, stripped of their complexity, they cannot really be used or understood in the way they were intended. Therefore, whilst striving for accessibility we have tried to preserve the integrity of the conceptual frameworks. For example, some of the concepts used are tied to theoretical ideas which are essential to understanding what we are trying to argue and how it fits with other ways of thinking about practice. We think it is important to give health and welfare professionals access to ideas from other disciplines and we must undertake the translation carefully, so that practitioners will have the foundations to read further if they so wish. To this end, we have provided a brief annotated guide to further reading and a glossary at the end of the book.

Rather than concentrate on one professional group, we have looked at broad and transferable situations in which knowledge is made, such as in encounters with service users, or in meetings and conversations with other professionals. Similarly, we have drawn on European and North American literatures. It is our contention that the ideas we present apply across services, occupational groups and western welfare regimes. Indeed, it is this general applicability that makes them so important for understanding health and welfare practice. However, clearly we have not been able to provide analyses of the specific organizational constraints or mandates of the different professions. Many of these (monitoring of performance, outcome measures, evidence-based practice, managerialism) are shared and they are all covered in other discipline-specific texts.

Part I maps out the conceptual ground and, in the first chapter, we argue that health and welfare practitioners are often confronted with competing versions of events, both lay and professional. This complexity and ambiguity cannot be addressed through evidence-based practice alone. There is a need to explore the ways in which protagonists in a situation put forward their 'truth claims', that is, how they warrant their position and attempt to undermine the claims made by others. We illustrate these arguments with a range of examples from practice. In Chapter 2, we examine arguments about the philosophical positions known generally as realism and relativism. At their simplest, these relate to questions about whether and how we can access 'reality'. We explore the implications of these different positions for health and welfare professions. However, we also seek to avoid polarizing the perspectives and to explore some of the subtleties of the debates. In Chapter 3, we put some conceptual meat on these philosophical bones and begin to build a framework to analyse practice in the way we have outlined. We introduce the different ways in which various academic and philosophical traditions have analysed talk and text and give some examples of empirical work relevant to professional practice. In particular we examine the ways in which facts may be assembled to convey a particular perspective and to do 'rhetorical' work.

Chapter 4 provides a bridge to Part II. We develop the ideas from earlier chapters by examining how plausibility is established in everyday conversations of various kinds. We argue that in all aspects of our lives we construct facts to achieve certain effects in dialogue with other people. We explore how people establish a 'credible voice', how they protect their accounts from challenge and how they attempt to undermine the accounts of others. By Chapter 4, you will probably be much more aware of your own use of these devices. You should also be able to reflect on how they may impact on the ways you make sense of cases as a professional and on how clients or patients referred to your service establish their own credibility (or not).

In Part II, we undertake the task of applying the concepts and methods to the institutional contexts in which health and welfare professionals work. Chapter 5 examines the ways in which people referred to our services negotiate the 'institutional talk' of professionals, by working to establish their credibility or authenticity. For example, they may be trying to present themselves as worthy of receiving services, to resist some form of non-voluntary intervention, or to defend themselves against allegations of abuse, neglect or criminal activity. All this depends on their ability to establish their own 'moral adequacy' through their speech. In Chapter 6, we shift our attention to explore how professionals in health and welfare agencies engage and interact with service users. Our approach goes beyond treating such encounters as concerned simply with establishing the facts, devising responses, or conveying factual information, to a standpoint where we regard professional talk as a means to establish authority and to conduct the business of the organization. In particular we look at professionals' strategies to maintain control of the interaction and at how clients may resist these. This raises important questions about the nature of professional power.

Chapter 7 shows how formal and informal conversations taking place between professionals, away from the encounter with the service user, can also have profound significance. We describe some empirical work in this area and ask you to reflect on the ways in which talking to your colleagues influences the interpretations you make about cases, and to think about what sorts of 'knowledge' you draw upon in so doing. We also argue that inter-professional talk can display, reproduce and reinforce aspects of professional identities. Talk about cases helps to differentiate particular professional identities from those of allied occupations.

In Chapter 8, we move away from talk to analyse various kinds of documents. Practitioners are accustomed to having their written records scrutinized as part of audit and accountability. Our approach is different. We are interested in how documents organize activity and are themselves organized by professionals. We refer to written materials as 'time-travellers', pointing to their capacity to simplify and 'freeze' events and transport them in a particular form into the future. We examine the ways in which schedules, checklists and proformas conceal information as well as ordering and recording it. They place particular demands on professional 'form-completers', which in turn have their own effects.

In Chapter 9, we have used the Louise Woodward case as an extended example to illustrate some of the ideas we have been using throughout the book. The case demonstrates that many situations cannot be resolved by the neutral application of formal knowledge. Rather, many diverse forms of reasoning must be drawn upon and these are illustrated in the judge's thinking during and after the trial.

In the final chapter, we reopen some of the debates and issues we raised in Part I. We explore how our approach to understanding practice relates to other frameworks, particularly evidence-based and reflective practice. We argue that the concepts we have used can help practitioners to read these literatures more critically and analytically. We do not suggest that they discard other ways of thinking about and understanding practice, but that they must engage actively with what they read and subject it to scrutiny. It is for this reason that we have used the verb 'practising' (reflexivity), as opposed to the noun (reflexive) 'practice' in the title of this book. We are suggesting that reflexivity has to be 'done', it does not simply exist. In the chapters that follow we hope to provide you with some concepts and methods to help you to practise reflexivity.

PART I

Developing a theoretical framework

CHAPTER 1

Arguing and thinking: implications for professional practice

Health and welfare professionals have important responsibilities towards service users. They are faced with difficult and complex decisions which can dramatically affect service users' lives: for example, they may have to decide whether to remove children from their parents in cases of suspected child abuse; or whether to recommend that a person with mental health problems remains in hospital, despite their wish to be discharged. They may have to make judgements about whether an older person who appears to be frail and 'at risk' should return home after a hospital admission, or whether a particular treatment should be made available to a patient, despite its high cost and consumption of tightly rationed resources.

The external pressures upon professionals to make good judgements and decisions have increased in recent years. There appear to be three principal reasons for this. First, public enquiries into child deaths, the publicity surrounding violent acts perpetrated by mentally ill people, scandals relating to the residential care of vulnerable children and adults, and more recently, concerns about surgical practice with young children have all fuelled doubts about whether professionals can really be trusted to police themselves. Health and welfare professionals, then, are no longer assumed to be working unequivocally in the interests of service users.

Second, the last two decades of the twentieth century saw major organizational and procedural changes in health and welfare services in the UK. This was linked, in part, to the political agenda of the 1980s and early 1990s: the 'marketization' of welfare. The drive to make public services conform to the principles of the market and commercial institutions led to an imperative to pursue maximum efficiency and 'value for money' through the rational analysis of inputs and outputs. This is perhaps best exemplified by the purchaser/provider division within contemporary welfare, as a result of which public sector organizations 'found themselves trying to deliver more for less, simply because they were given less and asked to do more' (Newman and Clarke 1994: 15). These changes led to increasing 'managerialism' in public services, exposing professionals to scrutiny *within* their own organizations, as well as from external bodies such as the judiciary, media, various inspectorates and government departments. Reaganite republicanism and Clinton's welfare reformism have led to similar developments in the USA and some cross-fertilization of ideas across the Atlantic (see, for example, Clarke 1991).

Third, alongside the ascent of market principles in health and welfare agencies there has been a growth in the language of 'consumerism', reflected in managerial and professional concerns about whether service users/clients/patients (or citizens) are receiving 'quality' provision, and in the implementation of complaints procedures. Whilst professionals have often been ambivalent or critical about some aspects of marketized welfare, it seems that the language of the new consumerism has been embraced; as Newman and Clarke (1994: 21) note: 'the language of quality, putting customers first and valuing front-line staff represents the possibility of reasserting a value base for public services'. Thus, over the past decade, the requirement for services to incorporate user perspectives and to measure satisfaction has become ubiquitous in policy and planning documents of various kinds.

Professional practice in health and welfare is, therefore, characterized by a greater degree of anxiety about its goals and outcomes, and by a perceived need to demonstrate to inspecting bodies, and a sceptical wider public, that practitioners and clinicians are 'doing the right thing' in the circumstances, and are using resources efficiently and effectively. This trend has been fuelled by Labour's 'modernization' programme (Department of Health 1998b, 1998c). The dominant answer to this uncertainty has been a technical, procedural, and often, bureaucratic one.

Within social work, for example, there have been introduced various schedules and proformas intended to improve, and render more consistent, the performance of assessments in child care and work with adults (Lloyd and Taylor 1995; for examples see Department of Health 1988a, 1999; Department of Health *et al.* 2000). This has been supported by legislation and policy change, for example the Children Act 1989 and the National Health Service and Community Care Act 1990. There can also be noted an increased focus on the evaluation of services, the measurement of outcomes of service inputs and the audit of health and welfare provision. In addition, in both health and welfare contexts, there is growing attention being paid to the concept of **evidence-based practice**, and within medicine, of clinical governance. It is suggested that clinicians, for example, aided by computer technology, would seek out research-based knowledge in order to improve their assessments and diagnoses and to make better-informed decisions about treatments and interventions (see, for example, Gray 1997; Ridsdale 1998).

It is easy to see why this approach may seem to be an attractive remedy to the multiple pressures affecting contemporary health and welfare practice. It seems to offer managers the security that those they manage have the best possible rational foundations for their decisions, it appeals to external evaluators of practice on the same grounds and to the champions of consumerism as a means to ensure both equity and 'best value'.

Whilst we would acknowledge the pressures which confront professionals and share these aspirations towards 'best' practice we want to urge caution about an unquestioning acceptance of a technical/procedural approach as the only answer to perceived credibility problems for health and welfare professionals. The attraction of such an approach lies in its appeals to scientific evidence, which, it is suggested, can offer greater authority to professional decision making. Professional judgement is thus cast as a careful, neutral process of weighing up information and applying its results to practice situations. Consistency and precision, it is argued, replace the ad hoc, arbitrary and 'common-sensical' processes – opinion-based practice (Gray 1997) – which allegedly have applied in previous decision making. Outdated knowledge, or lack of knowledge, and outmoded practices are replaced by up-to-date, factual information and more rigorous procedure.

Our concern is that such a search for certainty and truth can apply only to discrete components of professional activity, the remainder of which is characterized by uncertainty and complex qualitative judgements. We aim to demonstrate that, armed with the comfortable belief that they have sure and certain knowledge, health and welfare professionals may be less likely to reflect appropriately on their judgements and decision making, thus making error more, rather than less, likely. Health and welfare professionals need to acknowledge the uncertainty, ambiguity and complexity that lie at the heart of their practice (Parton 1998). From our perspective, health and welfare work is a messy and complicated business in which there are often no right or wrong answers. Workers are confronted by situations in which risk and uncertainty prevail. Our central argument is that, in the world of health and welfare practice, the pursued ideal of dependable scientific knowledge may well prove elusive and that other approaches which foreground understanding rather than explanation and prediction may more fruitfully be explored.

Using knowledge and making knowledge

The problem with evidence-based practice and the production of outcome measures is that they are concerned exclusively with how knowledge is used. They pay scant attention to how knowledge is *made*, produced or 'constructed', by professionals themselves. They do not allow access to the 'sense-making' processes of practitioners. For example, they do not explore how cases are actively categorized by professionals as this or that type of problem or one type of problem or another. It is to these complex reasoning processes that the concepts and methods introduced in this book are directed. They are not intended to replace other forms of knowledge or enquiry. However, if professionals are serious about practising 'reflexively', then we suggest that these processes are an essential component of 'practice wisdom' (Sheppard 1995) or 'clinical judgement'. The concept of **reflexivity** and the different ways in which it is understood are topics explored in later chapters. However, we want very briefly now to move away from using 'reflexivity' to denote a form of reflection or 'benign introspection' (Woolgar 1988a: 22) – a process of looking inwards, and thinking about how our own experiences may have influenced our thinking – to argue that there is more than this to 'practising reflexivity'. Practitioners also need to examine and become more explicit about the kinds of knowledge they use in their practice and how they apply these to make sense of events and situations they confront. This might be seen as a process of destabilizing taken-for-granted ideas and professional routines.

We propose that, instead of concentrating exclusively on a 'treasure hunt' or 'mining' (Kvale 1996) model for the identification and application of knowledge to health and welfare (hereafter HW) practice, clinicians and practitioners can fruitfully explore different approaches to knowledge use. The approaches we discuss open up to scrutiny the questions not only of what knowledge is generated but also how it is generated in day-to-day practice. This allows us to acknowledge the existence of competing versions of events, both lay and professional, and to explore the ways in which protagonists in a situation put forward their 'truth claims', that is, how they warrant their position and attempt to undermine the claims made by others. In effect, we are taking several steps backwards from evidence-based approaches because we are considering the processes of sense making and categorization themselves. These categorizations affect what *type* of evidence is deemed appropriate to the case.

In later chapters we look at the strategies employed by professionals and lay people to construct plausible accounts and to justify their (in)actions. Before we do so, we need, as it were, to construct a plausible account of why and how the concepts and methods introduced in this book can be useful to HW professionals. A consideration of a practice example will help to illustrate the difference between 'the quest for (a single) truth' approach and our own. The following comments were made by a ward sister on an acute medical ward.

Extract 1.1

Take Jessie. She came to us as a purely social admission. She'd fallen at home and is incontinent. She had turned against her home help, refused to answer the door to let her in. She didn't become ninety-one overnight, she's been old for a long time. She had been going downhill. She's been here ever since. She didn't have any medical problems.

(Latimer 1994 cited in Latimer 1997a: 143)

What are we to make of this description of 91-year-old Jessie? We could just accept it as the objective truth about Jessie: on an acute medical ward there is a very old patient who should not really be there (except that she has had a massive stroke), but is vulnerable and at risk living alone. The task for HW professionals might then be to work together to assess Jessie to see whether a return home is feasible and, if so, what is needed to secure this goal. For example, a different home carer or carers might be arranged who can meet Jessie's needs; alternative home support systems might be mobilized. If a return home was not wanted by Jessie or deemed impossible because of the risk in which it would place her, then alternative arrangements would need to be made in either a residential care home or nursing home. Decisions about Jessie's future might be made on the basis of **tacit knowledge** (Polanyi 1967) about what would be best for the patient in the circumstances (which would include the constraints placed upon the situation by resources), or by recourse to research-based knowledge about what is the best course of action in these circumstances: what sorts of care work best or are most appropriate for the old-old (the term frequently used in the gerontological literature for people over the age of 80)?

Alternatively, we might want to acknowledge that this is one way of describing Jessie, a patient on an acute medical ward, but not necessarily the only way of doing so and, indeed, it is a way of describing her that does particular things. The ward sister's account suggests that Jessie is 'out of place' on an acute medical ward – her problems are 'purely social' (note the emphasis here) rather than medical ('she didn't have *any* medical problems' [emphasis added]). Indeed, Jessie's problems are presented as being, to some extent, self-induced: it is Jessie herself who has rejected the services of the home help, placing herself in a vulnerable situation. This serves to imply that Jessie is perhaps less worthy of treatment than someone who is more cooperative with service providers. In other ways, her problems are deemed to be biological, part of the inevitable process of decline that accompanies old age. Her incontinence is part and parcel of this process of aging and decline. It does not warrant medical intervention (as it might do in a younger adult) because it results from this inevitable and unstoppable process of biological decline and therefore nothing can be done about it.

Using the twin devices of drawing on her age and her lack of cooperation, the ward sister is constructing a version of Jessie as less worthy of, less entitled to and less likely to benefit from treatment on an acute medical ward. In essence, the ward sister is arguing that Jessie should not have been placed with her and that she is now stuck with her despite the inappropriateness of this as a solution. Jessie is a 'bed-blocker', a problem for an acute ward because she is not fit to go home and there is nowhere else to place her. Jessie is thus a problem and a nuisance for nursing staff and the organization.

Seen in this light, Jessie is not deserving of respect as a person with rights, wishes and feelings that need to be taken into an account. Here we might add that the use of the patient's first name, rather than the more formal use of her title and surname, adds to the negative/dismissive tone of the ward sister and the making of Jessie into a problem. She is someone who is in the way, who needs moving on so that the 'real work' of acute nursing can occur with a 'proper' patient allocated to that bed. In effect, the ward sister is disclaiming responsibility for her – Jessie should not be her problem.

We are not suggesting that the ward sister is necessarily having 'bad thoughts' about Jessie. Rather, the specific institutional context of an acute ward has affected her descriptions, and her words have powerful effects. What is noticeable here is that Jessie's voice is denied. She, no doubt, would have a rather different version of the situation but her view is not acknowledged. The ward sister is attempting to put across the definitive version of Jessie. However, by offering this different reading of 'Jessie' (or rather of the ward sister's account of Jessie) we want to argue against the idea that there is only one way of seeing a situation which is the objective truth. In contrast we suggest that it is more helpful for practitioners and clinicians to work with the notion that there are multiple accounts of situations. This allows us to acknowledge more explicitly that the task for professionals is to make sense of these differing accounts and to determine for themselves which one of these is the most convincing rather than to assume their own objectivity.

Health and welfare practice and the problem of versions

We have argued that many of the judgements that HW professionals are required to make cannot be resolved by the neutral application of objective theory, or formal bodies of knowledge. In particular, we have suggested that professionals frequently confront competing versions of the same set of circumstances. In many cases, different interpretations of events may be offered by several members of the same family, by other professionals, by any number of interested parties, or by witnesses to events. In these situations, complex judgements must take place in which professionals decide whom they should believe and whose account they should treat with scepticism. In the case of Jessie above, the different versions are obscured by the particular account produced by the ward sister. The ward sister's story is perfectly accurate and 'factual' within its own terms of reference, but we have tried to show how it constructs Jessie in a particular way and hence facilitates certain courses of professional action, whilst making others less likely.

We should stress again that we are not suggesting that facts and evidence are irrelevant to professional activity, or that our approach renders them redundant. In making their judgements, practitioners need to concentrate their attention upon the objective facts before them. If a patient who has mobility problems and is unable to move about in bed has a pressure sore, it is essential that the nurse knows what treatment works best. That is, that she possesses or obtains formal knowledge about the management of pressure sores. Most HW professionals have similar needs for fairly stable and uncontested knowledge. For example, social workers and doctors assessing a case in which a child has been injured may need to refer to X-rays or blood tests in order to decide whether they believe a parent's story about how the injury occurred, or whether the child has a medical condition which could account for the injury. We are not suggesting that professionals abandon their knowledge base and instead simply choose arbitrarily between 'versions'. However, imagine either that the medical evidence in the child protection case is equivocal, or that you know that someone caused the injury, but that each parent is accusing the other. In these circumstances textbook knowledge is not likely to prove very helpful.

Let us stay with the example of child protection practice for the moment, as it is helpful in illustrating the kinds of professional activity that rely on other types of knowledge. As a consequence of high-profile child abuse enquiries during the 1980s (see, for example, London Borough of Brent 1985; London Borough of Greenwich 1987), practice in this area has been particularly affected by the quest for certainty. This has encouraged a preoccupation with establishing risk factors and determining 'dangerousness' and a proliferation of schedules and checklists aimed at prediction (see, for example, Dale *et al.* 1986; Munro 1998). If we can predict who is likely to abuse, runs the argument, then resources can be directed more efficiently and effectively at this group. Such an approach has its limitations, as several commentators have indicated, notably because it is much easier to establish in hindsight the existence of risk factors than it is to predict which particular people with a number of characteristics will commit significant harm to a child (Dingwall 1989; Corby 1994).

More problematic still is the fact that there is often no measurable, forensic or medical evidence to prove conclusively whether a child has or has not been abused. This is particularly so in suspected cases of emotional abuse or sexual abuse: indeed the Cleveland Inquiry demonstrated how problematic a reliance on physical evidence could be (Department of Health 1988b). However, it is also a problem in suspected cases of physical abuse where it can be exceedingly difficult to determine precisely how an injury has occurred to the exclusion of all other possible explanations.

Even where there is clear medical and forensic evidence, this will need to be carefully weighed and evaluated. It may help to ascertain what happened (for example by establishing how bruising would most likely have been incurred) and rule out other possibilities (for example that a fall is unlikely to be the cause of a particular pattern of bruising), but it is unable to determine other important issues such as who did it (for instance which of the parents was it, or could it have been someone else who had care of the child?), whether the child is still at risk (for example, do the parents acknowledge the harm?), and whether the child is likely to be protected in the future. An unquestioning dependence on external knowledge will not be helpful in such circumstances as it will offer neither conclusive proof nor categorical answers. It will not establish the right way to proceed (knowing that a bruise was inflicted by a parent does not lead to an invariant response within the child protection process) and it will not encourage a questioning and sceptical approach to a worker's own practice.

Generally speaking, in child abuse cases, social workers, alongside other professionals, are required to *appraise* the veracity of the statements made by the various participants. The social worker must piece together the various statements and so produce their own coherent professional account about what, in all probability, has occurred and what risks there are of further harm to the child. In short, the worker will be faced with a number of options and will need to make judgements about what should be done and to put together a case supporting and justifying their position. This might be a justification for a particular intervention or, in many cases, for non-intervention (see Department of Health 1995 for a discussion of the 'filtering out' of cases from the child protection system). This process, we suggest, involves not only the use of knowledge but also the production, the *making*, of knowledge.

Facts vs facts

We have suggested that many professional judgements involve an active choice between versions of events presented by different interested parties. These different versions are often intrinsically contradictory. That is, they do not simply state the same set of propositions from different perspectives but give instead different accounts of what may or may not have happened. They blame different people, or sets of circumstances and mobilize competing 'facts' in different ways. In social theory this is known as **incommensurability**, that is, the competing ideas are not measurable by the same standard. This means that no matter how hard a practitioner tries to obtain a consensus view, it will stubbornly evade them. They are left with no option but to judge the believability of each account against the others.

Sometimes HW professionals are confronted with only one account of a situation or set of circumstances, for example if a therapist is working with an individual, or if a psychiatrist, nurse or social worker is assessing a person who appears to have a mental health problem. In these cases too, as is shown in some of the examples below, professionals routinely make judgements about whether the person's account is plausible or morally persuasive. We suggest that without such judgements the professionals find it difficult to intervene. That is, professionals generate their own reading of the case which often differs fundamentally from that presented by the client or patient. We want to show here that this process is not dependent on the assessment of facts alone, but depends also on the complex processes by which plausibility, persuasiveness and morality are woven into the story presented to the professional and subsequently by the professional. An understanding of this is essential to the development of critical thinking in health and welfare.

We hope that the following examples will help to persuade *you* that *our* version of professional activity in health and welfare is convincing.

Multiple versions: working with couples and families

There are some situations in which competing versions are particularly likely to occur. Any work with couples or families may well involve attempts by individuals to recruit the professional into their own particular version of events. This is a fertile arena for individual parties to blame or to hold each other responsible for whatever is presented as the problem.

> The discourse of relational problems often takes the form of the teller describing him/herself as reacting to the unjustifiable actions of his or her spouse – 'You (actively) did something to (passive) me and I (having no choice) had to respond as I did' (Lannamann 1989).
>
> (Buttny 1993: 66)

At its simplest, this may involve one partner blaming the other for relationship problems, but children may also be involved and coalitions between different family members may be evident.

In the example below, a family are talking with a therapist (Th) about their problems. The father (Fa) and mother (Mo) are having relationship difficulties. The father thinks that the children's unreasonable behaviour is causing these. The mother, however, thinks that the problems in her relationship with her husband were already there and may be contributing to their difficulties in parenting their children. The teenage daughter Kirsty (K) has also taken a position. She has been spending time at her friend's house, and is comparing her own parents negatively with those of her friend. The therapist has just asked Kirsty how the friend's parents would respond if their children were ever rude to them (an accusation levied at Kirsty by both her parents).

Extract 1.2

K: They don't hit them or ground them or anything
Th: Right
Fa: But we don't hit you

K: Yeah you do

Fa: We do not

K: Yeah you do

Fa: I'll show you what hitting is sometime. There's no way I'd ever hit you two girls. I have to physically restrain you when you're kicking us.

K: You have

Th: Are there times that you're thinking of, because your dad seems very clear that he hasn't hit you and you're saying that he has, you remember when he's hit you?

K: He has, when I'm going out. He hit me

Fa: When did I last hit you?

K: He just says that. He grabs me and he hits me as well.

Fa: I don't hit you as well

K: Yeah you did

Fa: I suppose I hit you this afternoon did I?

K: No

Fa: Oh

Mo: And so do you think dad shouldn't hit you when you hit us, Kirsty do you?

K: I only hit you because you hit us

Th: But you get into physical fights with your mum and dad somehow

Mo: No you mean when we try to stop you from doing something you hit us. You were trying to get out of the house and I was trying to lock you in and you kicked me really hard.

(J. Stancombe, personal communication 1999)

We suggest that, in the absence of any medical evidence of 'hitting', or of confirmatory accounts from impartial witnesses, there is no way of the therapist knowing for sure whether Kirsty is hitting her parents when they try to restrain her, or whether she tries desperately to get away from home because her father is violent towards her. The purveyors of each version try to recruit the therapist into their particular account of the case. A judgement could be made between competing versions; however, this would be based on the therapist deciding whom she most believed, or on moral or political criteria such as a belief in child-centred practice (children and young people are vulnerable and therefore should be believed when they make allegations of abuse).

Competing versions: professional meets patient/client

The following extract is taken from an interview between a psychiatrist and a person detained in a prison psychiatric hospital in the USA. It has been analysed in detail by Mehan (1990). In the extract, the psychiatrist is making an assessment of the patient. We can see that the patient (Pt) is trying to persuade the head psychiatrist (HP) that he is being adversely affected by hospitalization. However, the psychiatrist reads his protestations as evidence of his continuing illness.

Extract 1.3

HP: Okay now Vladimir as I've promised you before, if I see enough improvement in you

Pt: How can I improve if I'm getting worse? I've been trying to tell you, I can tell you, day by day, I'm getting worse, because of the circumstances, because of the situation. Now you're telling me uh uh how can I until you see an improvement each time I get worse. So, it's obviously the treatment I'm getting or it's the situation or the place or or the patients or the inmates or either of them. I don't know which. I want to go back to the prison where I belong. I was supposed to only come down here for observation. What observation did I get? You called me up a couple of times. You say 'well take some medication'. Medication for the mind? I am supposed to take medication for, if I have some bodily injury. Not for the mind. My mind's perfect. Cause I'm obviously logical. I know what I'm talking about. There's no – and I am excited. Yes, that's the only fault you might find with me. I have a perfect right to be excited. I've been here for a year and a half, hum, and this place is doing me harm. I come in here, I, I uh, every time I come in here you call me I'm crazy. Now that's if there's something you don't like about my face, that's I mean, that's another story. But that has nothing to do with my mental stability. I have an emotional problem now, yes, which I did not have.

(Mehan 1990: 174)

The psychiatrist and the patient continue their conversation in this way for some time, with the psychiatrist insisting that the patient has a mental health problem and the patient insisting that his only problem is the psychiatrist. Ultimately the patient is asked to leave the room, and the head psychiatrist and two other doctors (DR2 and DR3) discuss the case.

Extract 1.4

HP: He's been much better than this, and he's now, he's falling apart, now whether this is some reaction to uh his medication, is certainly something I'll have to look at. However, uh, he was looking a lot more catatonic and depressed before and sometimes we find that, I mean, uh, antidepressants, you remove the depression and you uncover the paranoid stuff, and we may have to give him larger quantities of tranquillizers just to tone this down. So he's not looking ready to be able to make it back to prison.

DR2: He argues in a perfectly paranoid pattern. If you accept his basic premise the rest of it is logical. But the basic premise is not true . . . I think he's terrified of leaving.

HP: Um, the louder he shouts about going back the more frightened he indicates that he probably is.

DR3: This is known as Ganzer Syndrome

HP: Well not quite

DR3: Almost. Close

HP: Well I think what we have to do with him is, uh, put him on a higher dose of tranquillizers and see if we can bring the paranoid element under a little bit better control and see if we can get him back on medication. If he's taking it now, and I'm not even sure that he is . . .

(Mehan 1990: 176)

The extracts do not, in themselves, help us to decide which version we should believe. Yet both versions may be considered factual. The doctors' version mobilizes a set of psychiatric 'facts', about symptomatology ('he was looking a lot more catatonic and depressed before') and diagnostic categories (for example, Ganzer Syndrome) whilst the patient gives what is also a factual account of his experience which relies on a more social understanding of distress (for example, 'it's obviously the treatment I'm getting or it's the situation or the place or or or the patients or the inmates or either of them').

It is clear that the two versions are radically incommensurable. Mehan calls this 'oracular' reasoning, which he defines as follows: 'Oracular reasoning . . . is a process of arguing from and defending a basic belief. People maintain the truth or efficacy of a belief by denying or repelling evidence which is contrary to or opposes the belief' (1990: 161). They do not approach opposing views with an open mind.

Clearly, in this case, the patient's account is easily dismissed. He has a formal diagnosis of mental illness, and is also a prisoner. The psychiatrist has the formal power to adjudicate on the boundaries between normality and deviance and his version therefore 'wins'. We show in due course that ascribing deviant attributes (for example, she's mentally ill, a drug user, a neglectful mother) to a person is one of the ways in which professionals make decisions about the veracity of that person's version.

A further example of incommensurability is given in the following extracts. The first is taken from letters written by a child psychiatrist about the mother of Wendy (aged 8), a child with severe learning difficulties.

Extract 1.5

I found mother to be evasive and at times I thought she was deliberately covering up information. For example she did not know anything about her husband's experiences in early childhood and subsequently let slip that paternal grandfather was a very critical man and this has influenced her husband's attitude towards Wendy . . . She [child] has no speech, she does sign for some objects using Makaton. She is restless and ritualistic and does not sleep properly . . . She is incontinent and I was quite surprised how mother seems detached, leaving her in a smelly condition throughout the consultation until I prompted her. I found the mother detached and flat in her mood.

(Adapted from White 1997a)

The professional formulation here is clear: the mother is, in a number of ways, considered to be at fault. There is a common-sense presupposition that wives know in detail about their husband's childhoods and because she denies any such knowledge, whilst making some statements which appear to contradict this, the mother becomes defined as evasive. The description of the child's 'smelly condition' serves to reference the mother's culpable neglect of her parental duties.

The following account was written by the mother:

Extract 1.6

She [Wendy] climbs, jumps at windows, pulls out plugs . . . She seems to have tremendous mood swings, going from being completely wound up, almost wild to violent bouts of crying for which there is no explanation . . . She is still suffering terrible diarrhoea . . . and has had to be cleaned 3–4 times a day for the last 3 years . . . Wendy is so demanding that I am concerned about the other children. I feel I have no time for them and that they are really suffering, not only from this, but from the stress of living with a child who is so unpredictable . . . Wendy is a very confused little girl who desperately needs help. We love her.

(Adapted from White 1997a)

This is a powerful account in which the mother refers to her commitment to the child, and also talks about her fears for the other children. This and the psychiatrist's account are competing versions of the same case. Moreover, like the psychiatric interview in Extracts 1.3 and 1.4 above, they both mobilize different sets of facts. In later chapters, we will say more about the use of facts to produce accounts which are rhetorically potent, that is, which generate powerful effects and are difficult to resist.

Talking together: professionals and versions

We have shown that HW professionals are engaged in a range of activities that require the exercise of qualitative judgement. When we look at professional conversation in detail, the competing versions can often be seen, but the story will be delivered in such a way that some possible readings are edited out. Thus, messy reality becomes ordered in particular ways and some readings become buried. In the following extracts, a team of childcare social workers (SW) are talking about a case that has been referred to them (this transcript is discussed in greater detail in Chapter 7). The team leader (TL) begins by telling the team that an education welfare officer (Kate) has reported hearing a rumour that a teenage boy is reported to be 'shagging' (having sexual relations with) a 10-year-old girl, believed to be Sophie Byrne. It also transpires that Sophie has been found with a friend wandering around a local shopping precinct at 2 am.

Extract 1.7

TL: Kate managed to identify the child as Sophie Byrne through statements the children made and by reference to the accounts from [school] of Sophie being met by older boys from school. Actually, it looks as though from the onset Kate put two and two together from what the pupils at [school] said and spoke to the Head of [school] and she confirmed accounts of Sophie being met by older boys. The children often arrive late for school and are not really collected. Oliver is 7, is he 7? . . . There were no major concerns at the previous school. However, there had been one incident outside school where Sophie had been with a group of older boys who were smoking. That was when she was about 8. So what happened as a consequence of this, after all the checks had been done, it was allocated to Jan and Dawn was on the child protection bleep on that day. You can take it over now Dawn . . .

(Adapted from White 1997a)

The social worker continues the story describing the father's account:

SW: Mr Byrne initially said that he felt it was just boys talking, the concern about Sophie being shagged was just playground chit chat and he had no concerns about Sophie

(ibid.)

At this point the social workers seem to accept the plausibility of Mr Byrne's story and are reassured. However, the mother reacts to the suggestion that Sophie is being 'shagged', which is reported by the social worker as follows.

SW: Yeah Trish [team leader] we went out to talk to Mrs Byrne who gave quite a completely different view of things and basically is very worried about Sophie erm mainly around the Gemma Anderson family erm because she says that it's notorious round their way and she doesn't want her daughter mixing with them . . . Well anyway Mrs Byrne is obviously quite upset that Sophie is mixing with these children

(ibid.)

As a consequence of this reinterpretation, the social workers begin discussing previous history and focus on the risk to Sophie. The idea that she is being sexually abused by an older boy gains increasing currency. The father's version (Sophie is a bit of a handful but there are no real problems) becomes buried. The possibility that Sophie may be a 'naughty girl' is not discussed, although it is clearly available as a version. Instead, Sophie is interviewed and the possibility of a gynaecological examination is discussed. In this case, the social workers have made a case together. Although they are all agreeing with each other, their conversation has an argumentative quality (cf. Schwitalla 1986). There is almost an invisible audience to whom they are relating the case. This has the effect of solidifying their particular reading of the case and extinguishing any doubts. So, 'the original situation has now been "given" or "lent" a determinate character . . . which it did not, in its original openness, actually possess' (Shotter 1989: 149).

These data from diverse settings demonstrate that making judgements among different versions is a central and unavoidable aspect of professional practice. Such a perspective allows us to acknowledge more explicitly that the task for professionals is to make sense of these differing accounts and to determine for themselves which one is the most convincing.

'Facts' and their construction

In the examples above we have shown how the participants are attempting to claim their own version as true. We have also made it clear that, in stressing the existence of multiple versions, we are not suggesting that knowledge is redundant. Clearly, it is central to the work of HW professionals. Collectively, across their various specialisms, HW professionals need to understand illness and disease, mental distress, family relationships, children's development and a host of other issues and problems. Moreover, in order for 'truth claims' to be successful, they must appear to be factually correct, that is, they must achieve some congruence with objective reality as it is seen by others. Facts and their assembly by professionals and those for whom they provide a service are of fundamental importance. If an individual cannot support their case with facts, they will simply fail to convince anyone of anything.

However, as we have seen above, objective reality is often extremely malleable and people may assemble facts in a particular order to produce a certain reading of events. At its simplest, this might involve lying by omission – missing out a crucial part of a story in order to convince others of the veracity of one's own version of events. In professional practice, this might also involve asking questions or making observations that support one's own reading of a situation or one's own theoretical preferences and paying insufficient attention to other possible explanations (Sheppard 1995; White 1997b).

Within the social sciences, the view that there is a single reality which, given the right procedures, can be captured and explained, and the view that there may be any number of plausible explanations for the same phenomenon, have been characterized respectively as **realism** (or **objectivism**) and **relativism** (or **social constructionism**). Both standpoints have their avid supporters and critics. Indeed, it is easy for these positions to become ridiculously polarized, with each camp accusing the other of quite implausible beliefs. Our intention is to propose a sustained argument in favour of a relativist or social constructionist position. Before doing so we must define our terms precisely; we shall also clarify what we are *not* arguing. This will require a brief excursion, in the next chapter, into some philosophical debates. For those of you immersed in the complexities of practice, this may be rather unfamiliar and daunting territory, but it is essential that these positions and their implications for professional practice are explored before we engage in a more detailed exposition of our approach in subsequent chapters.

Summary

In this chapter we have explored the imperatives which currently exist for HW professionals to examine their practice critically and reflexively. We have argued that the contemporary preoccupation with evidence-based practice can only take the practitioners so far. In many circumstances professional judgements are just that – judgements. We have given examples of the various circumstances in which HW professionals must grapple with competing versions of events. The following points are crucial and will be developed in later chapters:

- Many judgements and decisions are based on the professionals' assessments of the veracity of particular versions presented to them. These assessments rely on reasoning processes which are often thought of as intuitive or based on 'gut feelings'.
- In arguing that in many circumstances there may be multiple valid readings of the same set of circumstances, we are not suggesting that facts do not matter. Choice between competing versions is not arbitrary.
- In social theory, the view that there is one incontrovertible, stable, independent reality, which given the right techniques we can capture and explain, is often known as realism, and is often associated with objectivism, positivism and the 'scientific method'.
- The view that there are rarely any neutral means by which to access reality, because human beings are always interpreting and reinterpreting what they find, is known as social constructionism, and its proponents are often called relativists.
- There have been a number of attempts to break down this either/or version of realism and relativism.

CHAPTER 2

Knowledge, truth and reflexive practice

Through a series of examples, we have proposed in the previous chapter that professional practice in health and welfare is not generally characterized by the pursuit of objective truth. Rather, it is more aptly perceived as the messy and complex business of trying to sort out, from among a variety of competing perspectives and multiple versions, what is occurring in a particular situation and what should be done in response. It may be that there are helpful signposts and clues in the form of medical evidence or expert opinion but these usually provide only partial answers at best. We concluded by arguing in favour of an acceptance of the 'malleability' of objective facts and the existence of competing versions of reality. This leads us into a more detailed exploration of what has become an often hotly contested debate between realist (or objectivist) and relativist (or social constructionist) perspectives. For reasons which we hope will become clear, we are unhappy about the distinction between the two as it is conventionally represented. However, as the terms are used ubiquitously, often as terms of derision by the opposing camp, it will help to clarify our argument if we examine the major elements of each of the positions, some of their more subtle components and the main criticisms that have been made about each of them. One of the claims that we wish to assert is that reflexivity is (or should be) an important component of HW practice and we conclude the chapter by exploring this issue and suggesting how the position we adopt in this book can assist in this endeavour.

The 'realist' (or objectivist) position

At the heart of the debate between the realist and relativist positions is the core question, how do we come to know our world? Those who espouse realism would respond to the effect that, 'there is a reality independent of the researcher [or social actor, or practitioner] whose nature can be known and that the aim of research [or knowledge acquisition, or professional practice] is to produce accounts that correspond to that reality' (Hammersley 1992: 43). The notion of the 'out-there-ness' of reality, that the world is separate from the knower, is central to realist thinking. For this reason, some (for example, Bernstein 1983) prefer the term 'objectivism' to describe this orientation to knowledge.

It is argued that we can come to know this separate, independent world through careful observations of it. For some, such observations are best carried out in the sanitized sphere of the laboratory where due care and rigour can more readily be applied than in the hurly-burly of the 'real world'. There, true scientific procedure and objectivity can be adhered to in order to produce impartial and incontrovertible facts about the world. Whilst the natural sciences are often perceived more readily to conform to these lofty ideals regarding knowledge generation, we can also find its proponents within the social sciences, perhaps most overtly within psychology with its **positivist** emulation of the procedures of the natural sciences. This is exemplified in Mary Ainsworth's laboratory explorations of attachment behaviours in young children in the Strange Situation Test (Ainsworth *et al.* 1978) or Milgram's controversial experiments into conformity and obedience (Milgram 1974).

Across the range of social science disciplines we can find various forms of realist approaches, in particular the use of quantitative methods to generate broad generalities about people and their circumstances, for example statistical information about the incidence of cancer across social groups, or the numbers of homeless people living on the streets. However, realism is not confined to quantitative methods; qualitative research can also be realist. A good example of this can be seen in 'naturalistic' ethnographic approaches. These are critical of the data produced by quantitative methods, claiming that 'by entering into close and relatively long-term contact with people in their everyday lives we come to understand their beliefs and behaviour *more accurately*, in a way that would not be possible by means of any other approach' (Hammersley 1992: 44). Naturalistic observations of social phenomena are said to get much closer to reality and to reproduce more faithfully its true nature. It allows us to see things/people how they *really* are. So, across many different types of research within the social sciences, we can see this fundamental belief in a **correspondence theory of truth**; that is, like a mirror, knowledge or truth should directly correspond to the reality it describes (Rorty 1979). Thus, from a realist perspective, knowledge acquisition has a veritistic dimension; that is, its orientation is towards truth determination (Goldman 1999). It is concerned to avoid error (false belief) or ignorance (the absence of true belief) to arrive at true and final descriptions of reality.

This understanding of knowledge is located within the **Enlightenment** tradition of western thought. The Enlightenment can be traced to the seventeenth century, and the work of French philosopher Descartes. It is characterized by a rejection of the traditional social order and forms of knowledge based on religious belief or superstition. Certain core themes can be identified within Enlightenment thinking:

> First, a concept of freedom based upon an autonomous human subject who is capable of acting in a conscious manner. Second, the pursuit of a universal and foundational 'truth' gained through a correspondence of ideas with social and physical reality. Third, a belief in the natural sciences as the correct model for thinking about the social and natural world over, for example, theology and metaphysics. Fourth, the accumulation of systematic knowledge with the progressive unfolding of history.
>
> (May 1996: 8)

Centrality was thus given to new secular forms of knowledge founded on experience, experiment and reason. *Science* was seen as the key to objective, value-neutral human knowledge; it would generate *universal* ideas about the nature of the world (including human beings); and by the application of science and reason *progress* would be achieved: 'the improvement of the natural and social condition of human beings' (Hamilton 1992: 21).

Objective, scientific knowledge would overcome ignorance, bias and prejudice and, by producing an understanding of social arrangements, would reveal their operation which in turn would generate social change. Through understanding, it is argued, comes the power to control both the natural and social worlds. Bruno Latour (1999) uses the metaphor 'mind-in-a-vat' to describe this enduring Enlightenment legacy, for it relies on some separation of the capacity for 'pure reason' (performed by a disciplined brain) from a connected 'body' continually rubbing against the complex (social) world. We return to this argument in due course.

Enlightenment themes have been carried forward into twentieth-century thinking about how we understand the social and natural worlds. In particular, it is evident that positivism can be seen as an heir to the Enlightenment project with its emphasis on observation (what we can see, feel, touch and so forth provides the best foundation for non-mathematical knowledge) and verification (the determination of the truth or falsity of statements about the world) (Blaikie 1993). As O'Brien notes, the positivist tradition within the social sciences suggests a 'progressive, cumulative, explanatory, "scientific" project . . . to explain, predict and ultimately control the social world' (1993: 7).

Within the positivist tradition, language is assumed to be a neutral medium for the transmission of knowledge and ideas. Jonathan Potter has suggested that such a stance treats language as a mirror: 'language reflects how things are in its descriptions, representations and accounts . . . they may be treated as accounts which are reliable, factual or literal, or, alternatively, the mirror may blur or distort in the case of confusion or lies' (Potter 1996: 97). In our example of Jessie (Extract 1.1) in the previous chapter, we can, from this perspective, regard the ward sister's description as reliable and factually correct: that is how Jessie is. Or, if we think it is untrue, we can suggest that it is biased and distorted or erroneous, that it does not describe 'the real Jessie', and that for some reason the ward sister has got it wrong. She might, for instance, be prejudiced against older people or lacking some important information. Where knowledge is accepted as objective it tends to be regarded as unproblematical and accepted at face value. When bias and error are assumed to have crept into the fact-finding process they are deemed worthy of scrutiny. It becomes important to determine how this infiltration might have happened and whether it is the result of deliberate intent. Thus bias and error tend to be explained psychologically (attributable to the personality of the fact-finder) or sociologically (attributable to the social milieu in which the facts are generated). There is thus an asymmetry in the way that 'the truth' and error or falsehood are treated within realist accounts.

There are several points to be made here about the relationship between HW professionals and (this kind of) realist knowledge. First and foremost, HW professionals have relied heavily on this kind of knowledge. Indeed, an 'objective' knowledge base has been seen as a defining characteristic of a profession (Parsons 1967; Johnson 1972; Baly 1984) and certain occupations, notably social work, have been extremely anxious about whether, alongside law and medicine, they too can demonstrate their fitness to be regarded as worthy of professional status on the basis of their particular expertise. In medicine in particular, we can see the importance placed on scientific experiments and clinical trials, and the centrality of the laboratory (the acme of science) in the generation of its knowledge. Moreover, it is possible to detect a certain wariness among some professionals towards embracing less scientifically formulated evidence as an acceptable basis for professional knowledge. Psychoanalysis is a prime example and we can note attempts to render psychoanalysis and its offshoots 'more scientific', that is more conformable to scientific standards (for a review of these attempts, see Stancombe and White 1998). Similarly, attachment theory, initially developed in the context of clinical work with children and young people, has drawn heavily on laboratory experiments with both animals and small children to produce a more scientific formulation of its core concepts and a typology of attachment behaviours (Holmes 1993; Burman 1994; Howe 1995).

Second, it could perhaps be argued that there exists a symbiotic relationship between the scientists and HW professionals: the former have relied on the latter to promulgate their work and to apply it in practice just as practitioners have depended on science to provide core knowledge. This has had important effects in terms of the ways that we think about how professionals (should) practise. We have come to associate it with a particular form of expertise. Practitioners are regarded as detached and neutral observers of other people's lives; they stand back to make assessments and form objective and dispassionate judgements about the nature of problems and their solution. They 'know best' because of their profound knowledge gained over years of tuition and study. Their very impartiality and separateness from the problem render them suited to making difficult and complex decisions which determine access to (scarce) resources and appropriate interventions in clients' lives. This designation of practitioners underlines the common approach among different professional groupings to problems, whilst masking possible inter-professional conflicts and rivalries centred on different knowledge bases, hierarchical organizational structures and the dominance of the 'biomedical model'.

At the same time we should also acknowledge ambivalence in certain quarters of the caring professions towards scientific knowledge. For example, social work's desire for a scientific knowledge base runs alongside, and often in tension with, a stance which claims that intuitive empathy and unconditional positive regard lie at the heart of professional practice. On occasion within HW there has existed scepticism and suspicion of the value of importing scientific knowledge into day-to-day practice. Health and welfare work has been regarded as a practical and pragmatic activity dealing with real issues – illness, disease, substance abuse, child abuse and neglect, and so forth – and therefore needing to be grounded in reality, to find real solutions to real problems. This suggests a challenge to the abstract, and sometimes abstruse, nature of objective knowledge and claims instead that more common-sense understandings of HW issues are more useful. Social workers in particular have often seemed susceptible to such arguments (Thompson 1995).

We do not want to formulate the key issue of the debate as being about the superiority of either scientific knowledge or common sense as a way of knowing about the world. Both not only adopt a realist perspective and assert the existence of a real world (which, as we show below, is not in dispute), but also assume that it can, with sufficient effort, be known and described using neutral language and descriptions (which is a much more problematic claim). We want to propose an alternative approach which regards the world as real, but knowledge as contingent. Indeed, it is towards this more 'subtle realism' (Hammersley 1992) that enquiries in the social sciences have been travelling. In order to explain this perspective, however, we need to explore the debates concerning 'social constructionism' (hereafter SC). Let us look first at what SC is before examining its implications for practice and addressing some of the criticisms made by its detractors.

The social constructionist position

As we have suggested, the objectivist position has been dominant in both scientific endeavours and professional practice in modern western societies where it became accepted that science and technology would contribute to industrial expansion and social and material progress. However, in the twentieth century, this optimistic view has been seriously dented by the experience of two world wars, the rise of Nazism and the Holocaust, the cold war, challenges to imperialism, the rise of nationalism, and concerns about global ecology. This loss of confidence in the steady march of progress has been reflected within academic disciplines, signalled by the coming to prominence in recent decades of more critical and self-reflective discourses such as Marxism, critical theory, feminism and postmodernism, to name but a few. Brown (1994: 13) suggests that 'these tendencies in academic knowledge have matured within the past decade to become an important intellectual movement [whose] unifying perspective . . . has variously been called social constructionism, the rhetorical turn, society as text, deconstructionism and postmodernism.' It is to the key elements of SC that we now turn.

Is there a real world out there? Beyond objectivism and relativism

At first glance, this might seem a rather strange, not to say foolish, question. Of course there is a real world out there – we continually bang into it in our daily engagement with recalcitrant objects such as cars which break down, household appliances which play up and furniture which gets in the way: surely these provide incontrovertible proof of the existence of real things? Similarly, death, violence and human suffering provide evidence of there being a real world in which at times events of horrific ferocity occur. There are things whose existence 'cannot be denied' (tables, rocks, blood, bones and so forth) and things which 'ought not to be denied' (war, poverty, disease, pain and such like). From any perspective, to argue against the existence of this material reality is nonsense. However, this is a commonplace accusation levied at those who expound social constructionism or who draw on similar ideas. However, we can find not one amongst 'the accused' who adheres to this bizarre 'there is no reality' form of 'universal constructionism'. As Hacking notes in his excellent debunking of the issues, to find a universal constructionist we would have to search for:

> someone who claims every object whatsoever – the earth, your feet, quarks, the aroma of coffee, grief, polar bears in the Arctic – is in some nontrivial sense socially constructed. Not just our experience of them, our classifications of them, our interests in them, but *these things themselves* . . .
>
> (Hacking 1999: 24, emphasis added)

Nobody makes such claims. If we were to argue that we are completely and absolutely disconnected from the world in this way, we should have to accept that our brains were encased in glass so incredibly thick that nothing could get in or out. This is another version of the mind-in-a-vat legacy (Latour 1999). Rather, the debate should turn on how we engage with the complexity that is reality, as Rorty notes: 'philosophers who get *called* relativists are those who say that the grounds for choosing between opinions are less algorithmic [that is, following a set of rules] than had been thought' (Rorty 1980: 727–8). From a social constructionist perspective, then, table-thumping and an invocation of death, biology or the Holocaust as evidence of objective reality are simply not relevant. They miss the point (see Edwards *et al.* 1995 for a refutation of what they call 'death and furniture arguments'). SC does not seek to deny that there are such things as grief, poverty, hunger, disease, genocide or a 'real world out there'. It declines to concern itself with the nature or essence of things (**ontology**), opting instead to focus on how we come to know about the world (**epistemology**). This means that SC is, as Gergen (1994: 72) would have it, 'ontologically mute. Whatever is, simply is'. However, 'once we attempt to articulate "what there is" . . . we enter the world of discourse' (Gergen 1994: 72). That is, we enter a world where the things that exist are represented and constructed through language as a set of concepts or ideas. For example, the feeling we understand as 'grief' exists as an embodied state, and would do so even if it were called something else and thought about in a different way. However, the processes and rituals we follow when grieving are culturally specific, and current ideas about stages of grieving, or about normal and abnormal grief, are heuristic devices which both reflect and construct our current understandings, and indeed experiences, of grief. These are part of the world of discourse.

War situations such as the one in Kosovo graphically illustrate how difficult it is to know 'what is really happening' and who is telling the truth. We are dependent for information on the antagonists, in this case NATO and the Serbian government, politicians and the various news media, which results in various claims and counter-claims about specific incidents and many different versions of events in circulation, making it difficult to know which is the authoritative account. Even if we were there to witness events for ourselves we would still only have a partial account which would not simply be based on our observations but would be coloured by our thinking about the situation and 'the side we were on'. What for many is the 'ethnic cleansing' of Kosovo Albanians is to others the flight to safety of villagers being bombed by NATO forces. Visual evidence will not necessarily resolve these differences of interpretation since we can call into question the authenticity of such evidence and deny its status as proof. That is not to say that it is of no matter which version is right and true, but in order to decide, we have to rely on judgements which are more moral and practical and rely less on objectivism.

Similarly, if we take the less emotive example of a firework display, it is clearly possible to render different accounts of such an event. We can treat it as a series of chemical explosions and seek to determine which precise combination of chemical compounds is needed to create an impressive constellation of colours and patterns in the sky. Alternatively, we can ignore these more technical concerns to focus on the artistry of the display, regarding it as a dazzling visual exhibition which appeals to our senses and evokes appreciation; or again we could treat the display as a noisy and terrifying spectacle which invites fear rather than appreciative awe. In another interpretation it could be constructed in terms of risk to health and safety. Can one of these accounts be said to be more objectively accurate than the others? If so, on what grounds can we make that determination?

Social constructionism contends that these are alternative ways of describing the same thing and that rather than trying to designate one of these as the truth it is more relevant to look at how each of the competing claims is made and at what is the context of the claim making. By what devices and in what terms are the various positions couched? How do people go about the task of making claims and appealing for support? The examples of the war in Kosovo and of a firework display raise two important issues. First, knowing is not a process of neutrality and detachment, there is no view from 'anywhere'. Equally, we cannot remove ourselves from the world we inhabit and our interactions with others, there is no 'view from nowhere' (Nagel 1986) but always a view from somewhere. Second, whilst there are circumstances in which multiple accounts can coexist in relative harmony (as between the firework maker and the appreciative spectator), there are times (and war propaganda is a prime example of this) where accounts conflict. In professional practice, too, this can be very evident where several different versions may compete for acceptance. This is a topic to which we return in subsequent chapters; before then we need to explore some other important aspects of SC, notably its position on language.

Language as action

Language is a key issue of difference between realist and social constructionist perspectives. Realists assume that language is a transparent medium for the conveyance of descriptions about the real world. Social constructionists, in contrast, argue that language is not necessarily a mirror on the world but 'a construction yard': 'descriptions and accounts *construct the world* or at least versions of the world, . . . [and] these descriptions or accounts are *themselves* constructed' (Potter 1996: 97, original emphasis). This is precisely what the 'Jessie' (Extract 1.1) and 'Vladimir' (Extracts 1.3 and 1.4) examples in Chapter 1 were intended to show: that language should be seen not just as descriptive but also as *performative* – it works to achieve particular effects: in the former case, to define Jessie as a 'problem patient' in the wrong place; in the latter to define Vladimir as someone in the right place despite, or rather because of, his protestations to the contrary.

An important point to make here is to emphasize the capacity of human beings for *artful* language performance. Various perspectives within the social sciences, notably **ethnomethodology, conversation analysis** and **discourse analysis** (see Chapter 3), have encouraged the study of everyday practices and emphasized the skills of ordinary people in talk and interaction. In mundane settings, people contrive (though not always self-consciously or successfully) to put across their point of view and to undermine the opposition. This can be illustrated by the following extract from a counselling session attended by Connie and Jimmy, an Irish couple now living in England, in which the counsellor invites each party to talk about the background to their marriage.

Extract 2.1

Counsellor: When before you moved over here how was the marriage?
Connie: Oh to me all along right up to now, my marriage was rock solid. Rock solid. We had arguments like everybody else had arguments, but to me there was no major problems. Y'know? That's my way of thinking but Jimmy's thinking is very very different.
Jimmy: Well being a jealous person um we go back to when were first datin' well we met in this particular pub. When we started dating we was in there, every single week we'd fight. We were at each other the whole time.
(Edwards 1997: 154–5, original transcription symbols removed)

Here we can see Connie portraying her marriage as very stable (the repetition of 'rock solid') at the same time as she suggests to the counsellor that her husband Jimmy will have a very different account. In contrast Jimmy presents the marriage as beset by argument and conflict from the beginning (by using phrases like 'every single week', 'the whole time'). Connie conveys the impression of a normal marriage ('like everybody else'), Jimmy of a pathological relationship which was always troubled and difficult.

If you were the counsellor, could you determine whose account is more factually correct? How could you be sure of the evidence provided? Or is this even helpful, after all even if one person's account is more accurate does it matter if the other person rejects it as fabrication? Taking sides and supporting one account at the expense of the other is likely to result in the unsupported party withdrawing from counselling. Instead, as the counsellor you would be faced with the challenging task of working out how to create dialogue and discussion between two people who are both committed to a particular version of events and determined to discredit the alternative account put forward by their partner. Both partners display considerable skill in deploying language to accomplish these twin goals. This theme around the performative aspects of language and the strategies that people employ in their interactions with others is something to which we return in subsequent chapters. The point to emphasize here is that how we perceive HW issues is not as transparent reflections of the social world but as socially constructed phenomena.

The example of mental health is pertinent here for it can be argued that we are not defining an objective truth but constructing a definition of someone according to the categories currently available to us generated within psychiatry and elsewhere. Words and behaviour which are designated as 'mental illness' may also be categorized in different ways within competing professionals discourses, as Jane Ussher notes:

> A woman who is unhappy, angry and withdrawn [or whose behaviour is interpreted thus] may be told by a psychiatrist that her hormones are in flux, by a psychologist that her cognitions are faulty, by a sociologist that her environment is responsible, or by a psychoanalytic therapist that she is repressing her unconscious desires . . . Who is right?
>
> (Ussher 1991: 103–4)

This serves to remind us of the many different ways that a mental health problem can be explained by competing paradigms. Yet we should also acknowledge that these competing professional discourses serve to exclude other possibilities. In modern secular societies with their medicalized definitions of mental distress we are unlikely to accept an interpretation which suggests that such a woman has been taken over by evil spirits and requires the attention of a shaman or an exorcist since these probably strike us as pre-scientific explanations and solutions. Rather, given the privileged status of psychiatry to define and treat 'mental illness' in western society, we are likely to have recourse to drug regimens, electroconvulsive therapy, or to some form of 'talking cure' in response to women's perceived mental health problems.

What interpretations such as these do is construct a world of meaning around the concept of mental health/illness. The definition and categorization of mental distress is, in Hacking's terms, interactive: these processes order and translate messy human conditions; in turn, human beings may themselves react to these orderings and classifications and hence redefine their own distress as an eating disorder, depression or psychosis (Hacking 1999). This looping effect of **interactive kinds** takes place even if the 'disorder' which the definition seeks to describe is caused by a 'natural phenomenon' (or what Hacking calls an **indifferent kind**) such as genes. Genes cannot, independently and of themselves, react to our definitions and understandings of them – they are indifferent. We, however, are not indifferent. We may learn to interpret certain actions and behaviours as evidence of mental illness, as the interaction between Vladimir and the psychiatrist (Extracts 1.3 and 1.4) indicates. Thus, rigid boundaries between the real and the socially constructed cannot be maintained. We must, therefore, go 'beyond [the artificial dichotomy of] objectivism and relativism' (Bernstein 1983).

Similarly, it has been argued that truancy is not an objective term that simply describes a universal phenomenon of pupils not attending school. It was brought into being in industrialized countries in the latter part of the nineteenth century through the institution of a system of compulsory education for children. Before then, schoolchildren probably 'bunked off' on occasion but the concept of truancy did not exist to define their behaviour. Only when schooling is made compulsory can the failure to attend school by certain children come to be regarded as a social problem – truants are perceived as not being under the regulation of parents or teachers and, as such, are a threat to the social order, a presence on the streets when they should be under adult guidance and control. There is then called into being a whole machinery to determine who is absent and how often (through registers and registration periods), truancy officers to check on children's *unauthorized* absences from school and a range of designated, legally sanctioned measures to bring about children's return to school. Truancy is not a universal phenomenon nor does it exist in a social vacuum but is brought forth in a particular historical and social conjuncture (Paterson 1989). However, all this historical contingency does not take away the fact that some children do skip school. This fact is real; it is its meaning that changes.

This brings us to another important tenet of SC thinking, namely that concepts, practices and social arrangements which may seem universal because we take them so much for granted are in fact historically and culturally specific, as both the above examples have shown. Vivien Burr suggests that for SC:

> all ways of understanding are historically and culturally relative. Not only are they specific to particular cultures and periods of history, they are seen as products of culture and history, and are dependent upon the particular social and economic arrangements prevailing in that particular culture at that time. The particular forms of knowledge that abound in any culture are therefore artefacts of it, and we should not assume that *our* ways of understanding are necessarily any better (in terms of being nearer the truth) than other ways.
>
> (Burr 1995: 4)

This applies also to science which should not be regarded as separate and different from the social world of human interactions. Since the publication of Thomas Kuhn's seminal work (1962) many studies have been undertaken under the broad rubric of the sociology of scientific knowledge (SSK) which have challenged science's traditional image as the bastion for the production of hard facts that are 'impersonal, empirically warranted, rigorously tested' (Potter 1996: 18; examples of SSK include Knorr-Cetina and Mulkay 1983b; Gilbert and Mulkay 1984; Latour and Woolgar 1986; Latour 1999). Such studies have focused instead on 'the breakdown in the conventional distinction between observation and theory, the stress on the way scientific claims are organized together in interconnected networks, and the emphasis on scientific practice and its communal nature' (Potter 1996: 40). The importance of these studies (discussed in Chapter 10) lies in their assertion that rather than science being seen as the archetype for the generation of objective and universal knowledge, we should recognize that it, too, is social. Scientists, just like other social actors, seek to persuade peers and an external audience of the correctness of one theory and the incorrectness of other theories, as exemplified by debates over genetically modified organisms, the safety of beef or the existence of global warming. That is, scientists engage in rhetorical transactions to secure funding, carry out their studies and explain and account for their work. For example, scientists have devised particular conventions for the presentations of their arguments which Gilbert and Mulkay (1984) have designated an **empiricist repertoire**, a formal way of writing which 'writes out' the author of a study and produces 'an impersonal, method-based, and data-driven account of findings and theory choice' (Edwards 1997: 58).

Social constructionism and uncertainty

For those who adhere to objectivism, the notion of historical and cultural relativism is intensely problematic because it raises the prospect of the uncertainty of knowledge. If knowledge keeps changing and not all truths can be fixed, how do we know that what we think is right? How does this affect our ability to function successfully in our social world? Can we and should we just believe anything? However, this, too, represents a sensationalist misreading of what the foremost thinkers in the field are trying to say. For example, pointing to the complex, interactive, social nature of scientific endeavour is not the same as saying all science is false, or that there is no such thing as reality. Rather than seeing the study of 'the making of scientific knowledge' as an extreme form of relativism, Latour encourages us to see it either as a more 'realistic realism' (Latour 1999: 15), or as 'sturdy relativism', by which he means that science can claim to be *relatively* sure *at this moment* about things it describes. For Latour, mind-in-a-vat 'objectivity' has, at its heart, a paradox:

> Why, in the first place, did we even need the idea of an *outside world* looked at through a gaze from the very uncomfortable observation post of a mind-in-a-vat? . . . And why burden this solitary mind with the impossible task of finding absolute certainty instead of plugging it into the connections that would provide it with all the relative certainties it needed to know and to act? Why shout out of both sides of our mouths these two contradictory orders: 'Be absolutely disconnected!' 'Find absolute proof that you are connected!' Who could possibly untangle such a double bind?

> (Latour 1999: 12)

One of the advantages of the SC approach to knowledge as situated, local and provisional is that it makes it possible to subject this knowledge to a much more thoroughgoing scrutiny. If we believe something is true and universally applicable and cannot be changed then that is it, end of story. If, however, we acknowledge that there are a multiplicity of ways of understanding and making sense of the world, then these 'discourses' are opened up for examination. Potter suggests that accepting the construction metaphor of language is productive on pragmatic grounds: 'if we treat descriptions as constructions and constructive, we can ask how they are put together, what materials are used, what sorts of things or events are produced by them, and so on' (Potter 1996: 98). We open up for discussion and debate areas and topics that the mind-in-a-vat form of 'unrealistic realism', with its claims to absolute objectivity and infallibility, closes down or does not even regard as topics worthy of discussion.

The consequences of constructionism

We have said that there are many misunderstandings about realism and relativism and we have tried to erode some of the boundaries between them. However, works which invoke the two terms are commonplace and we need to revisit some of the main criticisms levied at so-called relativism.

The abyss of relativism

One of the major criticisms of SC has been that, once the concept of objective truth is abandoned as the benchmark for evaluating statements and accounts, then we are plunged into 'the abyss of relativism', that is, a situation in which 'anything goes'. Alan Megill suggests that it is usually thought of as being the view that 'there is no neutral way of choosing between the (two or more) sets of background principles and standards of evaluation that could be used to evaluate (assess, establish) the truth of the competing knowledge-claims in question: in brief, no neutral authoritative view is to be found' (Megill 1994: 4). If we have any number of competing accounts and no objective criteria for establishing their validity then how can we make any meaningful distinction between them? For example, could it not mean that a parent's claim to have merely chastised their child appropriately for a misdemeanour is just as valid as the charge by childcare professionals that the parent has caused the child significant harm? It is argued, then, that a sort of stalemate ensues in which no version can be accorded precedence. For the HW professional this is deeply troubling because it provides no secure base from which to act or so it is alleged.

Undecidability: the problem of judgement

A second and related issue is the charge against SC of 'quietism', which Barbara Herrnstein Smith defines as 'the (supposed) politically disabling consequences of a rejection of objectivism: the supposed refusal to make value judgments, the supposed disinclination to take sides on political issues, and, accordingly, the supposed passive support of – or, in the current phrase, "complicity" with – all or any present regimes' (Smith 1994: 289). How could we uphold ethical standards if all we have is competing moral claims and no way of distinguishing between them? If there are no objective grounds upon which to argue in favour of a particular moral stance then is it not the case that injustice, inequality, oppression or abuse cannot be decisively challenged? White has noted that, 'Patently cruel child rearing practices (or even infanticide) could be treated as acceptable so long as the account of the parents was internally consistent' (1997b: 742). Similarly the claims by any social group of discrimination and unjust treatment could be (dis)regarded as simply one among many versions of a state of affairs.

Fighting back

Social constructionists of all persuasions rebut these charges and deny that epistemological relativism is synonymous with moral and political inertia. Richard Harvey Brown (1994) responds as follows to the 'fear of relativism':

> First, fewer atrocities in the history of the world have happened as a result of excessive tolerance than as a result of absolutism. Which is worse, the possibility that evil will be tolerated in the name of cultural relativism, or the promise that future atrocities will be justified by some group's assurance that they are absolutely right? Whereas tyranny is or depends on absolutism, in a democratic polity we are and must be relativists in practice because we exercise judgement as citizens in shaping or finding ethical truth. Democratic practice requires prudent judgement, and such judgement presupposes critical, even deconstructive, reflection on critical experience that is inherently contingent.
>
> (Brown 1994: 27)

Ironically, then, when 'objectivists' invoke the Holocaust, and accuse relativists of 'fence-sitting', they fail to recognize that genocide is a consequence of absolute certainty in the rightness of one's doctrine. Mass destruction does not result from contingency and 'not knowing', but from the illusion of absolute certainty.

Whilst Brown has referred more broadly to the political sphere, we might equally apply this in the more specific context of HW and recognize the importance of a democratic practice which takes account of varying perspectives, acknowledging different viewpoints and making careful judgements of them. So, we can make judgements, but we cannot rely on finding objective certainty or a single truth. Rather, we need a different, more debated and contested engagement with the problem of judgement. For example, Knorr-Cetina and Mulkay propose:

> The belief that scientific knowledge does not merely replicate nature *in no way* commits the epistemic relativist to the view that therefore all forms of knowledge will be equally successful in solving a practical problem, equally adequate in explaining a puzzling phenomenon or, in general, equally acceptable to all participants. Nor does it follow that we cannot discriminate between different forms of knowledge with a view to their relevance or adequacy in regard to a specific goal.
>
> (Knorr-Cetina and Mulkay 1983a: 6)

This is an important point for professionals in HW because it emphasizes that we need not fear that a relativist position suggests that our decisions will be simply random and arbitrary. In child abuse cases, for example, we will not dispense with medical evidence but rather subject it to intensive scrutiny, weighing it up against other information at our disposal. Similarly, with regard to our acceptance of western biomedicine we are likely to take a position of 'sceptical trust' where we go to medical practitioners for consultation and treatment but reserve the right to question the content and the process of our treatment, that is whether what was offered seemed effective and whether how it was offered seemed satisfactory. Or we may seek out 'alternative', 'complementary' practitioners if we so choose.

In addition, 'sturdy relativism' does not imply a society bereft of moral standards. Rather, it asserts that these standards are not fixed and immutable but in the process of being continually renewed and reshaped within a given culture. Again, whilst we may claim that child abuse is intrinsically wrong, it is clear that over the past century our views about the nature and extent of the practice have undergone considerable change (see Hacking (1999) for a sensible and thoughtful review of social constructionism and child abuse). But this does not prevent the making of meaningful value judgements. For Smith, judgements will be made on the basis of 'contingent considerations', that is, a careful appraisal of what is at stake, the possible alternatives and probable outcomes. These 'figurings, weighings and weightings' will take place 'in the light of historical evidence and judicial precedence . . ., broader communal interests and communal goals, and [our] own general values, beliefs, prior experiences' (Smith 1994: 303). Smith insists that there are no automatic guarantees and we need to do what we can to ensure the making of good judgements by monitoring and evaluating the structures, processes and practices of judgement making, in effect developing 'everyday critical practices'.

In their stereotypical forms, realist and relativist perspectives have aroused fierce debate which at times may be said to have generated more heat than light. For example, Goldman (1999) accuses social constructionists of 'veriphobia', an aversion to the truth, and is scathing of their claims. But we have shown that it is equally possible to put forward a case in favour of epistemological relativism by refuting objectivism's 'view from nowhere' (Nagel 1986). It is perhaps worth noting that these debates are not a simple indication of some *fin de siècle* (or millennium) malaise where doubt and uncertainty prevail: they can be traced back across the history of western thought to early Greek and Roman philosophers such as Aristotle and Cicero (Billig 1987; Fish 1995). Indeed, it has been suggested that these two positions on truth and objectivity are fundamental oppositions within western thought, as Richard Rorty indicates:

> There . . . are two ways of thinking about various things . . . The first . . . thinks of truth as a vertical relationship between representations and what is represented. The second . . . thinks of truth horizontally – as the culminating reinterpretation of our predecessors' reinterpretation of their predecessors' reinterpretation . . . It is the difference between regarding truth, goodness, and beauty as eternal objects which we try to locate and reveal, and regarding them as artifacts whose fundamental design we often have to alter.
>
> (Rorty 1982: 92)

In other words, these debates are not new and it may be distracting to worry too much about whether they should be designated postmodern or not. That is why we have chosen the looser formulation of social constructionism which is less politically charged and can more readily encompass the longer historical trajectory of the 'rhetorical turn'. What is important to us here in the assertion of our position is whether a degree of 'sturdy relativism' (or 'realistic realism') inevitably prevents us from achieving rigour in our analyses of HW practice. We contend that this is not the case. We assert that by acknowledging multiple accounts and by analysing how they are constructed to warrant particular claims and to undermine others we can in fact achieve a more rigorous approach to professional practice. We can achieve a greater degree of *reflexivity*.

Reflexivity

What exactly do we mean when we talk about reflexivity? It is a term much used in the social science literature whereas in HW, especially in nursing and social work, the term **reflective practice** has become something of a buzzword. Should we regard the two terms as synonymous or essentially different? At one level they seem to be capable of being used interchangeably. As we said in Chapter 1, it has been suggested that reflexivity is regarded by some as little more than 'benign introspection'. Woolgar suggests that, 'this kind of reflexivity – perhaps more accurately designated "reflection" – entails loose injunctions to "think about what we are doing"'

(1988a: 22). In the social sciences this has resulted in add-on pieces to research reports which give the 'inside story' about how the research was conducted, whilst in HW this has led to a focus on the learning process and the keeping of learning diaries to document how particular aspects of practice have been dealt with. At times, these can have something of a confessional nature. It is not that there is anything wrong with such a focus (it is better to do this than to practise without reflecting on one's actions), but it can be argued that it does not take the process far enough. If we are going to stand by our assertion that knowledge is socially constructed then we need to recognize that this must also apply in our own work.

This means that we need to undertake a process of 'epistemic reflexivity' in which we subject our own knowledge claims to critical analysis. In the social work context White has suggested that:

> epistemic reflexivity may only be achieved by social workers becoming aware of the dominant professional constructions influencing their practice. For example, within contemporary child-care services these pivot around notions of parental dangerousness and fragile childhoods. This does not mean that these constructions have to be rejected wholesale, simply that workers should be explicitly aware of the need to consider the consequences of their analyses and formulations.
>
> (White 1997b: 749)

We are not interested simply in what we have done and how we have gone about things when we reflect on our practice, we must also concern ourselves with the (tacit) assumptions we are making about people, their problems and their needs when we apply knowledge about child development, mental health, learning disability and so forth. This helps us to focus on the ways that

> the identities and needs that the social welfare system fashions for its recipients are *interpreted* identities and needs. Moreover, they are highly political interpretations; and, as such, are in principle open to dispute. Yet these needs and identities are not always recognized as interpretations. Too often, they simply go without saying and are rendered immune from analysis and critique . . .
>
> (Fraser 1989: 153–4, emphasis added)

Summary

In this chapter, we have examined issues in relation to knowledge and truth and explored the realist and relativist positions on how we come to know the world. In its objectivist, mind-in-a-vat form, the realist perspective is characterized by an adherence to the correspondence theory of the truth in which a mirror is held up to the 'real world'. From this perspective, language acts as a neutral medium for the description of things and events. In contrast, the relativist perspective asserts that language constructs the world that we experience. Our understandings of mental health, for example, are historically and socially constructed. They shape our understandings of the signs and symptoms of mental illness and exclude other possibilities, in particular understandings which appear to be based on tradition, superstition or pre-scientific thought. We then discussed the conventional criticism of social constructionism: that it renders us incapable of judging various competing positions and thus opens up the prospect of moral as well as epistemological relativism. The dangers of absolutism were pointed out alongside the assertion that a relativist position about the way knowledge of the world is constructed need not lead to apathy, quietism or nihilism.

We have tried to encourage you to think in less polemical terms about realism and relativism. Saying that we cannot with certainty know everything about a particular person, situation or event is not the same as saying that we can know nothing, or that there is nothing to know. In essence, what we have been suggesting in this chapter is that quests for absolute certainty and truth tend to close down discussion and encourage a blinkered approach to practice – they encourage a very *unrealistic* realism. When HW professionals feel defensive about their practice, as they do currently, it is easy to see truth and certainty as the only viable solution. We have argued for a different approach in which the complexity and ambiguity of practice are acknowledged. The concept of reflexivity was explored to suggest the importance not only of reflecting upon practice and how it is carried out but also upon the knowledge claims which (implicitly) underpin that practice. As we proceed to set out our argument in greater detail we hope that you may be convinced that reflexivity can open up new and fruitful ways to examine HW practice.

CHAPTER 3

Analysing talk and text: building a conceptual framework

In the previous chapters we built an argument for a different approach to the understanding of practice wisdom in health and welfare. We argued that, by using some of the insights from social constructionism, we may open up for analysis aspects of professional thinking and decision making which escape regulation and audit in the traditional sense. The discussion in Chapter 2 introduced the relevant philosophical and theoretical positions that bear on our work. However, we need now to explore the ways in which some of these ideas have been applied empirically.

This chapter explores concepts and methods, taken from a number of disciplines and academic traditions, which may be used to analyse conversation and written accounts of various kinds. After introducing the various frameworks, we present some ideas which we hope will help readers to examine in more detail their processes of decision making, and those aspects of their practice which they take for granted or may consider to be intuitive or based on 'gut feelings'. Using a number of examples taken from empirical work, we shall ask you to suspend your judgements about whether the particular versions of events presented are true or false, and ask you to consider instead why an account is or is not persuasive. The ideas we present are intended to be an essential supplement to rigorous observation and the careful application of theory and knowledge, and not a replacement for them. It is not knowledge and theory themselves that are the problem, but their innocent and unquestioning use.

Before continuing, we should like you to reflect upon the strategies that you employed the last time you tried to persuade someone either to do something or to believe your version of events. It is likely that you are not fully aware of the complex reasoning processes involved in crafting an argument, although we all employ these techniques routinely. For example, it is likely that you tried to put facts together in specific ways which supported your argument, that you attempted to convey your reasonableness and your capacity and willingness to listen to other viewpoints (which you had, of course, considered carefully, but rejected). For example, you may have taken care not to interrupt the other, and to display your interest in their arguments. You may also have tried to convey your expertise in relation to the subject under discussion, either by making others aware that you were a direct witness to the events in question, or by making some other reference to your particular skills, experience or knowledge.

Some of these strategies are generally well known and we may look for them routinely, but not always consciously, in making judgements about things we are told. However, there are other, rather more subtle strategies available which are not generally considered in day-to-day encounters. In this chapter, we introduce some concepts which can assist in analysing conversation and argument. In order to examine the kinds of 'intuitive' phenomenon we have described, it is necessary to draw upon 'microanalyses' of conversation or written accounts (such as letters, or case files). These are detailed dissections of people's talk or of the documents they produce. For example, attention may be paid to the specific words used and their order, or to the sequencing of phrases, or to the 'turns' which people take to hold the floor in a conversation. In this book, we have drawn on a number of different conceptual frameworks, for example sociology, ethnomethodology and **narrative**, conversation and discourse analysis. These frameworks have a range of philosophical, disciplinary or methodological orientations. There are sometimes subtle, but very important, differences between them. However, the frameworks share a particular orientation to language, treating it not as a mirror of reality, but as a means to construct, or cause us to see that reality in a particular way. At the same time, people use language in skilful ways to 'make' knowledge, that is to diagnose, categorize or order cases. This was illustrated in the case examples in Chapter 1.

The various traditions share this orientation towards language, but there are points of disagreement between proponents of the various schools of thought. This chapter summarizes the main features of each school before going on to consider some examples of analyses of talk and text which often draw on aspects of different frameworks.

Analysing Discourse and discourse

We need first to examine some of the terms we have been using and to attend to the particular ways in which they are being used in this book. To begin with, let us return to the title of this chapter and consider what we mean by 'talk and text'. The meaning of the word 'talk' in the title is straightforward: it refers to any conversation, even talking to oneself. A little more needs to be said about the use of the term 'text'. Text may, of course, refer to written material, such as case files, medical notes, nursing records, policy documents, or the law. However, it is possible also to view talk, or conversation as a text, that is as a piece of language which can be analysed, rather as one might analyse a novel for its internal order and for the ways in which words have been used to particular effect. This is made possible by the use of detailed transcripts of sequences of 'talk' which have been previously audiotaped. We say more about the various types of transcript and their use in due course.

First, however, let us consider why we have used the term **discourse** in the heading to this section, in both upper and lower case. The term 'discourse analysis' is often used as though it related to just one conceptual framework. However, it can mean a number of things. It may refer to language used within organizations or in encounters with service users, as this is displayed in talk, or written texts such as case notes (discourse). It may also refer to ways of thinking (Discourses) about particular phenomena, such as terminal illness, childhood, bereavement, sex, race, the family, or mental health, and how these reflect particular historical, political and moral positions. We have used the term 'Discourse' to refer to these broad societal influences.

These kinds of distinctions have led a number of commentators to sub-classify discourse analysis. For example, the use of upper and lower case in the heading above is intended to differentiate between discourse as talk in action and Discourse as a body of knowledge (Walker 1988). Walker contends that Discourses (forms of thought and knowledge, which may be, for example, theories or political ideas) are reproduced within discourse (talk) at 'the point of its articulation' (Walker 1988: 55). Therefore, when analysing any conversation it should be possible to look for Discourse(s) and also to examine how words are assembled and used (Miller 1994).

There is some debate over which level of analysis is most important, and about whether the specialized conceptual and methodological frameworks used to analyse one level can properly be used as part of a more eclectic approach. These arguments generally concern the particular ways in which people as actors in society are viewed within each tradition. In turn, they relate to longstanding questions within social theory about the nature of the relationship between the individual and society. These questions can be crudely summarized as follows:

- Do individuals create society through their actions or is it an entity greater than the sum of its parts which imposes certain things upon them? This is often known as the structure (society and its institutions, including language) versus agency (people and their activities, talk and interactions) debate.
- How do everyday events taking place between individuals within homes, organizations, clinics, hospitals and so forth (including professional encounters) relate to the 'big' institutions of society such as the state,

government, the law, the economy and, increasingly, the international institutions and corporations. This is known as the micro/macro divide.

- How is control exercised over the individuals in society? In other words, what is power, and where does it come from?

Let us now examine the ways in which these questions are dealt with within the various frameworks upon which we are going to draw. The summaries that follow are not by any means an exhaustive collection of the different kinds of discourse analysis: such an enterprise would run to several volumes. Our purpose here is to introduce to a professional audience some controversies, concepts and methods from social science. We must therefore strike a balance between doing justice to complex debates and providing focused discussions relevant to your practice. For those who want to know more we recommend Heritage (1984), Silverman (1985, 1993, 1997b), Buttny (1993) and Potter (1996).

Rediscovering the 'actor': ethnomethodology and conversation analysis

Ethnomethodology is a rather obscure, technical-sounding word which refers simply to 'folk' (ethno) 'methods' (ways of doing things): in other words to those complex forms of shared knowledge, upon which we all draw in 'doing being ordinary' (Sacks 1984). Ethnomethodology, then, is a kind of qualitative research which provides a means to analyse and explore the ways in which people make sense of and reproduce ordinary social practices.

Let us look in some detail at the opening section of Harold Garfinkel's seminal text on ethnomethodology where he describes his 'respecification' of sociology:

> The following studies seek to treat practical activities, practical circumstances, and practical sociological reasoning as topics of empirical study . . . Their central recommendation is that the activities whereby members produce and manage settings of organized everyday affairs are identical with members' procedures for making those settings 'account-able' . . . observable-and-reportable, i.e. available to members as situated practices of looking-and-telling.
>
> (Garfinkel 1967: 1)

What Garfinkel is saying here is that ethnomethodology seeks to move away from adjudicating on whether a particular practice is right or wrong, to look instead at how that practice gets done and what makes it work. This may sound a little strange at first, but it is central to what we are trying to do in this book.

In ethnomethodology, **accounts** assume a new significance, as all social action involves both an act (or an utterance) and a subsequent (or prospective) account of that act. Thus, what people say cannot be taken as an unproblematic reflection of what really happened. Accounts *of* events also usually embody some kind of account or justification *for* the action taken. The way in which the account is constructed will be determined by the context in which the talk takes place. In the selection of account, therefore, social actors will draw on shared understandings about how a competent individual (HW professional) should properly behave under a given set of circumstances.

This kind of understanding can yield insights into professional practice. For example, discussing the particular problems associated with assessment of risk in cases of self-harm, Varley and White (1995) note that the act of self-harm is a breach of accepted norms of behaviour; it is therefore 'accountable'. This is particularly so when the individual is also a parent. Drawing on insights from Harvey Sacks' study of a suicide prevention centre (Sacks 1967), the authors note:

> Where a woman has child care responsibilities, a dual accountability results. She must explain the act of self-harm and also account for the breach of the normative rules of parental responsibility. We are not suggesting that individuals contrive to produce inaccurate accounts, but that their version will be governed by common-sense notions of how to demonstrate 'despair and loss of hope', so that others will judge it to be understandable in the circumstances. The aim is to construct the act of self-harm in a socially meaningful and morally adequate way.
>
> (Varley and White 1995: 145)

Varley and White argue that standard assessment schedules fail to take into account the imperative to produce a moral account of the action taken. Once 'accounts' are seen as socially meaningful, assumptions about unmediated access to an authentic version appear naive.

This does not mean that we are arguing that it does not matter whether a child has actually been injured, or whether a person really has a dependency on alcohol which has caused them to become ill and to lose their home and family. There are different requirements for different aspects of practice. There are times when we are doing decision making and intervention, and there are times when we are thinking about what we have done or what we should do. Of course, these processes can go on at the same time, but the ideas we put forward in this book are intended to add rigour to practitioners' understandings of their own day-to-day judgements. We shall argue in this book that by following ethnomethodology's example and adopting a policy of 'indifference' (Garfinkel and Sacks 1970) as to whether an account is true or false and looking instead at professional talk as a 'practical accomplishment', practitioners may find a new form of reflexivity. Sometimes, there is a strong argument for forgetting about what we know and concentrating instead on *how* we think we know it and how we *do* the process of knowing. We provide some examples of this kind of work later in the chapter.

Conversation analysis

Conversation analysis (CA) grew from ethnomethodology's focus on the detail of what people actually do. The recognition that language was about more than description and that it actually performed things led to a search for empirical methods which could record and analyse instances of talk. The attention in CA is on a particular aspect of active meaning making: the sequential features of talk, that is the turns people take, the pauses in the talk, the way new topics are introduced and so forth (see Sacks *et al.* 1974). Conversation analysis uses detailed transcripts which attempt to represent as much of the 'real-time' talk as possible. Often, unconventional spellings are used to indicate regional accent, pauses are recorded, as are laughs, coughs, outbreaths and what are known as non-lexical vocalizations (such as erm, or ahh) (see West 1996 for a discussion of transcripts and transcription in research). Some examples of these transcripts appear in later chapters and the transcription symbols are listed in the appendix. These methods have facilitated the detailed analysis of particular types of encounter, such as those taking place between doctors and patients, to show, for example, the precise ways in which doctors keep control of the talk through their sequential conversational strategies (see, for example, Hughes 1982).

Returning to the central questions from social theory we referred to above, in ethnomethodology and CA, the actor is central. It is what individuals do and say in their encounters with one another that creates 'society'. Some exponents, particularly of CA, go further and argue that any concept of structure is redundant, since *all* 'order' must be produced anew *within* each encounter. Therefore, the particular social categories to which a person belongs (race, class, gender) are not important to the conversation analyst or ethnomethodologist. The ethnomethodologist is interested instead in what takes place in the encounter itself. If we cannot see it, observe it, capture it in transcript, it is simply, for all practical purposes, irrelevant. For example: ethnomethodology 'conceives social settings as *self-organizing* and for just that reason has no further need for the received concepts of "social action" and "social structure"' (Sharrock and Button 1991: 14).

Here we can see that although ethnomethodology is concerned with the active processes of meaning making, and hence is of considerable use to us in our enterprise, some of its claims are not without their problems. For example, understanding the dominance of some ideas is particularly important in exploring professional practices, but that understanding cannot be gained via the principles of ethnomethodology. For instance, the preoccupation with the assessment of risk in childcare social work is not invented anew in each encounter (Sibeon 1994). Ethnomethodologists accept that there are often multiple and competing accounts given and perspectives held by different 'members', or by the same individual in different contexts. We agree, and have also argued that HW professionals often confront multiple versions of events. However, if this is the case, the 'unsaid', or the 'could have been said if circumstances had been different', may become extremely significant (McHoul 1994), reflecting, as the ethnomethodologists would accept, different dominant contextual expectations (or 'background expectancies'), but also, surely, wider Discourses (contemporary morality, dominant knowledges, or sets of ideas which originate outside the encounter) (Jayyusi 1991). For example, the word 'mother' carries a set of cultural prescriptions and proscriptions which are worthy of attention in both social research and professional practice. In short, in its separatist form (which undoubtedly has its place) CA is strong on the analysis of talk in sequence but weak on the analysis of the power of certain phrases or forms of thought which predate the encounter, which brings us to the work of Foucault.

Foucault, Discourse and micro-power

We have pointed to the strengths of ethnomethodology as a means of analysing taken-for-granted aspects of professional practice. However, we have suggested that perhaps it gives the 'actor' a little too much freedom (it is too voluntaristic). There is often insufficient attention given to the power of certain dominant ideas and their supporting organizational and institutional frameworks. The work of the philosopher, historian and social theorist, Michel Foucault (see, for example, Foucault 1973, 1976, 1980) has become ubiquitous over the past decade, and for good reason. Foucault shares with CA (although they are uneasy bedfellows) a focus on language as doing more than just describing objects and events. Language structures, constructs or produces them. However, Foucault has a radically different idea of the actor. For Foucault, the actor is 'decentred'. This is a confusing word, often misrepresented as meaning that people do not think, make choices, or feel. This is a misreading. Rather, Foucault's point is that certain ideas (regimes of truth) have the capacity to make us think, feel and do particular things. We are 'constituted through discourse'. Let us provide an example. We are both mothers, and we routinely make judgements about whether we are good enough mothers based on standards of behaviour, thought and emotions which 'mothers' are supposed to display or possess. These norms are propagated by the media, agony columns, books, health visitors, midwives and so forth (see, for example, Rose 1985, 1989, 1998; Burman 1994). We therefore judge ourselves and self-police against standards of behaviour derived from developmental psychology in particular. We are 'inscribed' with the discourses of late twentieth-century 'sensitive' mothering.

This does not mean that mothers do not sometimes feel angry with their children, or that they are always there to listen, or that they never fail. Rather it means that they know they are failing. They know what it means to be a mother. However, this is mothering in the here and now. It bears traces of earlier ideas about mothering, but it also has its own quality. This is what Foucault means by the decentred subject – we are all inscribed with ideas about what it is to be a person, a mother, a nurse, a social worker, a judge or a paediatrician, which are historically contingent. We can resist these inscriptions, but in so doing we will inevitably produce some more. As HW professionals we are also crucial to the dissemination of these ideas, as we ourselves pass judgement on the psychological health and emotional adjustment of others. Of course, just as the actor in CA may be seen as too free, so the actor in Foucault's work may be seen as too constrained in the 'iron cage' of discourse (or rather Discourse).

This is not the place for detailed theoretical debate, for our purposes we want to argue that we can look at extracts of talk and text and analyse them using all kinds of different lenses. We can look at the taken-for-granted practical reasoning, the detailed sequential features of the talk, and the bodies of knowledge or moral categories on which the participants draw (Miller 1994). This kind of layered synthesis brings us to the 'new' **rhetorics**.

Performance and rhetoric: talk in action, action in talk

Drawing on the kinds of conceptual frameworks illustrated above, then, discourse analysis is a heterogeneous phenomenon. It is not one thing, but many. We now turn to a body of work which has become known as **discursive psychology**. A number of psychologists have become concerned with the neglect in traditional psychology of the subtleties of language use, and particularly its ambiguity and contestability (Billig 1987; Billig *et al.* 1988; Shotter 1993; Antaki 1994a; Potter 1996; Potter and Wetherell 1995; Edwards 1997).

Discursive psychology draws on concepts and methods from microanalyses of talk, such as CA, and also on the idea that certain forms of thought or knowledge can become dominant and can cause us to see phenomena in particular ways (for instance, as a child at risk, or as a person failing to 'come to terms' with their grief, or as a 'bed blocker'). Discursive psychology has been particularly concerned with what Edwards (1997) calls the action-performative features of talk, and of storytelling, and with the intrinsically argumentative (or discursive) nature of language (here a debt is owed to the philosopher Mikhail Bakhtin: see Bell and Gardiner 1998). Although they draw on CA and ethnomethodology, the discursive psychologists are unashamedly eclectic and are particularly interested in 'could have been said if circumstances had been different' features of **everyday talk** and written accounts, which ethnomethodology sometimes neglects.

This makes their work very useful for the reflexive analysis of professional activity. Derek Edwards summarizes this aspect as follows:

> It is not only that descriptions could have been otherwise; usually there is a fairly specific 'otherwise' that is at issue. That is to say, descriptions are selected and assembled with regard to *actual* alternatives, and sometimes specific counter-descriptions. They are not merely different from otherwise possible descriptions, but have a *rhetorical*, argumentative quality with regard to what somebody else might say (Billig, 1987). This is a feature, not only of overt disagreements between people, but of discourse in general. We can always inspect a piece of discourse, even the most straightforwardly uncontroversial and descriptive . . . and ask: what is being denied by that assertion?
>
> (Edwards 1997: 8)

This attention to the argumentative nature of language is important and it is evident in all of the examples from practice we presented in Chapter 1. When we talk of 'rhetoric' or 'rhetorical potency' in this book, we are using it in the same sense as in the extract above. That is, we do not mean to imply that a rhetorical expression is untrue or intended quite deliberately to deceive, as is sometimes meant, for example, when journalists refer to 'political rhetoric'; rather we are referring to words and phrases which do a particular job of persuading, usually by mobilizing *facts* in a specific order, with certain emphases, or which draw on culturally dominant ideas and moral judgements. Rhetoric is, put simply, powerful talk (Potter and Wetherell 1995: 82).

Narrative and storytelling

In the discussion of discursive psychology above, we have referred to the 'storied' or **narrative** nature of people's descriptions of events or circumstances. 'Narrative analysis' is itself a heterogeneous field and it is worthwhile our introducing some of the different kinds of narrative analysis here. First, what specifically is a narrative? Mishler (1986) defines it as a particular kind of 'recapitulation', which preserves 'the temporal ordering of events', that is, which presents events as the antecedents or consequences of each other. Clearly, these kinds of consequential accounts must attribute cause and effect in particular ways. On a similar note, a concise summary of Labov's (1972) work on the structure of narrative is provided by Atkinson:

> Labov suggests that narratives consist of ordered utterances that reflect the temporal order of a sequence of events, and he derives an elementary structure for narratives. The basic structural units are: Abstract (optional – a prefatory summary); Orientation (locates the story in terms of persons, places and times); Complication (what happened, expressed as a sequence of events); Evaluation (conveys the point of the narrative, and the point of view of the narrator; Result

(or the resolution of the story); Coda (optional – a closing summary, or recapitulation signalling a closure of a story sequence) . . .

(Atkinson 1995: 103)

In this final recapitulation we can assume that the storyteller either sums up their own reading of the events, reaching some kind of conclusion, or signals what issues remain unresolved in the story. Most commentators agree, then, that narratives allow individuals to construct a version of reality in which they attribute cause, offer explanations and attempt to convince the hearer or reader of the plausibility of their version of events. The detailed definitions of narratives which have been generated have considerable usefulness in analysing narrative form. However, there are some dangers in using classifications of this kind in isolation. For example, Edwards asserts:

> The temptation for analysts using [Labov's] scheme is to start with the categories and see how the things people say can be fitted into them, and, having coded everything as one category or another, to call that the analysis, and then compare it to other findings. In that role, as a coding scheme, these kinds of structural categories impose rather than reveal, obscuring the particularity of specific details, and how that particularity is crucial for the occasioned, action-performative workings of discourse.

(Edwards 1997: 276)

It is with these rhetorical, or action-performative, features of professional and client narratives that we are concerned here. We have treated narratives as the products of contingent, but not unlimited, choices, and will go on to show how (not necessarily self-conscious, but partly habitual) decisions about 'where to start a story [are] major and rhetorically potent [ways] of managing causality and accountability' (Edwards 1997: 277) in professional talk and encounters with service users. This focus builds upon the general agreement outlined above that narratives, by definition, embody some sort of chronology, with certain events being presented as the antecedents of others.

Applying the frameworks

We can assume that, as HW professionals, we rely on the same kinds of sense making processes we use routinely in our lives when we decide whether we trust and believe others. Likewise, other HW professionals and users of our service also mobilize skills (or 'rhetorical strategies') in persuasion. These strategies may not be evenly distributed in the population. Some people are better persuaders than others. The remainder of this chapter looks at the empirical application of the ideas we discussed above to examine some of the ways in which accounts are made persuasive, or are undermined. In so doing, we want to underscore the moral dimensions of practice in HW.

Strategies for arguing and persuading: constructing deviance

In professional practice in HW, decisions about whether an action is 'normal' or 'deviant' are central. We are using these terms broadly, and would include decisions about someone's parenting ability, their adjustment to chronic illness or bereavement, their mental health status, their ability to make decisions about their lives, their relationships with others and so forth. This bears upon our discussion in two ways. First, in order to define someone as deviant, the HW professional must either observe particular behaviours or be told about them by others. In turn, the professional must go on to construct their own story about the individual(s) concerned. Second, the ascription of deviant status to an individual is a major way in which their version of events can be undermined and invalidated, as is shown graphically in some of the examples in Chapter 1. Some of the time, the degree of fit between a particular story and the objective truths of a case may be overwhelming, or it may be so poor as to be ridiculous. However, most of the time, for HW professionals, this is not the case. Decisions rely on judgements about plausibility. So how do people 'do' plausibility?

Dorothy Smith, in her 1978 seminal sociological paper on the ways in which people use language to signal deviance in another, makes the following observations about her practice as a social scientist, which we think also apply to many professional assessments:

> The ordinary working situation of the social scientist presents her with a special difficulty. It is a normal feature of her data that the events with which she is concerned have travelled into the past and cannot be checked over. The perceptual decay of the phenomena she would describe and explain, make her singularly dependent on records, descriptions etc., of various kinds.
>
> (Smith 1978: 23)

Smith recognizes that these records or descriptions are already organized in particular ways. She draws on studies of professional practice, particularly in psychiatry and youth justice (see, for example, Cicourel 1968), to argue that considerable informal work goes on before, and during, a person's involvement with welfare agencies through which they gradually become defined as in need of a service.

In the interview analysed by Smith, a student is describing to a fellow student, who is acting as interviewer, the behaviour of one of her friends, K. The following are typical extracts.

Extract 3.1a

My recognition that there might be something wrong was very gradual, and I was actually the last of her close friends who was openly willing to admit that she was becoming mentally ill . . . We would go to the beach or the pool on a hot day, and I would sort of dip in and just lie in the sun, while K insisted that she had to swim 30 lengths . . .

(Smith 1978: 28)

Extract 3.1b

K is so intense about everything at times, she tries too hard. Her sense of proportion is out of kilter. When asked casually to help in a friend's garden, she went at it for hours, never stopping, barely looking up . . .

(Smith 1978: 29)

Extract 3.1c

A little while after the girls began to share the apartment, they had to face the fact that K was definitely queer. She would take baths religiously every night and pin up her hair, but she would leave the bath dirty. She would wash dishes, but leave them dirty too . . . We began to notice that she could never do two things at once, such as: watch TV and knit, or knit and talk, or eat and talk, or eat and talk and listen. If she talked her food would get cold, she would start when everyone else had finished. Or she would ask, when is dinner ready, and when told in about 10 minutes, she would go off and prepare herself something entirely different

(Smith 1978: 30)

Clearly, we are being invited by the student (Angela), and indeed by the interviewer who supports Angela's version, to believe that K is mentally ill. Like the ethnomethodologists, we should like you to suspend judgement for the moment and to concentrate instead on the internal organization of the account being presented. Some of the key concepts are described below. We shall be using them again later in this book.

First, note that certain expectations are set up early in the account (see Extract 3.1a). It is suggested that K was becoming mentally ill but that Angela was the last of her close friends to accept this. This has the effect of casting Angela as a witness to events, who is reluctant to see what is clear to others (that K is mentally ill). In making this statement Angela reinforces the plausibility of her version, signalling that she had to be confronted with overwhelming evidence before making her judgement. She makes explicit references throughout the interview to K's behaviour as odd or queer. Moreover, as she has the privileged status as witness to the events, she would be difficult to challenge unless the challenger had also been present on the occasions she reports. Angela defines herself and the other significant players as K's friends, which amplifies the force of her account. This definition sets up the expectation that she and they had K's best interests at heart. Angela includes K's other friends in the account as independent verifiers of her version. She uses the first person plural 'we' to signal the collective view that K's behaviour is deviant and odd.

In Smith's terms, these procedures help to **authorize** Angela's version. This gives Angela **definitional privilege** – the power to define. It is her behaviour and not K's which provides the norm (for example, 'We would go to the beach or the pool on a hot day, and I would sort of dip in and just lie in the sun, while K insisted that she had to swim 30 lengths'). As Smith points out, none of the behaviours described by Angela intrinsically provides evidence that K is mentally ill. Smith notes that some descriptions of K's behaviour may indeed be read as strengths (swimming 30 lengths, bathing every night) were it not for the skilful work of the teller of the tale. By the careful assembly of the facts of K's behaviour, as readers or hearers we are led to perceive her responses 'as arising from a state of the individual and not as motivated by her by features of her situation' (Smith 1978: 38). Contextual information is assembled so that K's behaviour does not appear understandable in the circumstances or motivated by her rational analysis of the situation.

Smith calls these strategies **contrast structures**. In a contrast structure, the first part of the statement sets up an expectation, in this instance provided by Angela who has the power to define, while the others signal deviation from this expectation. For example:

1 'We would go to the beach on a hot day'. This identifies the context of the action and hence allows the reader to make predictions about what sort of behaviour is appropriate.
2 'I would sort of dip in and just lie in the sun'. This provides an example of normal behaviour as prescribed by the person with definitional privilege.
3 'While K insisted that she had to swim 30 lengths'. Here, K's behaviour, which may otherwise be considered appropriate activity for a pool, is contrasted with the norm set by Angela and is also presented as obsessional by the use of the words 'insisted that she had to'.

Examining the extracts above, these structures can be seen elsewhere, for example:

1 'When asked casually to help in a friend's garden'. It was only a casual request.
2 'She went at it for hours, never stopping, barely looking up'. She took it far too seriously.

As we show in later chapters, contrast structures are ubiquitous in professional accounts and are also employed by the users of welfare services to make persuasive their own stories about deviance in others.

Harvey Sacks' work on **membership categorization devices** (see, for example, Sacks 1972a, b) can usefully supplement Smith's analyses and there are many overlaps with the notion of contrast structures. Sacks' work in conversation analysis has been highly influential in sociology, discourse analysis and related fields. Sacks argues that when we assign individuals to particular social categories, such as mother, father, child, old person or dying person, we mobilize a set of culturally prescribed expectations of proper behaviour. So that, if 'mother' is synonymous with care and nurturance, when we use the term 'mother' and follow that with a description of non-caring behaviour, we will ascribe deviance to that person. We can mark them as morally deficient. The behaviour associated with a particular category is known as **category-bound activity**. Often, membership categories occur in pairs, for example, mother–child, husband–wife. These clusters set up behavioural expections about how one part of the pair will relate to the other. For example, a mother may be expected to be nurturing towards her child, and the child may be seen as dependent upon the mother. Such pairings are called **standardized relational pairs**.

Hester (1992) has shown how membership categorizations are used routinely in referrals to statutory welfare agencies (see also Jayyusi 1984). If we return to the extracts in Chapter 1 we can see some examples. For instance, in relation to Wendy (Extract 1.5), the child with learning difficulties:

> She is incontinent and I was quite surprised how mother seems detached, leaving her in a smelly condition throughout the consultation until I prompted her.

In this statement, rather than use the person's name, the child psychiatrist uses the membership category 'mother'. This establishes an expectation of certain category-bound behaviours (caring, nurturance). These are not forthcoming, and the description of behaviours which precede and follow the categorization 'mother' have the effect of assigning the woman to the subcategory 'neglectful mother'. Almost endless subcategories can be generated in this way (see Hall (1997) for a discussion of subcategorization in social work).

Membership categorizations can also be seen in the Sophie Byrne case (Extract 1.7). You will remember that a team of social workers are discussing the possibility that Sophie (aged 10) is being sexually abused by an older boy. We can see how the team leader is signalling Sophie's deviation from the category-bound expectations of childhood. In this case, however, adults are cast as culprits ('the children often arrive late for school and are not really collected'). This is because one of the category-bound expectations of childhood is vulnerability and passivity.

> The children often arrive late for school and are not really collected. Oliver is 7, is he 7? . . . There were no major concerns at the previous school. However, there had been one incident outside school where Sophie had been with a group of older boys who were smoking.

Membership categorizations not only tell us about professional norms but also expose taken-for-granted cultural beliefs about expected behaviours, and hence open these up for debate.

From deviance to moral judgement

Returning to Smith's analysis of the interview with Angela, whilst the subtle rhetorical work in the account could lead us to believe that we are hearing a neutral account of K's descent into mental illness, there are clearly other possible readings. Smith notes that the account could be seen as kind of communal freezing out process, and that K's 'odd' behaviour may thus become understandable in the circumstances. She notes that these two possible readings appear to be mutually exclusive, or incommensurable. Whilst thinking of one reading it is almost impossible to see the other. The two versions produce a 'figure–ground' effect.

Smith notes that under normal circumstances further questions may be asked of Angela in order to check certain features of her account. This option is no longer available to her. It seems that, when she first heard it, Smith took the student interviewer's version of the story at face value: that is, she took it as an account of K becoming mentally ill. She did not question the account or seek clarification. On reading the transcript, however, she began to see the alternative 'freezing out' version.

As Cuff (1993) points out, this alternative reading depends on certain inferences about the moral positions of both Angela and the interviewer. That is, it depends on us seeing them, not as friends of K, but as enemies or rivals. Cuff draws on the work of Garfinkel (1967) which suggests that in everyday interaction people display a 'natural attitude', that they treat the accounts and requests of others in good faith. They do not routinely seek to discredit them or demand further evidence, as they might if they were, for example, scientists undertaking an experiment or lawyers in court (this kind of rigorous scepticism Garfinkel calls the scientific attitude, or scientific rationality). For everyday purposes, then, accounts are treated by others as true *unless there is some evidence of bias or partisanship*.

Cuff (1993) takes Smith's work considerably further by analysing how members (of society) who are telling a tale in circumstances in which they may be construed as partisan, such as when giving an account of the break-up of their own marriage, routinely anticipate the charge of bias and construct their account accordingly. The capacity to produce an account that will be heard as 'morally adequate' is crucial to the believability of that version. So, in reaching decisions about the veracity of a particular version of events, we tend to rely not on a rigorous process of questioning and clarification, but on our sense of the person's moral position in relation to the topic under discussion.

It might be argued that all this is irrelevant to the subject matter of this book. Is it not the case that professionals go about their business using scientific rationality, a rigorous questioning of versions? Our answer is, sometimes yes, but often no. For practical purposes, in order to decide when such question/answer sequences are necessary, professionals must draw on the same set of criteria used by lay people in their everyday encounters. If they never took people's accounts on face value, they would spend a great deal of time on very few cases and would irritate their clients beyond measure.

Moreover, what is considered to be a morally adequate version may well be affected by certain professional preferences, ideologies or discourses. For example, remembering the struggle between Vladimir (Extracts 1.3 and 1.4), the prison psychiatric patient, and his psychiatrist discussed in Chapter 1, if one were a practising psychiatrist, one might find the doctors' version more convincing. Vladimir is, after all, a prisoner (a membership category associated with untrustworthiness) who has been diagnosed as mentally ill (does not know his own mind). However, if one were an advocate employed by an anti-psychiatry, 'survivor' organization, one might well read the interview as evidence of oppressive medical practice.

The judgement may also be affected by the gender of the person giving the account or by their age, or rather by the set of cultural ideas associated with those groupings. Read the following extract and think about how you would feel about it as a professional dealing with this family.

Extract 3.2

We have fights, sure. When [he] starts harping on about something and doesn't stop, one really gets down. Then we have an argument . . . First comes the screaming, back and forth, then maybe some flowers go flying . . . but I don't call this assault. There was no hitting with fists or in the face . . . It was more like this (acts out slaps and shoves). It was just a reaction . . . you start shoving . . . react like a human being . . . Maybe sometimes you spit in [his] face . . .

(Hyden and McCarthy 1994: 553)

This account appears to be referring to a marital row in which the female party 'slaps and shoves' her male partner. However, we have changed the gender of the 'speaker'. The bracketed words read 'she' and 'her'. The account was in fact given by a man convicted of assaulting his wife. Knowing this, you may hear it as the assailant's attempt to excuse and minimize his behaviour. If the account were given by a mother who was describing a fight with her 10-year-old son, your view may change again, particularly if you had responsibilities for the protection of children. These different readings result from cultural expectations and not from the flow of words on the page. They result from inferences about moral character. Moral adequacy, as Cuff (1993) points out, is often assessed by reference to membership categorizations and subcategorizations and the range of morally sanctioned behaviour associated with them. However, as we show in later chapters, some moral judgements are easier to make than others, and some people are more skilled than others in constructing their account in a morally adequate way.

Summary

This chapter has put some empirical flesh on the theoretical bones of Chapter 2. We have introduced a number of different analytical frameworks which can be used to analyse talk and text, and have looked at examples of empirical work on the construction of versions. We have encouraged you to think about people's accounts of their experiences, paying attention to the internal features of the accounts and what makes them persuasive. This is not because we think HW professionals can adopt the privileged position of qualitative researchers and simply refuse to choose between competing versions. Rather, by bracketing judgement temporarily, other phenomena, which may inform it, are exposed and new lines of questioning may thus occur to you. The analytical devices discussed here, which will be built upon in later chapters, can also help you to reflect on your work in new ways.

We have introduced the following analytical concepts:

- Definitional privilege
- Contrast structures
- Membership categorization devices
- Category-bound activities
- Standardized relational pairs
- Moral adequacy.

By examining how these devices are deployed in various constellations within spoken and written accounts, we can start to understand the ways in which language works to construct a version of events.

Finally, we have argued that the traditional distinction between facts (as true) and rhetoric (as persuasion and propaganda) must be dispensed with. The most rhetorically potent phrases may also be true, and will certainly involve the assembly of facts. We have also argued that, for HW professionals, 'judgement' as a cognitive process of decision making is often dependent on being 'judgemental', that is on making assessments of people's moral worth, or at least on the moral adequacy of their accounts. If this is to be a reflexive process you need the right tools for the job.

CHAPTER 4

Conversational strategies: lessons from everyday talk

We have argued in the preceding chapters that facts are made rather than simply described. They are not objective descriptions of things, events and states of affairs existing 'out there' conveyed by the transparent medium of language. Instead we have suggested that language has a 'dynamic and pragmatic character' (Wooffitt 1992: 12). Describing and providing factual accounts are therefore social activities in which 'everyday language is seen as constitutive of everyday life rather than a detached commentary upon it' (Wooffitt 1992: 12). In all aspects of our lives we construct facts to do certain things, to achieve certain effects in dialogue with other people. In describing things verbally or in written form (for the time being we will focus on the former) we make choices about how we say things, even if we do not feel that this is a very conscious, well thought out process because it comes so easily to us.

This prompts us to take a different approach to descriptions and factual accounts. If we take the stance that facts are mere descriptions then we are not really interested in how things are put into words; we want to focus on *what* is being said or written and to read off from this some information about the world. On the other hand, if we take the view that facts are made and that what matters are the circumstances in which they are produced, that is if we suggest that knowledge is much more provisional and local, then we become interested in the production of these local knowledges and *how* they are accomplished in a particular time and place. However, as suggested in the previous chapter, we would also argue that people enact their encounters within particular discursive frameworks, for example about 'normal' and 'deviant' parenting behaviour. When a friend tells us about a 9-year-old child regularly being left alone by her mother, our discussion about the rights and wrongs of this, the implications for the child and what should be done about it are framed in terms of our prior understandings of 'good mothering' and children's 'needs' generated from our personal and professional experiences. We draw on this knowledge to make our judgements and to make pronouncements about what ought to be done.

In this chapter, we want to take forward our discussion of the issues by focusing on some of the strategies that people employ to make their descriptions and factual accounts believable. We begin by looking at talk in general, how people go about the task of persuading others in their everyday social interactions. We want to argue that there are some strategies and devices that are used very generally within ordinary talk. In the following chapter we explore how these devices and strategies are deployed by service users in the arena of institutional talk, that is talk which occurs in particular occupational settings, between colleagues, between members of different professional groupings as for example in multidisciplinary health and social work settings, and between professionals and lay people, for example in doctor/patient encounters, counselling sessions, courtroom questioning, interviews, advice sessions and so forth.

The dynamics of description

In Chapter 3 we drew attention to the use of contrast structures in Dorothy Smith's discussion of 'K is mentally ill' to define 'normal' and 'deviant' behaviours (Smith 1978). In this chapter, we want to explore some other ways in which facts are made. We should perhaps begin by emphasizing that fact making involves choosing how to put things from amongst a huge variety of possible ways of describing something. Emanuel Schegloff illustrates this with the following example:

> Were I now to formulate where my notes are, it would be correct to say that they are right in front of me, next to the telephone on the desk, in my office, in Room 213, in Lewisohn Hall, on campus, at school, at Columbia, in Morningside Heights, on the Upper West Side, in Manhattan, in New York City, in New York State, in the North East, on the Eastern seaboard, in the United States, etc. Each of these terms could in some sense be correct . . . were its relevance provided for . . .
> (Schegloff 1972: 81)

This example illustrates that there is no definitive description which comes from the notes themselves. Instead there is a potentially inexhaustible list of ways of describing the location of the notes and it is the situation in which they are being described that will determine whether the precise location on the desk or a much vaguer description is more apposite. For example, if Schegloff were asking someone to collect the notes on his behalf then he would need to describe their location quite precisely whereas if he were away from home and being casually asked about the location of the notes for his current project, it might be more appropriate to say 'back home in New York'. As Hutchby and Wooffitt note:

The implication is that even when speakers are describing the most routine and commonplace events or states of affairs they have a wide range of alternative words and combinations of words from which to choose. This means that on each occasion when speakers produce a factual report they have selected which referential item or descriptive utterance they wish to use. If any factual reference or statement involves a process of selection, we can ask: what are the tacit reasoning procedures which led to this specific formulation of a fact at this point in the interaction?

(Hutchby and Wooffitt 1998: 203)

An important point, then, is that accounts are variable and context-dependent but we also need to recognize that the same set of circumstances may generate alternative versions, as our examples in previous chapters suggest. People often disagree about their descriptions of the same events or state of affairs. You will probably have no difficulty in identifying some examples in which friends or members of your family have put forward quite different accounts of the same thing. At times, quite heated exchanges can occur as versions are disputed and details corrected: parent/child encounters seem to be a fertile area for the generation of contested versions. Often what adults consider interesting, entertaining or worthwhile will be written off as 'boring' and 'rubbish' by their offspring and vice versa (at least in our experience!). The existence of different versions is brought out in the following exchange between two friends, Gladys and Emma, who are discussing Emma's arrangements to have her daughter, Barbara, and grandchildren to stay at Thanksgiving.

Extract 4.1

Gladys: Everything OK for the weekend?
Emma: Ah I'm gonna cancel the kids. I just don't feel up to it Gladys.
Gladys: Aw
Emma: I just . . . Four days of 'em I just I'm really kinda shot and Bud says to cancel it so . . .
Gladys: Well what about poor Barbara she's looking forward to Thanksgiving.
Emma: Well I don't know I'm just not up to it I'm gonna talk to her I just don't feel up to it really to cook a big dinner en have them
Gladys: Oh I don't know I think it would do you good dear I really do
Emma: Do you?
Gladys: An' I think it would be good for Bud to be with those boys. And to see them and play with 'em.
Emma: He said to cancel it. So I guess I should do what the great white father says I don't know.
Gladys: Well dear . . . you know best about that dear.

(Adapted from a transcript by Gail Jefferson,
cited in Potter 1996: 62–3)

This is a rather uneasy exchange for Emma who signals her intended change of plans but does not receive the supportive response from her friend that she might have hoped for. Emma probably wanted to hear her friend say something like 'oh dear, what a shame, but if you don't feel up to it, it's probably best to put it off'. Instead, Gladys expresses a negative 'aw' which prompts Emma to provide more detail to justify her decision. Gladys' response to this is to refer to 'poor Barbara' who will be disappointed at the cancellation. There is a subtle implication here that Emma is letting her daughter down by cancelling the visit. This is not something that Emma wants to acknowledge ('Well I don't know') and she persists in arguing in terms of her own health and the impact the visit will have on her. She rejects the invitation to consider the situation from her daughter's perspective. Gladys then discounts Emma's argument, claiming that the visit would have the reverse effect ('Oh I don't know I think it would do you good dear I really do'). Emma seems more disposed to listen at this point ('do you?') and Gladys presses home her advantage by introducing other beneficiaries of the visit: Bud and (implicitly) his grandchildren. Emma then presses her point about Bud ('He said to cancel it'), passing the responsibility to him. In doing so she refers to him ironically as 'the great white father', an interesting choice of words because it is suggestive of Bud's authority within the family to make key decisions whilst at the same time he is refusing a (grand)fatherly role and responsibilities. Emma's 'I don't know' here seems to indicate her dilemma: should she do what her friend thinks is right or what her husband says? Gladys is perhaps aware here that she has pushed things as far as she can. Her response is not 'well take no notice of what Bud says' but 'Well dear . . . you know best about that dear'. This is a much more muted statement which avoids making any comment which might be perceived as casting aspersions on Bud or the nature of Emma's relationship with him. The use of the term 'dear' twice in the same sentence seems designed also to provide a conciliatory tone. At this point in the conversation Gladys declines to engage further in attempts to convince Emma and concedes the argument to Emma (and Bud). Gladys steps back from any further efforts to influence the decision about the visit although she has not indicated either that she is persuaded by Emma's argument.

Taken as a whole, we can see that Emma has to work hard to account for her decision to cancel her daughter's visit. Gladys did not find the excuse of Emma's tiredness convincing and introduced a counter-argument about the benefits to all concerned. Gladys succeeds in unsettling Emma's account for a significant part of the exchange but cannot easily deal with the introduction by Emma of an external constraint and concedes that Emma and Bud will determine the matter between them. In putting forward their opposing descriptions of the Thanksgiving visit as a 'good' or 'bad' thing, each speaker is trying to suggest that the alternative account is invalid. As Wooffitt states:

by producing one descriptive utterance from a range of potentially usable items, speakers 'bracket in' or index certain particulars of the referent of the description, and, at the same time, 'bracket out' other aspects of the referent. Thus, any description is a selection which brings to the recipient's attention specific particulars of the state of affairs being described.

(Wooffitt 1992: 15)

This discussion about competing versions is taken up again in later chapters in relation to **institutional talk**.

'Neil you've got shoes on': the action orientation of description

Not only are accounts variable and context-specific but they also have an action orientation, that is they are designed to do something, as the following exchange between a group of students indicates.

Extract 4.2

Becky: Oi. Ssshh. It could have been that
Neil: No that's not making a noise
Alan: Something outside it was definitely something outside
Diane: Neil you've got shoes on
                                  (Adapted from transcript, cited in Potter 1996: 108)

Diane's remark, 'Neil you've got shoes on', is not a simple description of Neil's attire. Although constructed as a statement, it contains an implicit suggestion that, in response to the suspicious noise outside, Neil is the most appropriate person to go and investigate. It does not need to be framed explicitly as a request or instruction for the students in the scenario and us as readers to understand what Diane intends by this remark. As Potter also suggests, the action being done by this remark is quite sensitive. It is a potentially dangerous situation and Diane has to offer an account which does not open her up to a charge of laziness or cowardice. By focusing on who is appropriately dressed to go out Diane diverts attention towards practicalities and away from possible criticism that she is prepared to put someone else into a risky situation whilst keeping herself safe. Potter goes on to claim that, 'One of the principal reasons for doing actions indirectly by way of descriptions is that the actions are sensitive or difficult in some way' (Potter 1996: 109). We might also add that it is probably easier for Diane, as a woman, to take this line than it might be for Alan, since investigating to see whether there is an intruder or burglar is probably considered in our culture to be 'a man's job'.

Similarly in the previous exchange between Gladys and Emma, although they disagree about whether the visit by Emma's family should be cancelled, they are very careful in the way that they express this disagreement so as not to fall out about the issue. For instance, when Emma says 'Four days of 'em' this seems to be a shorthand way of saying that 'it's not just a weekend but four days which is a long time. It will be hard work having visitors for that long and I don't feel up to it'. Gladys' response about 'poor Barbara' implies that Emma ought to consider her daughter's feelings, putting them before her own tiredness, but it is said in a subtle way, and one designed to indicate that Gladys is not being insensitive but rather that she is sensitive to other considerations. In many ways this interaction between the two friends is typical in that overt confrontation and hostility are avoided. Emma and Gladys attempt to persuade rather than badger and upbraid each other. In general we try to present ourselves in a good light in our conversational interactions: we want to be taken as fair and responsible, not as offensive and untrustworthy. How we establish our credibility so that we are seen as responsible fact-givers is addressed next.

Establishing a credible voice

A key issue for participants is establishing their credibility. How do we know that someone is telling the truth? How do we know that we can trust what they say? We can to some extent judge by appearances (or we think we can), as we make assumptions about people on the basis of how they look. This may mean that we alter our dress in order to increase our chances of being believed in certain circumstances. What we would wear for an interview or court appearance may be radically different from how we would dress to achieve credibility in less formal situations. We know as well that 'appearances can be deceptive' and that we can easily stereotype people on the basis of their appearance and assume negative attributes about them, using these to justify our decisions (see Silverman and Jones (1976) for a discussion of these issues in relation to recruitment and selection). Whilst appearance is one way in which we attempt to determine what people are like, what they say is also highly significant in establishing credibility. There are several ways that this can be done, and some of these are examined briefly here.

Disinterested vs interested parties

A primary task for a participant in a social interaction is to assert their credibility with the other people involved. Presentation of self is therefore more than a matter of appearance, it is also about what we say and do. In talk, people try to present themselves as objective and unbiased, as some-one who can be trusted to give an accurate, literal account. An important way to accomplish this is to assert that you stand outside a situation and therefore can see all sides of the argument without bias and prejudice. In a recent examination board discussion about a 'failing' student this was precisely the stance taken by the external examiner. They argued that the fact that they did not know the student at all meant that they were able to reach an unbiased decision. Knowing the student and having a positive view of them were presented as inhibiting judgement, introducing emotion into the process and therefore a handicap to decision making. An alternative reading might have been that knowing the student could help by contextualizing their actions and making sense of their response to the situation. Had this been the case, the student might have been seen not as 'failing' overall but as someone who had failed to produce coursework of a satisfactory standard in a particular set of circumstances. This in turn might have had the effect of focusing more on the pieces of work and the circumstances of their production than on a 'blaming' of the student. However, neutrality is a stance that is highly valued in post-Enlightenment society because it is suggestive of a rational, scientific approach. We can see its influence in other areas, for example in television news coverage where balance and even-handed neutrality are supposed to pertain. In everyday talk people will often present their version as factually correct, that is as *the* rather than *a* version, as this talk show exchange illustrates:

Extract 4.3

```
 1  Caller:  Uh, what was supposed to happen yesterday, it
 2           was an org- it was an organised lobby of
 3           Parliament by the National Union of Students
 4  Host:    Mmm
 5  Caller:  And the idea was to make the public of
 6           England, an' Great Britain aware of
 7           the loan proposals.
 8  Host:    You say it was an organised demonstration by the
 9           National Union of Students
10  Caller:  No it was it was
11           an organised march, which
12           was supposed to go . . .
13  Host:    Well you can organise a
14           lobby or a march it still amounts to a
15           demonstration . . . d'you think it got out of hand?
```
                    (transcript cited in Hutchby and Wooffitt 1998: 108–9)

We can see here that the caller presents a particular account of an organized lobby of Parliament as part of a campaign against student loan proposals. The caller rejects the term 'demonstration', presumably because it sounds more confrontational and open to 'getting out of hand' than a lobby which sounds not only organized but also low-key, an attempt at persuasion rather than a show of force. The talk show host tries to unsettle this version by calling it a demonstration and by pushing the caller to shift from a neutral description to an opinion as to whether 'it got out of hand'. By use of terms such as 'it was an organised lobby' and 'the idea was' the caller presents their account as accurate and factual and removes agency from the National Union of Students and the caller. In doing so the account is rendered more authoritative and, if the event 'got out of hand', responsibility should not be attributed to the National Union of Students.

In many instances, however, the role of objective outsider cannot be claimed and this gives rise to what Edwards and Potter (1992) have called the **dilemma of stake**: how do we establish our credibility and fend off charges of bias and interest when we are patently involved in a particular set of affairs? Being involved not only establishes our claim to knowledge but also lays us open to accusations of bias. There may be special difficulties in establishing our credibility in circumstances where we are regarded as odd or deviant. One tactic is to account for our 'deviance' as normal and ordinary. For example, in an interview for a Scottish radio station series on American life and culture, a gun-owner and member of the US National Rifle Association (NRA, which campaigns vigorously against gun control) passes off gun ownership as ordinary and necessary and dissociates himself from 'the wilder fringes of the gun movement' as the following extract demonstrates. Bob is the radio interviewer and Ted the NRA member:

Extract 4.4

```
131   Bob:  I was hearing some reports in some recent local
132         newspapers about some citizens' militia organization in
133         Oklahoma starting up I mean are these rumours
134         conspiracy theories (.) the wilder fringes of the anti-gun [control]
135         movement
136   Ted:  . . . the idea of militias and what not they're they're
137         the fringe groups they're the minority . . . you're
138         gonna have wild folks in any group that you put
139         put together and we don't condone or . . . agree with what
140         they believe in . . . as I said the average
141         citizen believes in realistic laws and obeys 'em and
142         we're not out there trying to overthrow the government
```
                         (Adapted from McKinlay and Dunnett 1998: 41)

Similarly, in their study of punk subculture Widdicombe and Wooffitt (1995) identified that punks portrayed themselves as ordinary people doing mundane things such as going into pubs and being unfairly discriminated against by publicans. In his study of paranormal experiences Wooffitt (1992) found that respondents were at pains to emphasize that they were ordinary people who just happened to have experienced something extraordinary, such as encountering a poltergeist. Often this was done by employing the device of 'I was just doing X when Y', in which the speaker would describe some mundane activity in which they were engaged (Wooffitt 1992: 118–19; see also Wooffitt 1991) when something unusual or terrible happened. In essence his informants were saying, 'believe us because we are just ordinary people with no axe to grind about this. We were as surprised as anyone at having this experience. It happened quite out of the blue.' This adds to the authenticity of the account and offers the account-giver a means to ward off challenges claiming that they are mad or ultra-suggestible unlike the rest of us who are (allegedly) much more sane and rational.

Stake inoculation

Presenting oneself as independent and fair is a good way to assert one's credibility as a fact-giver, but in some situations being involved and 'having an axe to grind' makes this less easy to claim. Where someone knows they will be suspected of being partisan they may adopt the strategy of **stake inoculation** (Potter 1996) to try to protect their credibility. In Extract 3.1 in the previous chapter, for example, Angela was able to put together a compelling case in order to argue that K was mentally ill, but in doing so she acknowledged that she was K's friend and that she had observed her behaviour closely. This could mean that her evidence was the more believable because it was gathered first-hand, but it could also mean that her evidence could be undermined by her proximity to K. What if Angela and K had fallen out? If this were the case, then perhaps Angela was merely wreaking revenge by discrediting K? What if Angela and her friends had victimized K? K's behaviour could be construed as an understandable response to a process of being frozen out by Angela and co. In order to defend herself against such possible charges Angela adopts the strategy of stake inoculation in which she tries to assert her credibility and to resist its being undermined by the careful way she constructs her story. She claims firstly that she took a long time to reach her conclusion about K, she is not the sort of person who is prone to hasty judgements but someone who makes them carefully after weighing the evidence ('My recognition that there might be something wrong was very gradual, and I was actually the last of her close friends who was openly willing to admit that she was becoming mentally ill'). Nor is she the type to collude with others against a friend. Her judgement was one that was independently arrived at by a number of friends ('Trudi and I found ourselves discussing [K's] foibles in her absence. I still tried to find explanations and excuses – I refused to acknowledge the fact that there was anything definitely wrong with K' (Smith 1978: 30). Moreover, Angela can provide other independent commentators on K's behaviour. Her mother had observed some of K's behaviour and reluctantly concluded that she acted strangely, for example in negotiating what she would have for breakfast and then taking the food the mother had prepared for herself (Smith 1978: 29). Whilst Angela's mother is not a completely disinterested bystander nonetheless she is an adult who for these purposes could be passed off as trusted adult outside the circle of Angela's friends. Similarly and additionally a family friend of K's is invoked later as an independent corroborator of K's odd behaviour which she can helpfully contextualize by admitting that 'K had seen a psychiatrist some time back' (Smith 1978: 31). Any suggestion of collusion and spitefulness is thus resisted. Angela is a fair and reasonable witness to K's deteriorating mental health. Other fair and reasonable people can corroborate her story. Fair-minded listeners will recognize this gradual accumulation of evidence which eventually forces Angela and others to accept K's mental illness. It is the evidence that pushes them into this opinion, they simply tuned into the facts in front of them and found an explanation for them.

This way of tracing the trajectory of a person's shifting approach to an issue is a good way to head off the accusation that someone is too biased to give a credible account. This is particularly the case with a controversial issue or one that commands limited public credibility. If we take the issue of foxhunting as an example of the former, the preferred strategy for protagonists is usually to trade facts and figures about the size of the fox population and appropriate methods for managing that population. This is the objective argument based on properly gathered facts by appropriately credentialled fact-gatherers. However, whilst these facts may be sufficient to convince supporters, they do not always work as well in changing the hearts and minds of opponents. The latter are wont to dismiss carefully crafted arguments with the rejoinder that 'they would say that, wouldn't they?', dismissing opposing evidence as biased, distorted or just plain wrong. A useful tactic at this stage in the argument is to produce a 'convert': someone who, for example, used to support the pro-hunting lobby, indeed hunted themselves, but has changed sides. This can add great potency to an argument because the arguer is able to present themselves as particularly well qualified to comment on the topic. They are someone who knows all the opposing arguments, who has given careful consideration to both sides of the case and perhaps engaged in much soul-searching before shifting position on a particularly emotive issue. Here it is usual to emphasize the rationality of this decision based on the quality of the evidence that has caused the shift in opinion, which projects an image of thoughtfulness and integrity on the part of the convert and offers a defence against possible charges of fickleness or lack of probity. This is what happens with Angela and K, where the former presents herself as reluctantly coming to the conclusion that K is mentally ill. As Smith suggests:

If something is to be constructed as a fact, then it must be shown that proper procedures have been used to establish it as objectively known. It must be seen to appear that way to anyone . . . The rhetoric of the fact is here that Angela is constrained to recognize it. It is a fact independently of her wish; she does not wish it and yet she is 'forced to face' it.

(Smith 1978: 27–8)

In other circumstances where stake cannot be disclaimed, it may be more sensible to **claim stake**, to acknowledge the possibility of bias before someone else points it out in an attempt to undermine a claim to credibility. An example from a newspaper article is indicative of this: 'It surprises me how horrified men are by fatherhood. As the World's Worst Mother I feel I have some insight into this' (Julie Burchill, *The Guardian*, 31 July 1999). The columnist in question is on record as having left her child with the father in order to pursue another relationship. Readers may therefore regard her as being on somewhat shaky ground in writing about men's lack of commitment to fatherhood. By referring to herself as 'the World's Worst Mother (note the capital letters here to emphasize rather than hide the point) she pre-empts any charge that she is hardly qualified to make such a judgement. Because of the widely publicized details of her life, Burchill cannot easily claim neutrality on the subject. She can, however, disarm her potential critics by openly acknowledging her stake. In doing so she can claim some integrity as someone who is not trying to hide their position but is open about it and able to reflect on what impact it might have on her views. Whilst it is not as strong a position as trying to bring off a stance of neutral impartiality, it may help in defending one's credibility in situations where this is likely to be attacked.

Category entitlement

The concept of **category entitlement** expresses the idea that 'certain categories of people, in certain contexts, are treated as knowledgeable' (Potter 1996: 133). If someone has witnessed a particular event we treat them as being more knowledgeable than someone who may have heard about it through that witness or through a third party. Sometimes we invest in people the entitlement to be knowledgeable on the basis of their membership of a particular category: doctor, lawyer, or war correspondent for instance. We may trust our GP to make the correct diagnosis or a news reporter to give us an accurate story about war or famine although we may be much more sceptical about the claims to truth-telling of groups of professionals in general (for example, doctors, social workers, police officers and politicians) in the wake of newspaper exposés and public enquiries. Rather than assuming knowledgeability on the basis of being assigned to a particular category we need to look instead at how category entitlements are worked up in social interactions. As Hutchby and Wooffitt suggest:

> Categories do not merely provide us with convenient labels which allow us to refer to persons: they also provide a set of inferential resources by which we can come to understand and interpret the behaviour of persons so designated . . .
> (Hutchby and Wooffitt 1998: 214)

Edwards and Potter (1992) provide a useful example of the ways in which category entitlement can be disputed in their discussion of 'Chancellor Lawson's memory'. This relates to a situation in which a dispute arose between a group of journalists and Chancellor Lawson (Chancellor of the Exchequer in the late 1980s) as to precisely what had been said at an off-the-record press briefing about proposals to change benefits for pensioners. Lawson's (alleged) comments, taken to be highly sensitive and controversial, were seized upon by the press and headlined in national newspapers. A dispute then raged between the Chancellor and the journalists as to what had actually been said and whether the briefing had been accurately reported. Were these reports by '10 fully trained shorthand-writing journalists', whose versions coincided because they had independently taken verbatim notes at the same meeting and were therefore beyond reproach? This was the substance of the journalists' defence which stressed their collective skills in taking down verbatim reports and their professional standing. Or were these mere 'hacks', whose stories coincided precisely because they had conspired together afterwards to fabricate a story with the express purpose of discrediting the Chancellor, as he alleged? (Edwards and Potter 1992: 63f). As Potter subsequently comments: 'the point is that category entitlements should be treated as things that can be built up or undermined rather than as frozen parts of a social system. Reporters can be tired old functionaries, gutter manipulators slavering after sleazy stories with their chequebooks, or heroic fighters after truth' (Potter 1996: 134). Just how they are portrayed will depend on who is doing the portrayal, in what circumstances, to whom and to what purpose.

By exploring the concepts of category entitlements and stake management and so forth we have tried to show how objectivity may be claimed or how stake may be managed by inoculation or open acknowledgement of interest. In all of these ways participants in social interactions attempt to advance their claims to credibility and to withstand counter-claims of bias and error. In many ways, we can see that people 'get their retaliation in first', that is they try to pre-empt criticism before it happens rather than waiting to see what sort of response they get. Having explored how people attempt to establish their own credibility as deliverers of 'true' accounts, we now want to turn to the issue of how people try to maintain the plausibility of these accounts. In other words, our focus now shifts from the teller of the tale to the tale itself and the devices contained within it to establish plausibility and authenticity.

Establishing a credible account

A primary goal for participants in social interaction is to construct a factual account that appears to be accurate and literal. One way to accomplish this may be through the use of devices which draw attention away from the producer of the account towards the facts which are being described. In written documents and formal spoken accounts it has been suggested that an 'empiricist repertoire' is deployed in which social actors such as scientists are written out of the account by the use of impersonal phrases such as 'it was found that' in preference to 'I/we found that' (Gilbert and Mulkay 1984). For example, a Nobel Prize lecture address began with the sentence: 'The trail which ultimately led to the first pulsar' (Woolgar 1980: 253). Here the scientist presents the research as a discovery trail in which a pre-existing entity 'the pulsar' is found during the course of a protracted process of investigation. This mode of expression serves to reinforce the notion of the scientist as discoverer rather than maker of knowledge. As Potter suggests: 'Data are treated as primary, both in the logical sense of forming the foundations of any theoretical ideas, and in the chronological sense of being identified before theory was developed from them' (Potter 1996: 153). Elsewhere Woolgar has referred to these approaches to fact construction as **externalizing devices** which 'provide for the reading of the phenomenon described by virtue of actions beyond the realm of human agency' (Woolgar 1988b: 75). They are typically to be found in scientific and technical contexts but not exclusively so. In 'K is mentally ill' (Smith 1978) Angela employs just such a device when she presents the case in terms of the accumulation of factual evidence which she could no longer ignore ('I was actually the last of her close friends who was openly willing to admit that she was becoming mentally ill (Smith 1978: 28). It is the weight of the external factual evidence that compels Angela to form her opinion. Similarly in his analysis of broadcast news reports Potter (1996) found that expressions such as 'the facts show' and 'the evidence shows' were frequently used to demonstrate the credibility of a particular stance on a current affairs topic: 'Facts show that there's no increase in drug use related to [needle exchange] programmes and there will likely be a decrease in HIV infection because of them. Anybody who looks at these facts as objectively as we have, I think, will come to the same conclusions' (CNN, 30 September 1993, cited in Potter 1996: 157).

Just as we found in our previous discussion that disinterestedness on the part of producers of accounts was difficult to sustain in certain circumstances, it is also the case that 'the facts' do not or cannot always be left to 'speak for themselves'. An impersonal presentation or one that assigns agency to the data will not always work. In such circumstances we may resort to other devices to make our accounts seem plausible. One of these is to produce independent corroboration. Here independence is crucial, it is no good if an account can be undermined by the counter-claim that its authors colluded to produce a flawed account, as we saw in the example of 'Lawson's memory'. Again, in 'K is mentally ill' (Smith 1978) several people witnessed K's behaviour and drew their own conclusions from it about what was wrong. Angela took some time to come to this consensual position and only with extreme reluctance. She is not therefore simply going along with the crowd but capable of exercising her own judgement when faced with the evidence. Her factual account is borne out by other such accounts.

Narrative and detail

A frequent occurrence within talk is the recounting of our own or others' experiences. In working up these narratives people demonstrate their artful and persuasive use of language. There are thus strong reasons for regarding fact and fiction making not as distinct but as sharing many similar features in their production:

> Factual and fictional stories share many of the same kinds of textual devices for constructing credible descriptions, building plausible or unusual event sequences, attending to causes and consequences, agency and blame, character and circumstance.
>
> (Edwards 1997: 263)

In working up a plausible account of 'what really happened' the use of detail can be extremely important: it can help to add authenticity to the speaker's pronouncements, as we can see from the following account of a paranormal experience.

Extract 4.5

I'd come home from a lab of some sort, I had so many I'm not sure which one it was, and now I crashed . . . That was approximately four o'clock in the afternoon, I was really dead tired. I was really dead tired, I fell into a very deep sleep that day . . . I remember, you know, it was a *really* deep sleep. But what woke me up was the door slamming. 'OK' I thought, 'It's my roommate,' you know my roommate come back into the room . . . I was laying on my back, just kind of looking up. And the door slammed and I kinda opened my eyes. I was awake. Everything was light in my room.

(Hufford 1982 cited in Wooffitt 1992: 139)

We can see that the person describing this experience is trying to make it as 'real' as possible. He tells us what he had been doing during the day, what time he got home, how he was feeling, what he did next. This makes this account sound authentic. It does not present as being fabrication because of the level of detail which sets the scene for the strange event. He was not, therefore, trying to have this experience but just doing X when Y happened (Wooffitt 1991). From the references within the account to lab work and a roommate we can infer that the account giver is a student, which is perhaps a membership category which would undermine rather than enhance credibility. However, the detail given mitigates against any response which dismisses it as a student prank or fabrication by making the account more credible. Indeed, the veracity of witnesses' accounts may well be judged according to the level of detail they can supply.

In situations where we want to persuade others of the plausibility of our account in the face of their disbelief, detail can be a useful device. It can also be used effectively in exoneration:

Extract 4.6

Lottie: Hello
Emma: Good morning.
Lottie: How are you?
Emma: Oh hi honey we haven't gotten together have we.
Lottie: Oh gosh no. Let's see Thursday night I
went into town I came back Friday it was late
Emma: Oh you went in Thursday night?
Lottie: Yeah, Earl had to get some stuff for . . . working on a picture so I had
to go up there to get it
Emma: You worked Thursday too?

(Adapted from NB:I:6::R:1 in Edwards 1997: 121)

Here we can see that Lottie is responding to Emma's 'we haven't gotten together have we' by launching into an explanation which accounts for her failure to contact her friend. She does not simply agree but offers a justification for her inaction. She not only acknowledges her blame but offers an exoneration for it. We might add here that vagueness about detail may well be used as a way of avoiding blame or recrimination, as we show in Chapter 5.

Active voicing

Speakers may add to the detail which they provide by including reported speech in their accounts. By doing so, they add to the immediacy and authenticity of the report, giving a strong sense of 'this is what really went on'. In this example the speaker reports what happened when she and her housemate came home to find a third housemate having a traumatic dream:

Extract 4.7

1   Joan and I walked into
2   the house and Ruth's
3   in the living room, um.
4   asleep. And we awaken her
5   when we go in,
6   and she starts
7   crying and bawling,
8   'Oh my God! I'm

```
 9   so glad you all woke
10   me up! I've been trying
11   to wake up and get out
12   of this room for so long
13   and I haven't been able to.'
```
(Wooffitt 1992: 160)

The use of the present tense and of reporting what the friend said when the two housemates woke her up makes this account more vivid and believable to the listener. Wooffitt (1992) describes as **active voicing** the use of the speaker's own reported talk or the inclusion of others' talk. On occasion, he suggests, speakers may report talk 'when in fact it is unlikely, or in some cases impossible, that the words so reported were actually said in that way' (Hutchby and Wooffitt 1998: 225). People tend to produce a composite account of what 'they' said to add strength to their claim, particularly when it is unusual and runs the risk of being derided. The purpose of active voicing is to strengthen the factual status of claims and to fend off any sceptical response.

Extreme case formulations

We have emphasized throughout this chapter that when we are talking to people we are not simply describing 'the real world' but trying to persuade the listener to believe what we say whether we are expressing an opinion, making a complaint, accusing someone else or justifying our actions. We want our views to be accepted as sensible and plausible, or better still to be adopted by the listener for themselves. Whilst in some circumstances it is a more profitable strategy to provide information in a low-key manner – this can after all make the account seem less emotional and more neutral – at other times we may want to maximize the impact of what we are saying by the use of **extreme case formulations** using terms such as 'best', 'worst', 'always', 'never' or 'everyone' (Pomerantz 1986). 'I never said that' is more emphatic than 'I didn't say that', just as 'my brand new dress is ruined' packs a greater punch than 'the dress I bought recently has got a mark on it'.

In the following example we can see how an extreme case formulation is used in a conversation in which the speaker (C) is telling his partner about how a week at work had gone in the absence of his co-manager (referred to as 'he'):

Extract 4.8

C: We got so much done and more than that but everyone had this feeling that we were accomplishing things, you know we all felt real progress going on, . . . it's just so amazin whenever he's around he's utterly disparaging of our efforts, and he's completely disruptive.

(Adapted from Pomerantz 1986: 224)

This account is structured to lay the blame for the difficulties at work with the co-manager by using 'everyone' and 'we all' to emphasize how cooperative and constructive the workplace is without the difficult co-manager: it ranges the co-manager against the rest of the staff group and places C firmly with the 'good guys'. As Pomerantz notes: 'the lay logic is something like: if others react the same way to the co-manager, then the co-manager is responsible for the difficulties' (1986: 224). According to Pomerantz, extreme case formulations are invoked not only to attribute cause to an object or person but also as a defence against challenge (for example, Julie Burchill's 'World's Worst Mother') or to invoke the rightness or wrongness of an action, event or state of affairs: 'everyone does don't they' as the response to someone in a suicide prevention centre questioning the fact that a caller has a gun at home (see Pomerantz 1986: 225).

Minimization is the other side of the coin: we may want to play down rather than play up an event or state of affairs. Someone might apologize by saying that they have 'just had a few' or that they are 'a bit late' to ward off the accusation that they are drunk or extremely late. If we are complaining about someone else or accusing them of doing something wrong whilst suggesting that we are in the right then an extreme case formulation can be an effective rhetorical device. In contrast to the injunctions of assertiveness training, accusations are often highly personalized, not focused on specific behaviours.

As Hutchby and Wooffitt suggest: 'in these cases it is not simply that people are trying to persuade their co-participants: they are also designing their talk in anticipation of a sceptical or unsympathetic response' (1998: 212–13). This is an important point and one that we need to bear in mind in relation to 'institutional talk', that is talk which goes on in encounters between professionals and clients or service users and those among professionals.

Summary

In this chapter we have developed our argument by suggesting how a microanalysis of everyday talk is relevant for the study of HW practice. We have looked at examples of everyday interactions to see how people construct their talk to persuade others of their credibility as an account-giver and of the authenticity of their account. The particular concepts and devices which we have discussed are:

- The action orientation of description
- Establishing a credible voice as an account-giver
- The dilemma of stake
- Stake inoculation

- Stake claiming/disclaiming
- Category entitlement
- Narrative and detail
- Active voicing
- Extreme case formulations.

We can now move on to look at how talk is enacted in encounters between professionals and service users drawing on these insights from everyday talk. These ideas form a launch-pad to analyse professional talk as a dynamic descriptive activity which is artfully constructed and performative.

Analysing talk and text in health and welfare

CHAPTER 5

'The appropriate client': service users constructing their case

Talk takes place in a variety of settings which include interactions between family members, friends, work colleagues and casual acquaintances. In the previous chapter we examined various devices used in everyday talk. In this chapter we switch our focus to 'institutional talk', looking first at what this term means before exploring the devices that service users (and clients, patients and so forth) use in their interactions with HW professionals. In later chapters we carry on this discussion by examining how professionals talk to service users and to each other as well as how they produce documentary records of these interactions and their decision making.

Institutional talk

In contemporary society a considerable amount of talk can be said to be institutional, that is it is talk which does the business of the organization, whatever and wherever that might be. It may take place in a courtroom, a classroom, an office or workplace, a doctor's surgery, a hospital, a prison, a social work office, or whatever. However, it is not the setting which makes talk institutional. Two colleagues having a chat about the previous night's TV programmes is an example of everyday conversation even if it is taking place in the workplace and in work time. Likewise, institutional talk can occur in the home as, for example, when a health visitor is undertaking a home visit, or it can occur away from the agency, for example an organised holiday for learning disabled people.

The study of institutional talk has been described as:

> the study of how people use language to manage those practical tasks, and to perform the particular activities associated with their particular institutional contexts

– such as teaching, describing symptoms, cross-examining, making inquiries, negotiating and interviewing.

(Drew and Sorjonen 1997: 92)

Drew and Sorjonen further indicate that, just as the location of institutional talk is not necessarily easy to prescribe, so the boundaries between institutional talk and conversation are not fixed. For example, we sometimes begin a work-related telephone call with some everyday talk, people may deliberately mix 'business and pleasure', and participants at social gatherings may lapse into 'work talk' much to the annoyance of their companions. However, whilst acknowledging the fluidity of these boundaries and the elements of similarity between everyday and institutional talk, a focus on institutional talk sets out to problematize the nature of encounters between lay people and professionals in various settings, and the ways that professionals interact with each other within and across disciplines. In particular it eschews the claim that professionals have power in these encounters because of their position of privilege and status within the social structure (see Zimmerman and Boden 1991). Instead, it is argued that it is important to study how the business of the organization is accomplished in interactions and how power relations are enacted.

This refocusing can help us to answer questions such as, how does a doctor do 'being a doctor' in encounters with patients? How does a lay person do 'being a patient'? What devices do lawyers adopt in their cross-examinations of witnesses? How do social workers and health visitors interact with service users? In trying to answer such questions what is of interest is the 'normal' business of doing institutional talk, that is the mundane everyday examples of interactions with patients, witnesses, clients, service users in order to identify the particular patterns which emerge in these activities. Studies of institutional talk begin from the premise that we need first to study how this ordinary talk is accomplished without making a value judgement about whether it is done well or badly. Indeed, some authors, for example Silverman (1997a), have suggested that there is a rationale behind the way that professionals raise issues with patients which may not be evident at first glance. There may be good reasons for what may appear to be 'bad' talk. (This is explored in Chapter 6.)

An important issue in the study of institutional talk is to acknowledge that encounters between lay (service users and so forth) and professional people may or may not be voluntary and consensual. The lay person may have chosen to seek advice from a doctor, a lawyer, a health visitor or social worker; they may feel obliged to do so, they have been referred by a third party (lay or professional), or they may be under compulsion to undergo professional scrutiny as in the case of a child protection investigation, mental health assessment or criminal prosecution. They may range from accepting this involvement to vehemently opposing it. In addition lay/professional encounters cover a multiplicity of purposes: information gathering, information seeking, teaching, assessing, interrogating, negotiating, advice giving to name but a few; and these purposes may be combined within a single encounter. Contacts between lay people and professionals may also be single events, irregular and infrequent contacts over a long period of time (for example with a GP), frequent and intensive over a short period (as in a child protection investigation) or frequent and intensive over a long period (as part of a child protection plan or in the treatment programme for a serious medical condition).

There is then no single type of institutional encounter between service users and professionals but a wide range of encounters. It may be helpful to think of them along a continuum, from those which are regarded as extremely formal (as, for example, a criminal trial or a traditional pedagogical setting) to those where a significant amount of informality can prevail (as in a community work setting). We should, however, be cautious about ascribing formality or informality on the basis of location. It will be preferable to establish when and how formality/informality are done in particular settings. Similarly we need to regard as topics for exploration how voluntary and involuntary interactions are accomplished, and how service users 'do' compliance or resistance in both types of encounter.

We have argued previously that there are two essential elements to interactions: one is the way we establish ourselves as a credible person who can be trusted to give the facts; the other is how to bring off our accounts as plausible and authentic. This raises particular issues in institutional interactions because of the circumstances in which lay people encounter professionals in HW and related settings. There are circumstances in which HW professionals are 'gatekeepers' for a range of scarce resources such as welfare benefits and health care services, and prospective service users may approach agencies in order to persuade them to allocate resources to them. They must demonstrate that they are a worthy recipient of such resources. For example, a patient may go to a GP with a clear idea of what they want (a sick note or prescription) and seek to persuade the GP's agreement as the following extract shows. However, they are unlikely to be able to go in and simply instruct the GP without risking rebuff.

Extract 5.1

Dr: Right. I'll give you something slightly different.
Pt: Give me the same tablets, doctor, 'cause etc.
Dr: Beg your pardon?
Pt: Give me the same tablets as I was on 'cause they were the only things as was ever any good to me.
Dr: Mm.
Pt: They were great. I would prefer you wouldn't change them.

Dr: Well, I think you'd better leave it to me to decide what you should have, don't you?

(Fitton and Acheson 1979: 73)

We can see here that the patient first makes a strong demand ('give me the same tablets') but the GP does not accept this, suggesting that he has perhaps misheard the patient ('Beg your pardon?') and the patient tries for a more conciliatory tone ('They were great. I would prefer you wouldn't change them'). The GP is unmoved by this appeal and reminds the patient of the appropriate doctor/patient relationship: the latter seeks help with a defined problem and the former prescribes the remedy. It is not what the patient likes or thinks is best which counts here, but the doctor's professional expertise and control over decision making.

In other circumstances, service users may be determined to resist the allocation of resources even when it is deemed by professionals to be appropriate, as for example in the case of older people who wish to retain their independence despite a deterioration in their capacity to look after themselves. Alternatively, lay people may need to defend themselves against allegations of abuse, neglect or criminal activity made by welfare or criminal justice agencies. All of these situations can create particular dilemmas for service users about how to present themselves and their case for maximum effect. In the sections which follow we examine some extracts of lay people's encounters with professionals in order to explore these issues of credibility and authenticity.

Establishing credibility

Credibility may be established in different ways depending on the circumstances. In relationship counselling sessions there is a serious issue of couples vying for credibility in the way they present themselves to the counsellor. Each partner seems to be saying 'believe me and don't believe my partner. I'm the one that's telling the truth, I'm in the right here and they are in the wrong'. In the next extract, for instance, Mary is responding to an invitation from a counsellor to her and her partner Jeff to indicate why they are seeking counselling. After some hesitation between them, Mary offers her version:

Extract 5.2

1	*Mary:*	Yeh um well. What happened,
2		Jeff started doing some exams which
3		lasted about four years. And before that,
4		this was when we were living in the
5		hospital, we were always doing some exams,
6		since we've met, at some point,

7	which has lasted some time
8	(pause)
9	Anyway Jeff was doing um a degree, that
10	lasted must've been about . . . we were
11	just coming to the end. Just last summer.
12	(pause)
13	And during that time I felt that um
14	he didn't pay any attention to me, that um
15	although we still had a s- we still had a had a fairly
16	good relationship, I didn't feel that there was
17	anything wrong, but at the time
18	I didn't really think anything too much about
19	these problems but it must have
20	all like come to a head. Then I felt like
21	he was neglecting me, he didn't wanna know
22	I was working too hard, um and then
23	I had the two children I felt I was being left on
24	my own uh and then I started
25	going round with my friends quite a bit
26	um just to get out of the house
27	(pause)
28	for some relief
29	(pause)
30	And then I met somebody else and um
31	I had an affair, uh . . . and then I

(Adapted from Edwards 1997: 278)

From this we learn that Mary has had an affair and we can infer that this is central to the couple's troubled relationship. Indeed, Edwards goes on to indicate that Jeff's version of the situation heavily emphasizes a 'happy marriage spoiled by a wife's sexual adventures' and Mary's 'irresponsible neglect' of her family (Edwards 1997: 279). Jeff's version (which is not provided in any more detail) would perhaps start with the affair and its dramatic, negative impact on the family. Mary chooses to start much earlier and to end with the affair. What does she achieve by doing this?

Primarily it allows her to present a context for the affair and to suggest longstanding relationship difficulties. Mary cannot claim total innocence as the affair is clearly an acknowledged fact between her and Jeff, but she can work to avoid being blamed as the guilty party by presenting Jeff not as the innocent victim in the situation but as a culpable partner. His long-term studies meant that 'he didn't pay any attention to me' (line 14) and then 'I felt like he was neglecting me' (lines 20–1) and more strongly still 'he didn't wanna know' (line 21). This neglect is then compounded by Mary working too hard (line 22) and having the children to look after (line 23) and being left on her own (lines 23–4). In response to this Mary began 'going round with friends quite a bit' (lines 24–5) with completely innocent intent ('just to get out of the house for some relief', lines 25–8). It is within this context of Jeff's preoccupation with study, his neglect of her, his leaving her to look after the children and Mary's increasing distress with the situation that she had an affair. Thus Mary intends to demonstrate to the counsellor that she is not some irresponsible 'homewrecker' or neglectful parent but a loyal and considerate partner and mother who has been made very unhappy over a number of years. Her attempts to do something about it just happened to lead to her 'meeting somebody else' (line 30).

We can see parallels here with Wooffitt's formulation of 'I was just doing X when Y happened' (Wooffitt 1991) discussed in Chapter 4. Mary presents a rather mundane and routine existence, with the affair as an unanticipated and unplanned outcome. In other words, this was not a callous and premeditated act but rather that of a long-suffering part-ner deprived of attention and assistance within the relationship. As we noted earlier in relation to 'K is mentally ill' (Smith 1978), taking a long-term view of a situation before reaching an adverse judgement or doing something for which one might be negatively judged in Mary's case is one way of appearing credible. Mary exonerates her actions by reference to 'the fact that' she did not initiate an affair without due cause but was precipitated into it by a long chain of negative experiences. In other words there is a long history behind the affair which needs to be taken into account before judgement is made of Mary's behaviour. Mary is thus able to acknowledge the affair without accepting blame, and to protect herself in advance from Jeff's counter-claims of her culpability. We can thus see this piece of talk as a piece of 'offensive' (designed to undermine Jeff's alternative description) and 'defensive' (intended to resist discounting or undermining) rhetoric (Potter 1996: 107). Mary's talk thus has a dual purpose.

You may have noticed how much space Mary was given to put her side of the story without interruption from either Jeff or the counsellor. It is quite usual within couples' counselling for the counsellor to give plenty of time to individuals to put their story (although presumably some partners would be less likely than Jeff to refrain from interrupting the account), but in other examples of encounters with professionals the client or service user is given less time and space in which to talk. For example, in his study of AIDS counselling Silverman (1997a) identifies two major counselling formats: the *interview* which consists primarily of questions by counsellors and answers by the 'counsellee'; and *information delivery* in which the counsellor holds the floor to give advice and the counselled person is on the receiving end. This issue of the space allowed to clients is explored further in the next chapter when we shift focus to look at professional talk.

Establishing credibility in a hostile environment

Whilst the counsellor in Extract 5.2 seems quite disposed to listen to Mary put her case without questioning her or casting doubt on her story, there are many circumstances in which the lay person needs to defend their credibility from being undermined in an environment which is much more sceptical or even downright hostile. We can illustrate this point about the very different climate in which someone might be compelled to operate and the constraints on 'allowable contributions' (Heritage 1997) by an examination of an exchange from a rape trial. In the following extract the counsel for the defence (A) is cross-examining a witness (W) who is also the complainant.

Extract 5.3

A: An' you went to a bar in (city) is that correct?
W: It's a club.
A: It's where girls and fellas meet isn't it?
W: People go there.
A: An' during that evening didn't Mr (defendant's name) come over to sit with you.
W: Sat at our table.

(Drew 1992: 489)

Here it seems that the defence counsel is seeking to imply that W had chosen to go to a place where 'girls and fellas meet'. Note that this formulation suggests a place where casual encounters are commonplace. A could have used the term 'men and women' or 'people' and put the focus on the purpose of going there as to meet friends or relax rather than suggesting a 'pick-up place'. Indeed, the witness responds by trying to deflate these suggestions with the much less emotive expression 'people go there'. Similarly she rejects the suggestion that she encouraged the attentions of the alleged rapist when he came to sit with her. The witness insists that the defendant merely sat at the same table. She implies that he either did so without invitation or at the invitation of someone other than her. The defence's case is that W 'asked for it' by choosing to go to the bar in the first place and by encouraging the defendant. The witness attempts to convey the impression that she was doing nothing out of the ordinary and that she did not encourage the advances of the defendant.

If we analyse how things were said as well as what was said, we are immediately struck by the lack of room for manoeuvre for the witness, particularly if we compare it with the previous extract from the counselling session. In the courtroom exchange the witness has a version to tell but is put in the position of having to respond to the alternative (negative) version of the defence counsel. The latter does not ask her an open question such as 'how did you first meet the defendant?', but proceeds to take her through a scenario (portrayed as 'the' scenario) with a series of leading questions which cast doubt on her motives and judgement in going to the club. One of the difficulties for the witness is that the format for questions is prescribed and rigidly applied within the formal court setting. It is difficult for the witness to break out of the format without appearing to be uncooperative. If she failed to answer or refused to do so, she could be instructed to respond by the judge, as in a different example of an exchange between a judge (J) and a witness (W):

Extract 5.4

W1: Your honour, I wish to say something.
J1: Just answer the question Mrs Fray.
W2: But he didn't/
J2: You must answer his question. You cannot just say what you like.
W3: Yes sir.

(Penman 1990: 28)

The witness' attempt to insert some information is rebuffed ('you cannot say just what you like') without any consideration as to its possible relevance to proceedings, despite her polite request. There are, however, serious penalties for those who fail to assist the court with its business or follow its procedures and who are deemed in contempt. The combination of the formality and unfamiliarity of the courtroom may seriously constrain the ability of the witness to put their point of view across. Moreover, the exchange between defence counsel and witness is by no means private. It occurs under the gaze of the 'overhearing audience' of judge and jury. In the case of the witness being cross-examined in the rape trial (Extract 5.3), it is this audience whom W has to convince that she is not sexually promiscuous, not someone who would make a malicious or vindictive allegation. Within this adversarial question and answer format the witness has to rebut charges of promiscuity and defend her integrity. In contrast, Mary (in Extract 5.2) is given a much more open platform and relative privacy in which to assert her credibility.

In Extract 5.3 W was able to offer a different version from the one put forward by the defence counsel. We noted earlier that detail can be an important way of accentuating the credibility of one's account by making it seem more 'real'. However, in a cross-examination it may be that detail can work negatively in that it can be seized upon by opposing counsel to put together a much less flattering version of a witness and their motives. One potential device to defend oneself from hostile or probing questioning is that of 'not remembering'. As the following extract indicates, witness (W) is reluctant to confirm information put to her by the defence counsel (A) because it may render her complicit in the sexual encounter with the defendant.

Extract 5.5

A: How many phone calls would you say that you had received from the defendant, between February and June twenty-ninth?
W: I don't know

W: I didn't answer all of them.
A: Scuse me?
W: I don't remember. I didn't answer all of them.

(Adapted from Drew 1992: 482–3)

In a hostile cross-examination (or other such interrogation) 'not remembering' may be an important way of staving off the attribution of blame. Drew comments:

> stating that one does not remember something can be a means of displaying the unimportance or lack of significance of that detail, and hence that it is the sort of thing one would not remember . . . 'not remembering' something attributes to it a kind of status as unmemorable because it was unnoticed.

(Drew 1992: 483)

The picture the witness is attempting to build is of her innocence: there was no reason for her to notice details about telephone calls and so forth because it is only with hindsight that it became relevant. Prior to the rape she did not particularly notice things because the situation seemed ordinary and unremarkable.

In a similar vein, Potter (1997) has suggested that 'I don't know' can act as a form of stake inoculation, in circumstances where one might come across rather negatively, or where it may be helpful to be vague and noncommittal in response. For instance, in her BBC TV *Panorama* interview with Martin Bashir, Diana, Princess of Wales responded 'I dunno' in response to questions about why she thought the Andrew Morton book about her life would change people's perception of her. Potter suggests that: 'For the Princess to accept that the book was part of a planned and strategic campaign to present a particular view of the royal marriage and her role in it would be potentially culpable. The 'I dunno's' present her as not sure of the role of the book, perhaps thinking it over for the first time' (Potter 1997: 157).

Devices such as 'I dunno' and 'I can't remember' are also frequently adopted by children in response to adult questioning when they are reluctant to speak or unwilling to implicate themselves or others in some wrongdoing. As adults we usually recognize these blocking devices although we may not necessarily have worked out effective means to counter them.

Credibility and entitlement

In welfare settings, establishing one's credibility is crucial in gaining access to scarce resources. A claimant may have to assert their worthiness and to defend themselves against charges of fecklessness and irresponsibility. For example, Donileen Loseke has suggested that in order to gain access to the women's refuge network 'the battered woman is constructed [by workers] as a person in dire need, as one who is not complicit in her victimization, and as morally worthy' (Loseke 1992: 46). As such she is then 'an appropriate client' in institutional terms. Those who fall outside this categorization are not and are deemed ineligible to enter a refuge.

Similarly, the following account by a client (CL) who has approached a Homeless Assistance agency demonstrates how clients attempt to portray themselves as 'appropriate', worthy of sympathy and therefore assistance.

Extract 5.6

> CL: Okay, I came down here alright with a friend. It wasn't some fling. My whole life has changed since I've come here, and you know what I mean I got hurt, I got robbed, I left a good job, good people. When I got hurt and had to go into hospital I didn't hear from my friend anymore. I could, nobody came, came to see me. I was just totally alone and I mean it was devastating.
>
> (Spencer 1994: 40)

This is a powerful piece of talk designed to establish the integrity of the client ('I came down here alright with a friend. It wasn't some fling . . . I left a good job, good people'). It relies heavily on the use of contrast structures: the good intentions and responsible actions are contrasted with ill luck ('I got hurt, I got robbed') for which the client is not responsible. These things just happened out of the blue. 'You know what I mean' invites the social worker to understand and agree with the account. A sense of crisis and catastrophe is invoked through the use of extreme case formulations: 'my whole life has changed', 'nobody came', 'totally alone', 'it was devastating'. This is someone who surely deserves the social worker's sympathy because they have not done anything wrong, misfortune has befallen them and they have been abandoned by a friend. Here the client implies that this is an abrogation of responsibility on the friend's part which adds to the sense of desperation. Taken all together, this is a client who is worthy of assistance.

Each of these examples (Mary, W and CL) is suggestive of how strongly credibility is linked to worthiness. To be believed as a truthful giver of an account is also to be accepted as a morally adequate person. A striking feature of each situation is the high stakes being played for. In the case of CL, material resources are at stake: being believed may well mean the difference between receiving help or not receiving help. In the other two cases, being blamed for the breakdown of a marriage or being publicly pilloried in court as a promiscuous woman, or even seeing the defendant acquitted, are highly sensitive issues. This theme of 'moral adequacy' is one that we want to take a little further, and one of the areas in which it has been explored to good effect is in relation to doctors' encounters with the parents of children with long-term illnesses and disabilities.

Establishing 'moral adequacy'

An early study of the 'moral adequacy' of parents was conducted by Baruch (1981, 1982) in which he compared Burton's study (1975) of parents of children with cystic fibrosis with his own research on parents of children with congenital heart disease. On the face of it the two studies revealed similar parental attitudes to the medical profession which is evident if we compare these two extracts:

Extract 5.7a

Parent: I went to the baby clinic every week. She would gain one pound one week and lose it the next. They said I was fussing unnecessarily. They said there were skinny and fat babies and I was fussing too much. I went to a doctor and he gave me some stuff and he said 'You're a young mother. Are you sure you won't put it in her ear instead of her mouth? It made me feel a fool

(Burton 1975 quoted by Baruch 1982 cited in Silverman 1993: 109)

Extract 5.7b

Parent: When she was born, they told me [she] was perfectly all right. And I accepted it. I worried about her which most mothers do, you know. Worry about their first child.

Interviewer: Hm

Parent: She wouldn't eat and different things. And so I kept taking her to the clinic. Nothing wrong, my dear. You're just making yourself . . . worrying unnecessarily, you see.

(Baruch 1982 cited in Silverman 1993: 109)

In both extracts the parents present an account in which they are the initiator of concerns which they took to medical staff only to be dismissed in a rather patronizing way and told not to worry. This could be taken as clear evidence of health professionals' failures in listening to parents, taking seriously their concerns and making early diagnoses of disabilities.

However, Baruch makes a radically different analysis of the data from Burton (1975):

Burton treats her findings as an accurate report of an external event and argues that parents' early encounters with medical personnel can cause psychological damage to the parents as well as lasting damage to the relationship with doctors. On the other hand, I see parents' talk as a situated account aimed at displaying the status of morally adequate parenthood. In this instance the display is produced by the telling of an atrocity story.

(Baruch 1982 cited in Silverman 1993: 109)

In other words, Baruch is arguing that parents need to demonstrate that they care deeply about their children and have their best interests at heart. He is not engaging in a debate about whether 'atrocity tales' such as these are true accounts of 'what really happened' but instead focuses on how these mothers demonstrate their moral adequacy as caring parents (see also Dingwall 1977; Baruch 1981). Several things may resonate for us after our discussion in the previous chapter about devices to establish credibility:

one is the use of active voicing ('I did X', 'they said Y') to add immediacy to the account (Wooffitt 1992). Both extracts convey a strong contrast between 'them' and 'us', that is parents, expert in knowing their own child, not being listened to by the avowed medical experts who dismissed them as neurotic mothers. The mothers also show their ongoing care and responsibility towards their child by emphasizing how regularly and frequently they sought advice and expressed concerns ('I went to the baby clinic every week'; 'And so I kept taking her to the clinic'). In addition in Extract 5.7b the mother emphasizes her ordinariness ('I worried about her which most mothers do, you know'). These are women who belong to the membership category of 'normal, nurturing, responsible mothers', undeserving of what they perceive to be dismissal by medical staff.

Similarly, Silverman (1987) has studied how mothers do 'moral versions of parenthood' in relation to adolescent children with diabetes, as the following example indicates. Here the mother (M) of Tessa aged 15 is talking to the doctor (D).

Extract 5.8

```
1   D:  How do you think she's getting on?
2   M:  Very well (   ) We only have rows about her tests
3   D:  (   )
4   M:  I mean she has to see you, I don't. She's a big girl
5   D:  She's in between. There's a bit of her wanting you to take an interest.
6   M:  Oh I do. For her own sake. She's growing up fast.
```

                                                            (Silverman 1987: 235)

Silverman suggests that this is an example of a 'no-win' situation for mothers. If they claim that they behave responsibly and guide symptom management they can be accused of 'nagging' and not fostering sufficient independence in their teenage children. Conversely, 'an emphasis on self-expression can be defined by others as uncaring "permissiveness" and mean that parents can be sharply reminded that "young adults" still need guidance and support' (Silverman 1987: 235). Here the mother refers to rows, backtracking when this might seem to be nagging, only for the doctor to challenge her shift of responsibility onto her daughter by making oblique reference to the fact that she ought to continue to 'take an interest'.

In our final example of doing 'moral adequacy' we can see how a mother (M) and father (F) respond quite differently to a comment by a health visitor (HV).

Extract 5.9

```
1   HV:  He's enjoying that isn't he
2   F:   Yes he certainly is
3   M:   He's not hungry cuz he's just had his bottle.
```

                                                            (Heritage and Sefi 1992: 367)

Here, the father seems to take the health visitor's comment at face value. He assumes that she is making a neutral observation about the baby's feeding and responds by agreeing. In contrast, the mother appears more alive to the possibility that this might not be such an innocuous comment. The health visitor might be implying that the baby is hungry, and if so, then clearly a responsible mother would have recognized it and have done something about it. Her 'He's not hungry cuz he's just had his bottle' defends her position as a morally adequate mother, that is someone who would know when her baby needed feeding and would have done something about it. She has earned this category entitlement. As Heritage and Sefi comment from their study of health visitor/parent interactions: 'the mothers saw their knowledge, competence, and vigilance in baby care as an object of evaluation and, moreover, by a person with officially accredited competences to judge their conduct' (1992: 366). This could lead to mothers being defensive in their interactions with health visitors or unwilling to ask advice about aspects of baby care in order to appear knowledgeable and competent.

In his research in the paediatric diabetic clinic, Silverman (1987) concluded that there were four key aspects to moral adequacy which staff looked for and parents attempted to demonstrate: managing the child's condition; monitoring in relation to testing, diet and injecting; providing a consistent, healthy diet; and being alert to potential problems. In childcare social work, moral versions of parenthood tend to centre on the concept of attachment which is used to interpret parent/child interactions and to assess the adequacy of parenting/mothering (Burman 1994; White 1996; Taylor 1999). In different areas of HW work moral adequacy is defined in different ways. It is important therefore to explore its components and how they are accomplished in the specifics of client/professional encounters rather than to assume their existence or similarities across a variety of contexts. You might like to pause here to think about the ways in which clients are expected to demonstrate moral adequacy in your agency.

Providing an authentic story

Having explored the issue of service user credibility, let us look now at the issue of how clients and patients work to make their stories sound authentic.

Constructing out-there-ness

We noted in Chapter 2 that there are certain ways of writing and speaking which render an account more neutral and detached. As Latour and Woolgar (1986) suggest, we use gradations of certainty in our talk. 'It is child abuse' seems more objective and certain than 'I think it's child abuse' or 'it could be child abuse'. The circumstances of users' encounters with professionals mean that we are unlikely to find examples of a full-blown empiricist discourse (Gilbert and Mulkay 1984); however, certain elements of it can be found in 'client talk', in particular the suggestion that pre-existing facts are gathered and knowledge developed by an inductive process. If we return to the example of Mary who is giving her version of her relationship problems, we can see that she does distance herself from events to create factuality:

Extract 5.10

13   And during that time I felt that um
14   he didn't pay any attention to me, that um
15   although we still a s- we still had a had a fairly
16   good relationship, I didn't feel that there was
17   anything wrong, but at the time
18   **I didn't really think anything too much about**
19   **these problems but it must have**
20   **all like come to a head.** Then I felt like
21   he was neglecting me, he didn't wanna know

(Edwards 1997: 278, emphasis added)

Here Mary sugests that she was not actively thinking about the relationship 'but it must have all come to a head'. This is presented as happening independently of Mary, without her active involvement or deliberate intent. She was just involved in the ordinary events of being a wife and mother and was unaware of her unhappiness. As Potter indicates: 'such constructions obscure the work of interpretation and construction done by the description's producer: "the facts" are, first, not being constructed as facts and second, their significance is not being generated by their producer, it is provided by the facts themselves' (Potter 1996: 158).

Authenticity through detail

In some professional/lay encounters clients appear to be rather 'low-key' in their presentation of information and make little effort to hold the floor. A striking feature of GP and initial hospital consultations is the way in which patients orient themselves to the diagnostic procedures of the medical profession. They wait to be asked for information and respond briefly, even when the doctor might wish them to give a more elaborate exposition of symptom development. Sometimes doctors have to work quite hard to get information: simply pausing to give patients space to talk proves insufficient and more direct questioning is needed. This is illustrated in the following example from an initial hospital consultation in a cardiography unit (see the appendix for an explanation of the transcription devices retained because they indicate the pauses in the talk).

Extract 5.11

1	Doctor:	Now your doctor's written to say that you've been getting
2		pain in your chest. Is that right?
3	Patient:	Yes.
4	Doctor:	Can you tell us about that?
5	Patient:	Well it's mostly over here, (when I get it).
6	Doctor:	Mm Hmm. What -under the right breast?
7	Patient:	Yes. (2.4) And then I mean if I'm doing anything, you know,
8	Patient:	I get so (0.6) tired, and you know (1.2) as if I (0.6)
9		haven't stopped all day.
10	Doctor:	Yes.
11	Patient:	Perhaps I've only taken the cleaner over (3.6)
12	Doctor:	And how long have you been getting that pain?
13	Patient:	Well (0.8) I started having the pains (something) about
14		two years ago (1.2) and I've had chest X-rays for it, (1.6)
15		and well (0.6) it's always been clear.
16	Doctor:	Yeah, right. (2.6)
17	Patient:	So . . . (4.6)
18	Doctor:	And has the pain always been in the same place?

(Hughes 1982: 363)

Much has been made in the literature of the 'asymmetry' in the doctor/patient relationship (see, for example, Hughes 1982; Mishler 1984; Frankel 1990; Maynard 1991) and it is an issue to which we return in the following chapter on how professionals deal with patients/service users. However, it is worth pointing out how the patient takes their lead from the doctor in this instance. They do not launch into a long-winded history of their signs and symptoms, instead waiting to be questioned by the doctor. Their responses are brief and little information is volunteered even when (as at line 16) the doctor gives the patient time to give a more elaborate answer. Given the brevity and the imprecision of the information offered the doctor falls back on a succession of prompts in order to acquire more information.

In circumstances where 'the facts' may be disputed or a person is anxious to extricate themselves from charges of culpability, a much greater attention to detail may be preferred. We saw this in Extract 5.2, where Mary gives an account of events leading to her affair, and it is evident also in a passage from Mary's account of her relationship with her partner Jeff. Mary is talking about a night out when she returned home at 1 am and then phoned Jeff, who was 'on call':

Extract 5.12

22	Mary:	I was at home and um then we had an
23		argument didn't we. Jeff said what do you think
24		what hour do you think this is and you

25	shouldn't be home this late and I said at
26	least I had the decency to phone yuh I coulda lied
27	and I didn't want to lie because I
28	thought there was no point in lying to him
29	I don't want to keep on lying well I never used
30	to lie but since I had this affair I did start
31	to lie obviously

(Edwards 1997: 145)

Mary uses active voicing to report what she and Jeff said in the course of their row. We are thus invited to believe her account as being authentic. Wrapped up in the account are all sorts of other signs that its recipients are asked to attend to: that Mary is trying to make amends to Jeff; that she is trying to behave differently now; that during the affair she did behave in an aberrant fashion by lying, but now she is trying to reconstruct her relationship with Jeff. Had Mary simply said 'I went out on Friday night and Jeff and I had a row about it' she would not have been able to accomplish nearly so much in terms of her own exculpation and her implicit blaming of Jeff for not trusting her. Mary thus conveys that she is trying to repair the relationship, whilst blaming Jeff for undermining her efforts.

In the next extract we can see another example of the use of detail as a means of exculpation and one which brings out the ways in which the discursive business of talk can be oriented towards minimizing the outcomes of actions or behaviour. This is a telephone helpline conversation between A (helpline worker) and B (caller):

Extract 5.13

1	B:	. . . Well, she ((*wife of B*)) stepped between me and the child
2		I got up to walk out the door. When she stepped between me
3		and the child, I went to move her out of the way. And then
4		about that time her sister had called the police. I don't know
5		how she . . . what she . . .
6	A:	Didn't you smack her one?
7	B:	No.
8	A:	You're not telling me the story, Mr B.
9	B:	Well, you see when you say smack you mean hit.
10	A:	Yeah, you shoved her. Is that it?
11	B:	Yeah, I shoved her.

(Sacks 1992a: 113, line numbers added)

This seems to be a case of 'pleading guilty' to a lesser charge, albeit outside a courtroom. First B gives the detail to establish what was happening, which involves the elaborate positioning of him, his wife and child in relation to the door. He then resorts to 'I don't know' (another example of vagueness in the face of questioning where detail might assign guilt) as he can offer little explanation as to why his sister-in-law had called the police whilst maintaining his innocence. In response to the probes from A, B rejects the suggestion that he 'smacked [his wife] one' which has extremely clear pejorative and blaming overtones in favour of the less emotive 'shoved'. The implication is that he sought merely to move her out of the way rather than to cause her harm. Any injury that occurred as a result of being shoved could be deemed to be accidental whereas smack shows intent to hurt. B therefore does his best to absolve himself from blame by acknowledging involvement but denying the charge of 'smacking her one'. Total denial is difficult to sustain (as it was for Mary in the case of her affair in Extract 5.2) but B makes a strong attempt to minimize his culpability.

In a similar context of male violence our reading of Hearn's research (1998) suggests that men draw upon the alleged support of friends and family to minimize their culpability. For example, a man imprisoned for various acts of violence towards women, including indecent assault, reported to an interviewer: 'And like my mate were with me when all this [indecent assault] has gone off. He's even turned to me and said, "You've done nowt"' (Hearn 1998: 155). We can see here the use again of active voicing to enhance the factuality of the statement and to deny the gravity of what the man did. We might also note the links here to Goffman's concepts of face and facework, where face means 'the positive social value a person effectively claims for himself . . . in terms of approved social attributes' and facework is 'the actions taken by a person to make whatever he is doing consistent with face' (Goffman 1972: 5). In the above instances we can see attempts to engage in facework designed to protect the fact-teller from being regarded negatively.

Extreme case formulations in client talk

In the previous chapter on everyday talk we noted that staying cool, calm and collected is often the better way to present one's version. It sounds more authentic and reliable if an account is presented in a measured way with supporting detail. In some circumstances, however, service users need to provide additional emphasis to indicate the level of their distress and the extremity of their need. Extreme case formulations are used routinely in such circumstances to strengthen the user's version. We might add here that the need to persuade a potentially reluctant gatekeeping agency of the worthiness of one's case or to dissuade an agency representative from intervening or providing unwanted treatment can encourage their use. Scarce resources may only be allocated to caregivers who are not just tired and a bit low but 'at the end of their tether', 'utterly unable to cope' or 'totally exhausted'. In a later chapter we will see that workers also use such devices to persuade a colleague or manager of the rightness of a particular course of action (see also Hall 1997).

To illustrate this point about extreme case formulations here are two examples. The first is taken from the exchange between Connie and Jimmy with a counsellor.

Extract 5.14

Connie: Jimmy's thinking is **very, very different**
Jimmy: Well being
a jealous person we go back to
when we were datin' when we were
dating first well we met in this particular pub
When we start'd datin' we was in there **every**
single week we'd fight. **We were at each other**
the whole time

(Adapted from Edwards 1997: 155)

Here Jimmy is putting forward his version of the relationship as troubled from the start. He emphasizes the consistency of the disharmony by his use of 'every single week' and 'we were at each other the whole time', signalling that this was intrinsic to the relationship. The force of the words is intended to persuade the counsellor that 'this is how it has always been', whereas his partner Connie's version is of a good marriage which has recently gone wrong.

The second example reintroduces Vladimir, whose exchange with the head psychiatrist was discussed in Extract 1.3. He is making the case for his release from the psychiatric unit and his return to prison.

Extract 5.15

I am supposed to take some medication for, if I have some bodily injury. Not for the mind. **My mind's perfect.** Cause I'm obviously logical, I know what I'm talking about. There's no – and I am excited. Yes, **that's the only fault** you might find with me. **I have a perfect right to be excited . . . Every time** I come in here you call me crazy . . .

(Mehan 1990: 174, emphasis added)

Vladimir uses several extreme case formulations to press home the point that he is not crazy. His difficulty is that, as the patient, he is not able to provide the authoritative assessment of his state of mind: it is psychiatric staff who have definitional privilege. Claiming a 'perfect mind' could be interpreted as counter-evidence of mental ill health, and becoming excited and extreme may serve to undermine his claims rather than to promote them. Instead of righteous indignation, medical staff may well adduce distress and deterioration in his condition. Rather than underlining worthiness, using extreme case formulations may have the effect of making a service user seem 'over the top' and thus may undermine their credibility and the authenticity of the account. They will not necessarily succeed in convincing professionals. Conversely, if service users are too low-key in their accounts they may come across as not really being in need. This is particularly likely to be the case in circumstances where resources are allocated on the basis of the client's story and where 'objective evidence' (such as the results of medical tests) is either not appropriate or not available.

Summary

In this chapter we have applied the analysis of talk set out in Chapters 3 and 4 to a study of institutional talk and, in particular, of service users' exchanges with professionals. We have noted that such talk occurs in a range of settings and has a range of purposes, and is consequently difficult to categorize. Our examples of talk have reflected this diversity since they have been drawn from formal set-piece encounters in the courtroom, surgery and clinic where lay people are led through an exchange by a professional such as a consultant or a defence lawyer to more free-flowing exchanges where the client or patient is given more space to put forward their version of events, as epitomized by extracts from counselling sessions. We have used these exchanges to demonstrate how lay people work to make themselves appear truthful and morally worthy. We also explored how users attempt to make their accounts plausible by the use of various devices: for example, providing detail, not remembering, and using contrast structures, extreme case formulations, and offensive and defensive rhetoric.

Implications for practice

We hope that as you have been reading you have been pondering questions such as, how is this relevant to me? How can it help me make sense of practice? – and coming up with answers. A point we want to underline is that talk between practitioners and clients is central to HW work, notwithstanding all the work that goes on behind the scenes (practical and administrative tasks, contact with colleagues and so forth). Yet, in our view, existing practice handbooks and research accounts of practice tend to treat client/practitioner interaction primarily as a means to an end: to seek out or impart information, to make diagnoses and assessments, to communicate decisions, and to offer advice and guidance. Talk itself is largely ignored. It is usually the facts that talk 'brings to light' or the thoughts and feelings engendered in the participants that are the focus of attention.

We argue that talk is not simply a resource (a neutral medium for supplying information) but a topic worthy of study in its own right. By problematizing talk we also problematize the client/professional relationship more effectively. We bring into focus the issue of 'moral adequacy', in particular the ways in which agencies expect clients to behave, and the ways in which clients 'do' (and resist doing, or fail to do) 'moral adequacy'. By analysing talk we can make better sense of welfare work.

Adopting this approach to talk does mean attending in a different way to the talk that occurs in your daily practice. You will notice how people say things and what they are trying to achieve. You will think about how else they might have said something and the consequences of that for them, for practitioners and for the agency. However, it does not and cannot mean that the process of listening and analysis takes over and becomes an end in itself. You still have to function as a practitioner, make judgements and take decisions. We want to argue that qualitative research methods are relevant to developing understandings of practice but we recognize the differences between the two endeavours. There will be constraints and limits to your explorations of talk. At the same time, we want to suggest that analysing talk is a helpful way of interrogating service users' talk and practice within your agency.

Exercise

Using either the extract below or a (brief) dialogue that you have had with a service user, produce a short commentary on the interaction, drawing on the concepts introduced in Chapters 3 to 5, and paying particular attention to the following:

(a) How is the non-professional person (patient, client, parent) trying to present themselves as credible and 'morally adequate'?
(b) How do they try to make their account seem real and authentic?
(c) Which of the devices referred to in recent chapters are being used?
(d) Do service users do anything different when they are talking to professionals from the way they interact in everyday talk?

An exchange between a client (CL) and a social worker (SW) about rent arrears

70   SW: Did the rent arrears sort of get to the stage where the council were
71   sort of threatening to turn you out?
72   CL: Yes.
73   SW: They did? And what happened? How did you manage to solve
74   that?=
75   CL: =Well, I went down to see them because my husband it's
76   difficult for him to get time off work now. And I went down to
77   see them and I said to them, you know explained to them the

78	situation and ehm I told them that I'd pay them thirty-two
79	pounds a week rent instead of the twenty pounds, so that was
80	just over ten pounds rebate arrears I was clearing off.
81	SW: Yes.
82	CL: And that when I went out to work, I'd be able to give them more,
83	say twenty pounds extra a week.
84	SW: Mm.
85	CL: On top of the thirty-two pounds you know.
86	SW: Yeh=
87	CL: =So that it would clear it up that much quicker and they
88	they were quite pleased at the thirty-two pound actually. Even
89	if I don't go out to work, that thirty-two pound will satisfy
90	them.
91	So we're able to do it. But next week, I don't know,
92	SW: Yeh
93	CL: Or the week after, I don't know.
94	SW: Well it's a bit shaky really=
95	CL: =Well the thing is I know that I've got to pay that money
96	every week=
97	SW: Yeh.
98	CL: Whether or not I've got the food money, even if I have to
99	borrow off Mum and Dad.
100	SW: Yeh.
101	CL: I've got to pay that rent every week, otherwise the kids won't
102	only not have a home.
103	SW: Mm.
104	CL: They'll not have a family anymore. So I've got to sort of
105	( )
106	SW: Isn't it depressing having all this kind of stuff?
107	CL: Well it does=
108	SW: =put a strain on you.
109	CL: It does, but I sort of mm=
110	SW: =Battle on=

(Stenson 1993: 68–9)

Doing professional authority: practitioners constructing accounts

In the previous chapter we explored ways in which insights generated from a close study of talk can be applied to service users' exchanges with HW professionals. In this chapter we shift attention onto an exploration of how professional practitioners/clinicians in HW engage and interact with users of services. We suggest that there is a rich and underexplored literature which can offer fresh insights into the nature of these encounters. This moves us away from treating such encounters as unproblematically concerned with professionals establishing the facts, devising responses or conveying factual information to a standpoint where we regard professional talk as a means to establish authority and to conduct the business of the organization. In particular we are interested in looking at the ways in which professionals attempt to maintain control of the interaction, and how clients might resist these strategies. This raises some important issues about the nature of professional/user relationships and of professional power, and we conclude the chapter with a discussion of these. We begin by looking at conventional approaches to professional practice so that we can bring out the differences between them and the approach we are suggesting.

Conventional approaches to understanding professional practice

Within mainstream approaches, we can identify two principal kinds of literature about the professions: macro, academic studies of the professions, and micro-level studies of practice. The first has tended to be preoccupied with defining the nature of the professions, the process of professionalization and the concept of professionalism. In particular there have been debates about whether the professions should be seen, on the one hand, as 'a positive force in social development, standing against the excesses of *laissez-faire* individualism and state collectivities, and on the other as harmful monopolistic oligarchies' (Johnson 1972: 12). These attempts to define the nature and functions of the professions in modern industrial societies have in turn generated lists of professional attributes, the positive version of which has emphasized altruism and a commitment to public service alongside a specialist knowledge base, regulated education and training, controlled entry and self-regulation of practice.

In the second literature which often is intended for a professional audience (either instead of or as well as an academic audience) the focus is on practice and the implementation of policy and procedures at the local level. The impetus behind micro-level literature has been a desire to reveal 'what really goes on in practice', sometimes with an intent to expose poor practice, failures to implement policy or the fallibility of procedures. This can then form the basis on which to make judgements about standards of performance, whether practice is 'good enough' and for recommendations about how to make improvements. Within these studies it is customary to draw on interview material with workers to demonstrate how 'the facts' about practice have been arrived at. For example, in his study of child protection social work Brian Corby asserts that: 'Group discussions with social workers . . . *revealed* considerable dissatisfaction with the case conference system' (Corby 1987: 70, emphasis added). This is another instance of empiricist discourse (Gilbert and Mulkay 1984) written in such a way as to suggest that 'the facts were revealed' and knowledge was discovered rather than made by the researcher. Corby goes on to identify a particular concern of social workers, namely that whilst they bear considerable responsibilities within the child protection process, they perceive themselves as having little influence in the decision making process. As evidence in support of this conclusion Corby uses the following quote from one of his respondents.

Extract 6.1

It always worries me at case conferences that the only agency who is going to deal with the situation if removal is decided upon is the social services – no other agency. Because they don't have to deal with the follow-through they, therefore, will take that step more easily than we will, because we know the problems of kids in care, but we're the only agency that knows that – that's why we're hanging back much more and that's why we're often the ones in the position of saying no.

(Corby 1987: 71)

One way of treating these data is to accept them as factual evidence in support of Corby's argument about social workers' unease with case conference decision making. But we can also shift our focus away from what is being said to an analysis of *how* it is said, as we have done in previous chapters. We can then see the way in which the social worker emphasizes the separation of social services from other agencies ('the only agency who is') and an 'us and them' situation. They also suggest that the social services department is more measured in its approach because it takes into account not just the situation which led to the case conference but also what might happen to the child if it were removed, thereby acknowledging that care may also be a damaging experience for the child. 'Saying no' to removal of a child is thus presented as a more considered and concerned approach that other professionals fail to appreciate. Within the account the social services' position is defended, indeed presented as the right one, whilst other agencies are criticized for their lack of appreciation of social services' difficulties and for their undue influence over a decision. Who are the responsible professionals in this version? Undoubtedly it is the social workers.

Thus, rather than treating this account as a definitive statement about what happens at case conferences, we can read it in a different way as an example of a social worker 'doing moral adequacy' in inter-professional working. If they were asked, other participants in the child protection process, including parents, would also engage in offensive (undermining other accounts) and defensive rhetoric (warranting their own claims) in a similar fashion. Here is a parent in the same piece of research describing their negative experience of a case conference: 'I was embarrassed more than anything because Tracy's headmistress and Tracy's teacher were there. My head was down the whole time – I was crying . . . if I'd been told they were going to be there, fair enough. I would have been all right, prepared' (Corby 1987: 79). The insensitivity of professionals is counterposed to the sensitivity of ordinary people such as parents, even those subject to a child abuse investigation in another example of a contrast structure. The client is thus 'sympathy worthy' (Spencer 1994).

In this kind of qualitative research, talk is often important but it is usually interview talk in which interviewees comment after the event on aspects of their practice. It is treated as the neutral medium by which professionals and service users communicate to researchers factual information about institutional practices, relations and systems based on their own experiences. Examples of this kind of talk tend to be used for particular purposes: as evidence to substantiate and amplify the facts about HW practice revealed by an author's researches.

An alternative reading of these accounts is to treat them as examples of professional and service user 'atrocity stories' about how they are badly treated either by a specific person or within 'the system' (Stimson and Webb 1975; Dingwall 1977; Baruch 1981). We looked at this topic in the previous chapter in relation to mothers of children with disabilities or long-term medical problems. Seen like this, they are suggestive of how professionals and non-professionals do 'moral worthiness' and attempt to bolster their credibility in the face of a potentially critical audience. However, they may not tell us as much about what goes on in encounters between service users and professionals as we like to think. After all, we know that people's accounts of what they say and do cannot be taken at face value as an accurate depiction of what they 'really' do or what 'really' happened.

It is for this reason that we want to suggest that there are materials and methods available to us which pay greater attention to the detail of encounters between service users and professionals and which can be fruitfully explored in order to illuminate professional practice. These materials use transcripts of tape recordings and detailed field notes to provide examples of institutional talk between professionals and clients. These are analysed using the approaches outlined in Chapter 3 and developed further in relation to everyday talk in Chapter 4 and service users' talk in Chapter 5. Here we focus on professionals talking. We are particularly interested in what they try to accomplish in their interactions with service users. How do they present themselves as credible professionals who speak authoritatively on behalf of their agency or profession? How do they demonstrate professional knowledge and expertise? How do they engage with service users? What devices do they employ in order to convey information, to elicit information, and to establish who is the 'appropriate client'?

The discussion that follows draws on a range of examples from HW and related professions. It should be noted that certain areas of professional activity have been much studied, notably doctor/patient talk (see, for example, Atkinson and Heath 1981; Fisher and Todd 1983; Mishler 1984; Silverman 1987; Davis 1988; Maynard 1991), courtroom exchanges (Atkinson and Drew 1979; Maynard 1984; Levi and Walker 1990; Penman 1990; Drew 1992), counselling and mediation sessions (Edwards 1995; Peräkylä 1995; Greatbatch and Dingwall 1998; Silverman 1997a) and classroom encounters (Sinclair and Coulthard 1975; Stubbs 1976; McHoul 1978; Mehan 1985; Edwards and Mercer 1987). There are far fewer studies of other occupations, in particular the interactions between nurses, health visitors and social workers and patients/service users (although see Baldock and Prior 1981; Pithouse and Atkinson 1988; Heritage and Sefi 1992; Stenson 1993; Latimer 1997a, b for brief published studies).

Before we begin our approach we should reiterate that we are not advocating a social constructionist approach as a means to tell us 'what really happened' in any objectivist sense (see Chapter 2). Rather we are suggesting that we can analyse transcripts and detailed notes and provide an interpretation of them. By 'reading' and interpreting we can make better sense of HW practice than we do if we treat talk and text as mirrors of the truth. The use of such materials also allows other analysts to have access to them and to make other interpretations if they so choose.

Establishing an institutional identity

In the mainstream literature on professions and professionalization it tends to be assumed that professional identity is something which is acquired outside and prior to the encounter with the service user through the medium of training and regulatory procedures. Our approach suggests that we can usefully look at how identity is constituted in talk, as Antaki and Widdicombe put it: 'something that is part and parcel of the routines of everyday life, brought off in the fine detail of everyday interaction' (1998: 1). In such an approach identity becomes a topic to be investigated rather than a resource to be used to explain some factor or other.

An example may help to clarify what we mean. In the following taped extract a teacher (T) is talking to a mother (M) and a father (F) about their daughter Donna who is also present but does not speak.

Extract 6.2

T: [begins by talking about not liking the tape recorder] . . . (hh) Right um Donna um I just took over Mister Jay's class um four weeks ago so, I don't really know a lot about Donna's work I've had a quick look at her work in the folder, and from her mark's she um, you seem to have, passed in the first part of the year and then really gone down in the last um, pieces of work which was a poetry oral? and a um a novel (2.0) a novel in another form that was putting part of the novel into another style of writing. Now um (2.0) in class (1.0) Donna's a little bit distracted? often? Down the back there, with um the girls that she sits with, though she does give in class when she's asked to, she does all her work, um I'm (1.0) would you like to- do you work with Donna at home with her schoolwork at all? do you see it at all or?

F: Not really no=

M: =(We very rarely) see her schoolwork

F: they generally disappear off to their bedrooms with their homework and um=

T: =Ye:es (2.0) Well um

F: We don't see much of (it)

T: Let me see yes I didn't mark this was all Mr Jay's (1.0) This is a summary, they had to summarize um this (1.0) um let's see where her, mistakes seem to lie. (3.0) Oh it seems alright. (3.0) Why did she only get four and a half for that. Hmmm. [. . .]

(Baker 1997: 133)

In this long turn, the teacher provides the parents with information about how Donna is doing in class (note the use of 'Donna is/does' to establish facticity rather than any more tentative framing of the remarks) before inviting the parents to comment on their contribution to her homework. We can read other things into this besides the obvious one of information-giving. The teacher also establishes herself in the identity of a 'teacher': someone who has 'first-hand and long-term knowledge of the student; can read other teachers' notations and make sense of them; observes what is going on, where, in the classroom; knows who the student's friends are; and knows what the parents want to know' (Baker 1997: 133). Despite not having taught Donna for long she nonetheless is able to establish herself in the membership category of experienced and competent teacher whose commentary on Donna's progress is to be trusted. Baker calls it an elaborate version of 'who I am/what I know/what my relevancies are [academic work, classroom behaviour and performance, influence of peers and so forth], and who you are/what you know/what your relevancies are, and what we want of each other' (1997: 134). The talk establishes teacher/parent roles and relations and strongly indicates that 'good' parents will be those who assist with and monitor homework in order to contribute to a home/school partnership – note the lack of conviction expressed by the teacher ('Ye:es (2.0) Well um') when parents justify their lack of oversight of homework by an argument that Donna's behaviour is typical either presumably when compared with her siblings or with teenagers in general and that a certain autonomy is to be expected ('*they* generally disappear off to their bedrooms', emphasis added).

Two points are important here. First, this is a moral construction which lays down the standards of being a 'good teacher' and 'good parent'; second, that identity can be seen as being locally situated and occasioned in talk rather than simply a set of attributes brought to an encounter. You will probably be able to think of occasions where, as a service user, you came across a professional who failed to bring off an identity as a competent practitioner. What was it about their appearance or performance that failed to convince you? Were they inappropriately dressed or did they not seem able to talk authoritatively and demonstrate a command of their work. Alternatively, you will be able to think of an occasion in which someone, encountered either in your personal life or at work, successfully brought off a professional identity. What was it about how they did 'who I am/what I know/what my relevancies are' that persuaded you of their professional authority and expertise? When you consult a doctor, for example, what is it that makes you trust them and decide to follow their advice?

Producing collective institutional identities

Another point to note is the way that professionals in certain circumstances may also draw on a collective identity, speaking of themselves as part of a profession or agency. In the following extract a social worker (SW) is talking to a couple (Lucy and Mark) whose children have been removed following a child abuse investigation. Mark is being prosecuted for alleged violence to one of the children.

Extract 6.3

SW: Going through the files, which obviously **I** had to,
Lucy: [Yeah]
SW: [to get the] court thing together (0.2) y'know it was that you too [sic] had had difficulties around (.) uncontrolled responses, towards the children
Lucy: Yeah
SW: Y'know this is how **I** feel that it is. **My assessment** is that (.) you two (0.4) aren't systematically injuring the children. I mean some people (.) do do that, some forms of child abuse entail that.=
Lucy: =Umhm (0.2)
SW: For you two it's like an uncontrolled response. Y'know, the kids are too much, th- the world's too much, and so (.) you lash out, hh at a moment where you just can't control it. .hhh Now it'sa- its- because of that, and because **I feel** that that that's (.) possibly workable with
Lucy: Umhmm
SW: that (.) **we** want to place as much support into the family to reduce the levels of stress you're experiencing, and work with both you and Mark
Lucy: umhmm
SW: to (continues with proposals)

(Adapted from Potter 1996: 192, emphasis added)

Here we can see the way in which the social worker does 'being a competent social worker' by establishing their 'relevancies': they are someone who has read the files, gathered relevant information and made an interpretation of it. They have used this to put together an assessment of the alleged abuse as an 'uncontrolled response' explicable in terms of stress, rather than, say, a sadistic injury to a child or an instance of habitual cruelty. They can interpret and define behaviour, stating what it is and what it is not, where it stands on a continuum of seriousness and what is an appropriate response. This is all done using 'I' to show that it is a professional judgement by a knowledgeable and authoritative social worker. There is then a switch into using 'we' when it comes to discussing the allocation of resources to support the couple.

Here it is important for the worker to show that they are not operating as a lone individual but as part of an agency which has given its backing to the assessment and the plan. In institutional talk this 'we' can often be important to show that decision making is a collective process. Professionals will often use 'we' to emphasize their membership of a professional group or agency as part of their armoury of defensive rhetoric, designed to advance their authority and credibility and to avoid being singled out for blame. Clients and patients will also back up their opinions by stating that they are shared with others.

Professional detachment

In general, professionals bring off their identity by a neutral, detached stance as evidenced in Extracts 6.2 and 6.3. Neither the teacher nor the social worker introduces any personal elements into the conversation or refers to their own experiences. Specifically, they do not divulge whether they are parents themselves, although this is the highly significant membership category for the service users. Indeed, a distinction to be made between everyday talk and institutional talk is that in the former it is common to invite and receive an empathic response: 'I know just what you mean', 'that happened to me' and so forth, whereas in the latter case there is usually an absence of 'second stories': 'For instance it is absolutely not the business of the psychiatrist, having had some experience reported to him, to say "My mother was just like that, too"' (Sacks 1992b cited in Silverman 1993: 134).

However, there are exceptions to this circumstance when an empathic response is an allowable contribution, primarily in institutional interactions of a quasi-conversational nature. For example, where a counsellor offers comfort to someone who is distressed, it may be acceptable to offer some personal information as a means to demonstrate empathy by the invocation of a common experience and a shared understanding. Indeed, self-help and support groups have burgeoned in recent years for the very purpose of providing the kind of practical and emotional support that 'detached' professional input is said to lack. These organizations are predicated on the assumption that shared experience is an important prerequisite for proper understanding of an issue and meaningful engagement with the client. The assumption underpinning this kind of work is that there is a fundamental difference between institutional and everyday talk and that in situations of crisis and distress the latter is superior.

The negotiation of professional identity

So far, we have indicated that professionals work to achieve an appropriate institutional identity in their interactions with clients in which they tend to present themselves as standing outside the situation, reviewing it in an objective and impersonal manner. However, it would be inappropriate to suggest that control over establishing a professional identity rests solely with the professional. Service users can and do accept the identity proposed by the worker. This is what the mother and father appear to do in Extract 6.2. They do not challenge the teacher's views even though they have grounds to do so on the basis that she has not been teaching their daughter for long. Instead, the teacher puts them on the defensive about their supervision of Donna's homework. They accept the teacher's authority to pronounce on their daughter's school performance and to take up the issue of homework. In Extract 6.3, Mark, although present, makes no contribution and Lucy's response is somewhat ambiguous. She begins with a 'yeah' and then opts for a couple of non-committal 'umhmm's. In doing so, she does not actively endorse what the worker is saying but nor does she openly disagree. She gives the appearance of acquiescence in the worker's designation of 'who I am/what I know/what my relevancies are'.

It is important to recognize here that this tacit acquiescence is local and provisional, it pertains within the limits of this encounter. It does not mean that once the meeting has ended Donna's parents and Lucy and Mark might not say something like 'who do they think they are, telling us how to bring up our kids?' One of the important insights offered by the approach we are suggesting is that it acknowledges and accounts for the shifting nature of consensus and alliances between professionals and service users. Just because clients appear to have taken in what was said and accepted it at the time does not mean that they will not take issue with it later or work to subvert it. For example, Logan conducted research with adoptive parents who, although they had previously consented to contact by the adopted child with their birth family, subsequently demonstrated reluctance to maintain contact when they were interviewed some time after the adoption had taken place. At this stage they produced moral accounts which justified their reluctance as being in the best interests of the child and adoptive family (Logan 1996). This apparent change of heart is puzzling only if we assume that what people say at a given time in particular circumstances is a fixed and enduring indication of their 'true' thoughts and feelings rather than a more provisional statement made as part of a local, situated negotiation.

Service users also challenge professional identity more openly by directly questioning a worker's professional authority or by bringing in *personal* attributes to measure the worker against. For example, in child care it is not uncommon for users to ask social workers 'have you got children yourself?' or 'do you think you are old enough to be telling me what to do with my kids?', making age and personal experience the primary qualifications for making judgements about parenting rather than professional training, knowledge and practice experience. This emphasis on workers' personal traits serves to detach the worker from their organization and challenges their individual claim to credibility. It may also cast doubt on the worthiness of an agency which allows such 'unsuitable' workers to act as its representatives.

In the following extract between a wife (W), husband (H) and two female divorce mediators (M1 and M2), both of whom are social workers, we can see an example of how a client challenges the institutional identity of the mediator.

Extract 6.4

```
1   W:   And er (.) I've had to go out to work. And my next door neighbour's
2        have said is Kathy: (.) this was when she was smaller not so much
3        no:w 'hhh when she was smaller was crying all ni:ght. (.)
```

```
4       You know. And (.) because he were – he'd come in and he was so
        drunk
5       he never heard her.
6       (0.3)
7  H:   You see ⌜you bring this up- hang ⌜o:n hang on love (.) you=
8  M2:         ⌊John's              ⌊( )
9  H:   =bring this up now:, it wasn't brought up at a::ll (.) when you know
10      when we went to cour ⌜:t for access.
11 M2:                       ⌊Ri:ght.
```
(Greatbatch and Dingwall 1998: 123)

In this extract we have another example of offensive rhetoric in which W attempts to undermine the moral adequacy of H as a parent. But what is of most interest to us here is the way that H treats M2's attempted intervention at lines 7–8. Both speak at once, M2 appears to embark on a comment on H either to W or to M1 or to both ('John's') to which H responds by saying 'hang on, hang on love'. As Greatbatch and Dingwall note, the term 'love' has particular connotations: 'In mainstream British English . . . women may use this term when addressing members of either sex, but normally men only use it when addressing females, and in all cases there is a strong suggestion of familiarity' (1998: 123). It strikes a note of informality which would be inconceivable in certain settings, notably the courtroom. It also emphasizes the social identity of M2 not as a professional mediator but as a woman. Greatbatch and Dingwall suggest that this usage has two possible effects: one is to soften H's injunction to M2 not to speak, the other is to upgrade his 'resistance to M2's bid for speakership and thereby further emphasizes the importance he attaches to his response to W' (1998: 124). We might also add that it serves to limit M2's professional authority in the encounter. She is not the one controlling the encounter at this point, H is. (There is a great deal of feminist research which has focused on men's control of conversation with women; see, for example, West 1979; Spender 1980; Tannen 1990; Wodak 1997 for a review of the topic).

Through this discussion we have tried to demonstrate that service users' compliance with an assertion of professional identity cannot be assumed; rather a negotiation takes place within the interaction. Clients resist professional control in a variety of ways, some of them more open than others. In some circumstances certain tactics may be more successful than others. Within the framework of a counselling session there may be more space for a 'counsellee' to take charge and prevent the counsellor coming in as in Extract 6.4. After all, the dialogue in the session is not a means to another resource but a means to solve relationship problems. In contrast we saw in the previous chapter in Extract 5.1 that service users may need to take much more care to defer to the authority of the professional when other resources are at stake (a prescription, a referral to a consultant, a request for a nursery place and so forth). Challenging the personal and professional identity of the practitioner may not be an effective way to portray moral adequacy and create sympathy.

Adversarial approaches are likely to be used with caution by service users, and we perhaps see them most where users are trying to resist the imposition of an unwanted service (a mental health assessment or a child abuse investigation are perhaps the most obvious examples). Compliance and challenge to institutional identity both work on the basis of 'us' (service user) and 'them' (professional) relations. They assume difference and distance. A third approach is one that we referred to in the previous chapter where we suggested (see particularly Extract 5.6) that clients sometimes attempt to undermine the perceived boundaries between professionals and clients by getting the professional onto their side. Using terms such as 'you know what I mean', 'you understand what's happened', 'you know how I feel about this', the user tries to incorporate the practitioner into their way of seeing things.

Indeed, it should be said that both practitioners and service users sometimes work together to blur the boundaries between friendship and professional intervention. In a televized documentary about childcare social work a mother whose children were being removed by the police and social workers was heard to say plaintively to the social worker, 'How could you do this to me, I thought you were my friend?' In HW welfare work where empathy and unconditional positive regard have the status of core values (social work, counselling and nursing are the most obvious candidates) it is hardly surprising that these boundaries become somewhat obscured as workers and clients work to play up non-institutional identities and play down institutional ones as a means to 'do business together'.

Fact making vs fact-gathering

We have explored how institutional identities are produced in the interactions between practitioners and service users in the previous section. We now need to turn our attention to another aspect of the business of institutional talk, that is the way in which facts are produced. Within HW, asking questions, seeking information, forming diagnoses or assessments and imparting information are essential elements of the daily routine. Whilst information is also sought from other informants, lay and professional, and documentary sources (for example files and reports – see Chapter 8), it is the interview with the client or patient which is fundamental to the diagnostic or assessment process in HW. The ability, therefore, to conduct interviews and to ask good questions is strongly emphasized. Gathering 'the facts' and information about feelings (the latter may not always be accorded such importance) is seen as intrinsic to the professional task. Kvale (1996) refers to this approach as 'the interviewer as miner' in which 'knowledge is understood as buried metal and the interviewer is a miner who unearths the valuable metal . . . knowledge is waiting in the subject's interior to be uncovered, uncontaminated by the miner' (1996: 3).

As you will expect from your reading so far, we want to unsettle this notion of fact-*gathering* (or mining) by suggesting that it is useful to regard facts as made rather than gathered. HW professionals do not simply gather facts randomly in a manner ordained by the facts themselves. They are not empiricists who simply collect 'all there is to know' and then sift through to determine what is relevant. They go into situations looking for specific things and with particular views about what is normal and acceptable behaviour. Upon this basis they make judgements about abnormal, deviant behaviour and decide when 'something ought to be done'. In their practice they are guided by checklists and proformas which classify problem behaviours and list signs and symptoms (for example the psychiatric classification schedule the DSM-III and III-R; see Thornton (1992) for a discussion). HW practitioners draw on implicit and explicit rules about relevance.

As indicated in our previous discussion about professional identities, HW workers shape information to construct an authoritative version of situations and events. We could see this clearly in Extract 6.3 where the social worker chose, from a range of possible interpretations, to account for an instance of child abuse in terms of uncontrolled responses. On this basis, they determined that the most appropriate intervention was not to remove the children but to provide support to the family to diminish the stress upon the parents. In other words, the 'facts' lent themselves to different interpretations and the worker selected one of these as the most fitting. In order to explore these issues we intend to focus on two particular aspects of the interview process – information seeking and information delivery – as these can help us to make sense of the fact making process that is contained within it and illustrate our argument effectively.

Information seeking

Health and welfare professionals seek information from patients and service users in a variety of settings and circumstances. Sometimes the duration of the contact is very short, as in the average GP consultation. In other situations the interview process will last some time and, indeed, may be conducted over a period of several weeks, for instance when a social worker undertakes a comprehensive or core childcare assessment (Department of Health 1988a, 1999; Department of Health *et al.* 2000). In cases of long-term illness or treatment, interviews with an HW professional may be a regular feature of a client's life. What characterizes the interview, regardless of its length or frequency, is its use of the question and answer format. Institutional talk within interviews is epitomized by a much more interrogatory style than is typical in everyday conversation. In institutional encounters, such as our contacts with a doctor, dentist, nurse or social worker, we expect to be asked questions. The 'deal' is that we give information which is turned into a diagnosis or assessment and returned to us as the definition of the problem and its solution.

Attention to the detail of talk has suggested that there are different kinds of questions that may be asked: real questions which genuinely seek information unknown by the questioner; 'exam' questions asked by someone who already knows the answer and is testing the knowledge of the person asked, for example by a teacher; and 'admit' questions asked in order to get the respondent to admit to something that they would rather not reveal, for example to a parent suspected of child abuse (Searle 1969; Hutchby and Wooffitt 1998). What sorts of question do you think are being asked in the following extract? A is the defence attorney and B is a witness and the complainant in a rape trial.

Extract 6.5

```
 1   A: . . . you have had sexual intercourse on a previous occasion haven't you?
 2   B: Yes.
 3   A: On many previous occasions?
 4   B: Not many.
 5   A: Several?
 6   B: Yes.
 7   A: With several men?
 8   B: No.
 9   A: Just one.
10   B: Two.
11   A: Two. And you are seventeen and a half?
12   B: Yes.
```

(Levinson 1992: 83)

Here we can see an example of a device that, in the jargon of conversation analysis (CA), is called **turn-type pre-allocation** being used in a trial. In essence this means that in certain formal arenas (courts and official ceremonies are the prime examples) there are strict conventions about who may speak, when and what they might say. We saw in the last chapter (in particular in Extracts 5.3 and 5.4) that witnesses must follow a restricted format and 'turns' are set down in a specific pattern: in the court, lawyers ask questions and witnesses must wait for the question and then answer it. They should not butt in, refuse to answer or digress in their reply. We can see also that the lawyer's questions are of the 'admit' type. From our understanding of such exchanges we can see how the defence lawyer devises questions which will portray the witness as a woman of loose morals by reference to her sexual activities and her age. At the same time the witness attempts a damage limitation exercise to preserve her moral adequacy ('not many', 'two'). We should also remember that in formal settings like the court the presence of an 'overhearing audience' of magistrates or judge and jury is also crucial. The lawyer is not asking 'real' questions seeking information, but ones designed to influence the views of those who will adjudicate on the matter in hand.

Much of HW work consists of less formal institutional talk in the surgery, interview room, ward, clinic and so forth rather than in the court or traditional classroom. Since there are not the same restrictions on the conduct of such exchanges the interactions may be conducted in a more conversational style. The interview proper may be prefaced with casual chat about the weather, or non-institutional talk may be introduced during the institutional part of the interaction (in much the same way as a visit to the hairdresser seems to encompass talk about holidays as well as the business of the haircut). In some circumstances, however, a formal style is preferred, using a short question and answer format. There may be various reasons for this: the interview may occur when time is limited and there is a need to get on with the business in hand, as is often the case in the GP consultation; to produce the effect of authority and gravitas (as in some medical consultations and ward rounds); or in quasi-judicial interviews to emphasize the investigative nature of the process (as in a child protection case). The next extract is dialogue taken from a consultation in a cardiac unit between a doctor (D) and a patient (P).

Extract 6.6

```
 1  D: Heaviness and breathlessness? //
 2  P: Yes//
 3  D: Where? Heaviness, where?
 4  P: Here.
 5  D: Yes.
 6  P: Here. Near this side more. Cross the top //
 7  D: You will get it on exertion?
 8  P: =Yes. A // (   ) And it ends up like pain ah – a
 9  D: =Yes
10  P: Heaviness in the throat.
11  D: Hmm.
12  P: I went to the doctor and explained to (0.8) it was (0.4)
13     one of the group I saw //
14  D: =Yes //   Yes //
15  P: =not my doctor// I've had him for forty-eight years.
16  D: Yes. Would you only get this if you exerted yourself?
```
(Adapted from Hughes 1982: 371)

This interaction is very much oriented to the business of defining symptoms and making a diagnosis. It is noticeable that the patient's reference to having had the same GP for forty-eight years arouses no comment from the consultant. In a less functional, more conversational exchange it might have prompted some form of response, but here the patient is quickly brought back to the task in hand of symptom description. Not only is there an absence of second stories (where professional people share information about themselves) but D is oriented to only very specific forms of 'first story', that is only to those aspects of the patient that are relevant to a possible cardiac complaint. This is very much a technical display by D. 'Who I am/what I know/what my relevancies are' is much more narrowly focused in comparison with Donna's teacher in Extract 6.2 who is interested not simply in academic performance but also in classroom behaviour and contributions as well as homework.

In certain circumstances, questioning may require greater tact and delicacy than that shown in the rather abrupt exchanges of Extracts 6.5 and 6.6. After all, much of the work of HW practitioners involves quite tricky areas of people's personal lives such as discussing allegations of child abuse, compulsory admission to a psychiatric unit, the investigation and treatment of serious illness or dealing with someone who has been bereaved. In such situations the interaction between practitioner and client may be tentative and punctuated by lengthy pauses. This is illustrated by the following example in which an AIDS/HIV counsellor (C) is interviewing a patient (P) at a genito-urinary clinic in a British hospital.

Extract 6.7

```
 1  C: Has your pa:rtner ever used a condom with you?
 2      (1.0)
 3  P: N:o
 4      (1.5)
 5  C: Do you know what a condom looks like?
 6      (0.5)
 7  P: (I don't)
 8      (0.3)
 9  C: (Did you) (0.3) have you perhaps- (1.0) the condom
10      shown to you at school?=Or?
11  P: No
```

(Silverman 1997a: 41)

The pace of this is radically different from that of the rape trial exchange in Extract 6.5. That comprised a volley of brief, often one-word questions and answers. It too could be said to be dealing with delicate matters, after all the defence lawyer is effectively accusing the witness of low morals, but there is no hesitation in the exchange. The 'admit' questions of the defence lawyer need to be expressed in a frank and explicit way. They are designed to blame the witness in front of an overhearing audience. It is very much an attacking style.

In contrast, the AIDS/HIV counsellor has a more didactic intent. The first question is perhaps a real one, possibly an 'admit' one but of a different

order. The thrust behind the counsellor's turns is an educative and pre-
ventive one: safe sex and the use of condoms protect against HIV/AIDS,
therefore it is helpful to find out whether the patient's partner uses condoms
and what the patient knows about them. An adversarial, antagonistic tone,
as in the rape trial, is unlikely to be effective in achieving the institutional
goal to promote safe sex. The counsellor therefore allows the patient a lot
of time to frame their answers and takes especial care at lines 9–10, rephras-
ing their question and pausing twice whilst saying it. This is not, after all,
a situation that lends itself to a simple injunction 'you must insist that
your partner uses condoms', since such a direct undermining of P's moral
adequacy is likely to be counter-productive. A much more cautious tone is
adopted and the underlying message about the protective value of condoms
is contained within a series of apparently factual enquiries about familiarity
with and use of condoms. The demands of the adversarial courtroom style
are quite antithetical to the delicately balanced relationship between counsellor and patient.

This suggests that there are no absolutes about good professional practice:
what works in one setting is not necessarily transferable to another. We
may also have strong reservations about the effectiveness of certain professional styles of questioning, in particular the defence cross-examination
of key witnesses in rape trials. Such a style may be highly effective in
protecting the innocence of the accused but, by the same token, it serves
to discredit, even to humiliate the complainant in a highly public fashion.
We would suggest that we need to subject interviewing to greater scrutiny
in order to understand better how it works, what is effective, why and
for whom.

This leads us to a vital point about the framing of questions. This is not
just an issue of the skilled use of **open, closed** and **leading questions** as some
of the professional literature on communication would seem to suggest.
Such a focus is predicated on the assumption that more impartial knowledge is gathered when clients are asked open questions so that they may
choose how to respond, than when they are asked closed ones which constrain their replies. In contrast, we are interested in the detail of how being
an effective defence counsel or AIDS counsellor is performed in everyday
situations. This is what Silverman (1997a) means when he argues that some
of the devices adopted by counsellors (for example their more tentative
style) do not necessarily indicate 'bad' counselling but can actually be
accounted for within the terms of the local situation of counselling people
who are undergoing AIDS/HIV testing.

Imparting information

The delivery of information is another vital aspect of HW work. Some
of this may be regarded as routine, such as the dispensing of a prescription

for a minor complaint. It may be a relatively straightforward matter of telling the patient what is wrong and the do's and don'ts regarding the taking of medication. As you can see from earlier examples, even this activity is worthy of scrutiny. However, in many situations, HW practitioners have to impart information of an extremely delicate nature. You will no doubt be able to think of examples from your own practice where this has been the case. You may have had to inform parents of your intention to begin legal proceedings to remove their child, or to tell someone that you were of the opinion that they should be retained in a psychiatric unit against their wishes, or to inform someone that they have a life-threatening illness, or about the death of a relative. Specific devices may be used in such situations in order to lead gently into the topic area and to soften the blow of the news. What are the devices that workers use? One has been termed the **perspective display series** (PDS) (Maynard 1991), which is a rather obscure term describing a very straightforward technique – in fact you are almost certain to have used it yourself on many occasions in your personal and professional life. Let us look at the example Maynard provides from an encounter between a doctor and a mother in a paediatric clinic for children with 'developmental difficulties'.

Extract 6.8

```
 1  Dr E:   What do you see? as – his difficulty.
 2  Mrs C:  Mainly his uhm – the fact that he doesn't understand
 3          everything and also the fact that that his speech is very hard to
 4          understand what he's saying, lots of time
 5  Dr E:   Right
 6  Dr E:   Do you have any ideas WHY it is? are you – do you?
 7  Mrs C:  No
 8  Dr E:   Okay I you know I think we BASICALLY in some ways agree
 9          with you, insofar as we think that D's MAIN problem, you know
10          DOES involve you know LANGuage,
11  Mrs C:  Mm hmm
12  Dr E:   you know both you know his – being able to underSTAND, and
13          know what is said to him, and also certainly also to be able
14          to express, you know his uh thoughts
15                                  (1.0)
16  Dr E:   Um, in general his development . . .
```
                                                (Maynard 1991: 468)

The use of a PDS in the above extract provides a way for the doctor to prepare the mother for bad news. The difficulty of this situation is probably compounded when it involves a child's mother, for here is someone who knows their child, who may have assembled a range of evidence to support a thesis that the child is improving. How can the doctor dash her hopes by producing a negative assessment that may be seen as a challenge to her competence to 'know' her child? As Silverman notes, 'the function of the PDS in such an institutional context is that it seeks to align the mother to the upcoming diagnosis' (Silverman 1993: 135). This is done by Dr E inviting the mother's opinion, giving a token agreement ('Right') and then reformulating what the mother defines as speech problem as one of language. Notice also the repeated use of 'you know' as Dr E tries to get Mrs C on board with his diagnosis, and the use of 'we' (line 8) to indicate that this is not simply Dr E's personal opinion but a shared professional one. Overall, Maynard suggests that 'a confirmation, reformulation and elaboration of the child's condition all occur, and, in several ways, coimplicate the recipient's perspective in the diagnostic news' (1991: 468–9); in other words PDS allows the practitioner to shape what they want to say according to the sort of preliminary response obtained from the patient or client, in Maynard's terms to coimplicate the client.

PDS is also a standard technique for giving feedback on performance. First ask the person how they think they have performed. You then have a better idea of what they are expecting from you and you can use that as a platform to put across what you want to say. The device is particularly useful as a preamble to giving 'bad news' or negative feedback.

Silverman also deals with this issue of delicate information delivery in his study of counselling for people testing for HIV/AIDS. His analyses of counsellor/patient talk suggest that counsellors employed different formats to put across information about transmission and ways to practise safe sex. A frequently-used format was a non-personalized delivery which avoided getting into the specifics of the patient's situation, focusing more widely on general ways that people behave and hypothetical situations that the patient might encounter. Advice was also put across in the guise of information delivery to make it more palatable to patients. Some of these aspects are evident in the following extract from a pre-HIV test interview between a counsellor (C) and a patient (P).

Extract 6.9

```
1   C:  .hhhh Now when someone er is tested (.) and they
2       ha:ve a negative test result .hh it's obviously
3       ideal uh:m that (.) they look after themselves
4       to prevent ⌈any further risk of=
5   P:             ⌊Mm Hm
6   C:  =infection. .hhhh I mean obviously this is only
7       possible up to a point because if .hhh you get into
8       a sort of serious relationship with someone that's
9       long ter:m .hh you can't obviously continue to use
```

10   condoms foreyer. .hh Uh:m and a point has to come
11   where you make a sort of decision (0.4) uh:m if you
12   are settling down about families and things that you
13   know (0.6) you'd- not to continue safer sex . . .

(Silverman 1997a: 113)

Professional power and client resistance

So far we have looked at how professionals establish their institutional
identity in their encounters with service users and described some of the
ways in which patients and clients might accept, comply with or challenge
that identity. Subsequently we have looked at some of the devices that
practitioners employ to seek out and deliver information about delicate and
highly personal aspects of users' lives. This raises some important issues
about who exercises control in practitioner/user interactions.

Common-sense views treat power as a possession, something that people
or groups bring into their dealings with others to exert control and exact
compliance or consent. Within this kind of thinking, politicians and busi-
nesspeople are seen to have power. In these politically correct times it has
become conventional to argue that white, middle-class men are the power-
holders and that women, black people and disabled people (amongst others)
are oppressed and powerless. Similarly, managers are deemed to have
power over workers, supervisors over supervisees and so forth. In social
work education and training, for example, it is customary to argue that
practice teachers have power over students because of their role in the
facilitation and assessment of practice learning, their (presumed) greater
knowledge and practice experience and their position within the agency
hierarchy. They are then enjoined to consider how they can exercise this
power positively and how they might empower the student. Thus, power is
treated as a sort of invisible parcel that a person or social group carries
around with them.

Our micro approach to how knowledge is produced locally in the day-to-
day routines of institutional talk suggests that we might take a different
position apropos the concept of power which moves away from the power-
as-possession stance and assumptions that gender (or any other social
identity) automatically confers power in any simple causal way. Indeed,
one of the great strengths of micro-sociological/discursive psychological
approaches is that they treat issues such as gender and power as topics to
be explored rather than resources to explain a particular phenomenon. Kathy
Davis (1988, 1991) provides an interesting illustration of what we mean.
As an avowed feminist, Davis undertook research into the power relations
between male doctors and female patients. She expected her findings to be
similar to those of other feminist studies of health care for women, namely

that doctors controlled women's fertility and reproduction; that doctors made overt judgements about women's sexuality and childcare skills; that women were not taken seriously in medical consultations; and that women's problems tended to be treated as psychological rather than physical in origin (Davis 1991: 75). When Davis studied the minutiae of doctor/patient talk her findings were quite different:

> Much to my surprise (and admittedly, chagrin), I was forced to conclude, . . . that the GPs were behaving in an undisputedly friendly and benevolent fashion. They displayed an unflaggingly sympathetic interest in their patients' problems, even the most trivial ones . . . In fact it was almost as though I had wandered into a conversation between two friends rather than an institutional encounter. It did not look anything like a power struggle.
>
> (Davis 1991: 76)

Just as Davis expected to find powerful, authoritarian behaviour on the part of the doctors so too she expected the patients to be 'scarcely able to hold their own, hapless and helpless in the face of the combined forces of institutional authority and male domination' (Davis 1991: 76). Instead she found patients who could be 'surprisingly recalcitrant and rebellious' and who 'routinely exercised power in all sorts of subtle, sneaky and even somewhat unorthodox ways' (1991: 76). From this Davis concluded that a top-down model of power was inadequate and that what was needed was 'a model which treats power relations as something to be negotiated by parties who both have access to some resources, albeit unequal ones' (1991: 81). The advantages of such an approach are that it moves away from regarding power as inevitably concerned with repression and coercion; it avoids treating those in the 'underdog' position as hapless and helpless victims' (it would suggest also that being an 'underdog' is worthy of investigation, not an attribute to be assumed); and it acknowledges that power is present in ostensibly pleasant and friendly interactions.

Rather than assuming that professionals have power in their encounters with clients simply because they are professionals, we need to shift the focus somewhat and ask different and better questions about power relations. How do professionals convey authority in their interactions with clients? How do they exercise control? What strategies do clients adopt to resist this control? Who defines 'the facts' and how? These seem much more fruitful avenues for analysis because they do not make presumptions about power and this seems to accord with the practice experiences of HW professionals. Patients are not docile and passive recipients of advice and treatment. They use the resources at their disposal to show their moral adequacy, to resist being undermined, to attempt to define 'the facts' and to make themselves worthy of sympathy.

We can explore this process a little further in the following two final extracts which detail interactions between a health visitor (HV) and the mother (M) and father (F) of a new baby in 6.10a, and a mother (M) and grandmother (G) in 6.10b.

Extract 6.10a

```
 1  HV:  Have you thought about the immunisations yet.
 2       (0.5)
 3  F:   Not rea:lly 'ave we?
 4  M:   N ⌈o:.
 5  HV:    ⌊The: ones on offer are diptheria (.)
 6       whooping cough (.) tetanus (.) polio
 7       and measles.
 8       (0.2)
 9       'hh And the (0.3) health authority
10       recommend (0.7) that unless there's a family
11       history on (0.4) the immediate side your
12       . . . brothers and sisters or your brothers and
13       sisters 'hh with a history of epilepsy
14  F:   Mm:,
```
[conversation continues on this topic in similar vein to line 63]

(Heritage and Sefi 1992: 399)

Extract 6.10b

```
1  M:   No: that's what they ( . . . ).=
2  HV:  =Babies loose [sic] a lot
3       of heat through their heads so =
4  G:   =Well she's ⌈always got a hat ⌈on (   )
5  HV:             ⌊b-              ⌊Bonnets are
6       worth having.
```
(Adapted from Heritage and Sefi 1992: 408)

Here the HV's relevancies are to assess current care, identify problems, offer advice, and pick up on health promotion issues like vaccinations. Both extracts demonstrate HV's professional identity through her knowledge of infant care and her assumption of the right to give advice, the stock-in-trade of her work. However, the response of the parents in each of the extracts is interesting. In Extract 6.10a the mother and father remain extremely non-committal about having their child vaccinated, they give what Heritage and Sefi call an 'unmarked acknowledgement', that is they merely issue a series of 'ums' (much as Lucy did in Extract 6.3). Their resistance is passive. They do not engage HV in argument or say that they refuse to consider vaccination, they merely side-step the issue.

This illustrates the limits of the health visitor's control and authority: she can advise and attempt to persuade but she cannot oblige the parents to comply. In the matter of vaccinations the parents have the right to decide.

In Extract 6.10b an alternative form of resistance is displayed. The health visitor gives advice but both the mother and grandmother put in a claim of competence: not only are they aware of the problem of the baby getting cold but they have already attended to the matter and routinely put a bonnet on the baby. The advice is therefore superfluous (although it does not stop HV persisting with her advice-giving in this instance). This is a more active strategy than the 'unmarked acknowledgement' but both are used as forms of resistance to the health visitor's advice giving.

From this discussion we want to suggest that a cautious approach should be adopted towards the issue of asymmetry in practitioner/client relations. It should not simply be assumed that professionals are inevitably dominant because of their 'power' and status. Instead we should explore how professionals assert their knowledge and relevancies and when and how clients attempt resistance of either an active or a passive kind.

Summary

Our focus in this chapter has continued the theme of institutional talk begun in Chapter 5. However, we have shifted attention away from clients to explore the topic in relation to HW practitioners. We have addressed three major themes: how professionals establish their institutional identity; how facts are made in relation to the seeking and imparting of information; and the issue of professional power and client resistance. In the next chapter we continue this exploration of institutional talk but concentrate on professionals talking to each other about clients and client issues.

Practice implications

Professional talk has been given very little attention by practitioners who tend to focus on what was said rather than acknowledging the performative aspects of talk. We argue that professionals' talk acts to establish institutional identity and authority. Even when you are giving information you may well be indicating what your service's expectations of clients are. We are not suggesting that you stop talking to clients/patients for fear of saying the wrong thing! That would neither be feasible nor desirable. But we are suggesting that you listen much more carefully to your own practice talk and that of others. How do you say things? Why do you say them in that way? How do you try to achieve compliance from service users? How does resistance manifest itself and how do you deal with it? What are the situations in which you feel 'powerless' with clients? Are there times when clients' voices are silenced or not listened to? These are not idle questions but ones of central importance to you as practitioners.

If talk is at the heart of HW practice then we need to understand it better. In our view, microsociologies and discourse analysis offer useful tools for this enterprise.

Exercises

EXERCISE 1

Analyse the following extract paying particular attention to the following:

(a) How does the professional establish their institutional identity?
(b) How do they seek or impart information?
(c) How do they produce 'the facts'?
(d) How does the service user interact with the practitioner? Who controls the encounter and how? Is there any evidence of resistance on the part of the client?

Extract 1

This is an extract between a female AIDS/HIV counsellor (C) and a male patient (P) who has visited a genito-urinary clinic several times previously for HIV testing. The original transcription conventions have been retained because they indicate the pauses and overlaps in the talk (see appendix).

```
 1   C: you can actually [create your own NSU by by stress
 2   P:                   [mm
 3   C: and worry
 4   P: mm I see I'm not the type of person to heh heh (  )
 5      [stress
 6   C: [yes but it might be [something you're submerging up
 7   P:                      [get stressed
 8   C: here you see
 9   P: mm[hmm
10   C:   [and (.) mixed up with that is is (.) the worry
11      about (.) what you hear on TV and radio and (.) and
12      what you read in the news[papers
13   P:                          [mmm
14   C: and magazines hh and so (0.5) mi there's a great
15      complete mixmatch of of (.) what's actually
16      happening to human beings at the moment in (.) in GU
17      medicine because they're still worried [about
18   P:                                         [mm
19   C: HIV as well as a sexually transmitted disease < so so it
20      might be one of these you know=
21   P: =mm
```

22 C: that that's creating the problem (0.5) so hh um
23   (1.0) I think what you have to do is (.) when you've
24   had your clean bill of health this time
25   (0.4)
26 P: yes
27 C: is (.) [[softly]] get on with <u>living</u>
28 P: I do live my life anyway so

(Silverman 1997a: 149–50)

EXERCISE 2

Put together a transcript of a piece of professional/service user talk drawn from your own or a colleague's practice. You could either tape this (if that is permitted within your agency and by the client) or you could make detailed notes as soon after the encounter as is practicable. Analyse the transcript using the questions in Exercise 1 and material contained in this and previous chapters.

Arguing the case: professionals talking together

Chapters 5 and 6 discussed some of the strategies employed by service users and professionals to persuade each other of certain things, or to control the talk in their encounters with each other. It seems self-evident that the meeting with a client/patient is the principal arena in which professionals make sense of the situations they confront. The whole idea of assessment and clinical judgement presupposes that, during their meeting with a patient/client, practitioners are actively categorizing and ordering the person's 'troubles' and that this will inform subsequent action. It is not surprising, therefore, that researchers, too, have been concerned to understand what happens in these encounters. In previous chapters, we have sampled the rich literature generated by this academic interest in professional/client interaction of various kinds.

In this chapter, we want to show how formal and informal conversations taking place between professionals, away from the encounter with the service user, can also have profound significance. Paul Atkinson (1995) notes that the usual preoccupation with the doctor/patient (professional/client) encounter creates the illusion that decisions are taken instantaneously, that they somehow arise out of the communicative strategies used by the professional, or from their spontaneous judgements about clients' responses to their questions. However, Atkinson notes:

> The analysis of doctor–patient interaction, conventionally conducted, cannot capture the more protracted and dispersed processes of work that are pervasive of modern medical organizations.
>
> (Atkinson 1995: 33–5)

The smaller number of studies focusing on the practical reasoning used by professionals, and on their ways of warranting decisions and judgements to *each other*, confirm that these processes exert a material influence upon process and outcome (see, for example, Bloor 1976; Pithouse 1987; Atkinson 1995; Hall 1997; Latimer 1997a; White 1997a). In this chapter we want to introduce you to some of this empirical work and to ask you to reflect on the ways in which talking to your colleagues influences the interpretations you make about cases. We shall examine the extracts of professional talk in a number of ways and on a number of different levels to show how it does several jobs.

First, we shall look for the subtle rhetorical strategies at play, that is, for the performative features of the talk: what work the talk is doing. You will recognize some of these strategies from previous chapters; however, we shall show that, in the context of inter-professional talk, they can have particular potency. They may open up new ways of conceptualizing the 'problem', but rather more often they seem to serve to reinforce a partial reading of a case. Second, we shall explore the operation of shared professional discourses. Or, we should say Discourses (see Chapter 3), for these are not simply local ways of thinking but are dominant forms of knowledge which often reflect broader societal or theoretical notions. When professionals talk to each other, these forms of knowledge or tacit understandings are often displayed. They provide the taken-for-granted components of practice. Sometimes, in multidisciplinary settings, we can see how certain knowledges associated with particular professions can be privileged, carrying more weight than those associated with other occupations. Third, following from this we shall show how inter-professional talk can display, reproduce and reinforce aspects of professional identities (Dingwall 1977; Rawlings 1981; Travers 1994; White 1997a, 1998a, 1999a). As all these aspects of collegial talk impact on professional sense making, it is important for a reflexive practitioner to be aware of them.

Argument and rhetoric: inter-professional talk as public reasoning

There is a dominant notion, both in professional education and in social research, that the case 'formulation' or 'diagnosis' arises from the ether in the encounter between the professional and the client. This notion does have some cogency: categorization and sense making *are* taking place in the encounter as professionals sift and weigh information, decide what questions to ask, make judgements about the veracity of the statements they hear, construct and assign moral character and so forth. Were this not the case, we should not have needed to write the last two chapters. However, this is not the whole story and we need to look at the way inter-professional talk is assembled and what are its effects.

Although it is based on a series of shared professional and indeed 'ordinary' social understandings (see Chapters 3 and 4), sense making in the encounter remains in essence an internal, private action. It might show itself in the choice of questions or in reactions to answers given, but in these settings professionals do not usually 'show their working'. However, the act of 'sense making' is given a public face in subsequent (or sometimes prior) discussions with colleagues and other professionals. These public airings are particularly fertile grounds for 'knowledge making'.

Charles Antaki (1994b), a discursive psychologist (see Chapter 3), has drawn attention to the very social nature of public reasoning. He argues for a shift in attention away from trying to understand individual cognitive reasoning processes, and towards looking for the ways in which people publicly account for their opinions and judgements. He argues that:

> everyday reasoning – at least, reasoning out loud – is often justificatory and always partial . . . ordinary reasoning can be much more a case of authorizing what one is saying than genuinely reaching an answer unknown at the start of the journey . . .
>
> (Antaki 1994b: 182)

In other words, in spite of speakers referring to other perspectives or alternative viewpoints, these are cited only to give greater rhetorical force to the 'ready-made' viewpoint or opinion, which is actually quite solid and not really up for negotiation. For example, in reciting their argument, speakers often 'answer' anticipated counter-arguments (this is similar to the notion of stake inoculation described in Chapter 4). These 'answers' may appear to be equivocations. They often claim uncertainty, but the effect of them, Antaki argues, is ironic. They actually mark certainty and rationality, and protect the speaker from challenge. Consider the following example:

> She appears to be perfectly happy, I mean she can't be a hundred percent happy, nobody is, but she appears to be happy
>
> (Antaki 1994b: 179)

Here, Antaki notes that the claim that someone is happy, is moderated and hedged by the phrase 'appears to be' and by the qualification that she cannot be completely happy because nobody is. However, the effect of this 'hedging' is to convey considered rationality, rather than wild speculation.

What has all this to do with professional practice? Surely professional talk has the flavour of formal reasoning, a genuine searching for truth after rigorous enquiry. Sometimes this may indeed be the case; however, as we show in following extracts, it is not the whole story. Moreover, particularly when only one professional group is involved in the talk (for example, doctors to doctors), a process of **co-narration**, where different speakers 'chip in' with affirming statements, reinforces the rhetorical force of what is a partial reading of a case.

Ascribing and fixing identities in professional talk

Joanna Latimer (1997a) has noted how identities are ascribed to service users through professional talk. We agree and shall argue that the processes of public reasoning referred to above have the potential to produce fixed patient or client identities for people referred to HW services. The examples are taken from childcare social work, paediatrics and 'geriatrics', all of which show how a variety of linguistic strategies are used to mark certainty and uncertainty and to fix identities and stories in particular ways.

Example 1: The use of reported speech

This rather lengthy first example enables you to see the cumulative rhetorical quality of the talk. We looked briefly at a small part of this extract (adapted from White 1997a) in Chapter 1 (Extract 1.7). Now that you have a range of conceptual tools at your disposal, it is appropriate to examine it in more detail. The transcript is taken from a social work allocation meeting, which is a weekly forum, in which the team manager attempts to allocate to an individual social worker referrals requiring further action. The social workers are discussing a child, Sophie Byrne, aged 10, about whom various concerns have been raised. The case here has been divided into four parts corresponding to the social workers' reports of the accounts of the various parties involved in the case. The use of reported speech (Leuder and Antaki 1996; Hall 1997) is a powerful way of marking certainty and uncertainty in talk. The extract begins with a discussion about the origins of the referral.

Extract 7.1

Part 1: Reporting the referrer's story
TL: This is really worrying . . . Right. Sophie Byrne is ten she lives [address] and
it was referred by, people will probably *remember* the referral cos it was
referred by Kate Cross [education welfare officer] which is a bit of a con-
voluted referral but we get there in the end. Kate had been talking to the
Head of Year about Mike Brooks, about Mike's absences from school. During
this conversation it transpired that Mike's course tutor had been told by two
other pupils at the school, that Mike was shagging a ten year old called
Sophie . . . Kate rang the local school and located Sophie Byrne at [name]
School. Staff at [the school] told Kate that three teenage boys collected
Sophie from school one day last week. *Recently,* Sophie's mother went to
pick her up from school and Sophie wasn't there. Sophie's mother in the
past has requested ed. psych's (educational psychologist) help for Sophie
and Mum finds her behaviour very difficult to deal with. One morning last
week, [the team leader is reading from the file] which is now about three
weeks ago, Sophie's parents found her wandering around the precinct at
2 am. Kate had no further details. Mike is actually staying with the Anderson
family. Nobody knows why he is staying there. Kate managed to identify the
child as Sophie Byrne through statements the children made and by reference to the accounts from [school] of Sophie being met by older boys from
school. Actually, it looks as though from the onset Kate put two and two

together from what the pupils at [secondary school] said and spoke to the Head of [school] and she confirmed accounts of Sophie being met by older boys. This had happened the week before last, which as I say is about three weeks ago . . . The children often arrive late for school and are not really collected. Oliver is 7. Is he 7? . . . There were no major concerns at the previous school. However, there had been one incident outside school where Sophie had been with a group of older boys who were smoking . . .

At the beginning of this extract, the team leader sets the tone with the statement, 'This is really worrying'. She tells the team that an education welfare officer (Kate) has reported hearing a rumour that a teenage boy (Mike) is reported to be 'shagging' (having sexual relations with) a 10-year-old girl, believed to be Sophie Byrne. We are told that Sophie's mother finds her behaviour 'very difficult to deal with' and it also transpires that Sophie has been found with a friend wandering around a local shopping precinct at 2 am. The story has conventional narrative format (see Chapter 3). For example, it is heavily temporally marked (for example, 'one day last week', 'recently', 'one morning last week', 'about three weeks ago'), giving it an unfolding dramatic quality. The deductions of the education welfare officer are afforded a factual status (for example, 'Kate managed to identify', 'she confirmed') and thus are used to 'authorize' (Smith 1978; see Chapter 3) a particular reading of the case. The boy's circumstances are portrayed as rather suspect and surrounded in mystery: 'Mike is actually staying with the Anderson family. Nobody knows why he is staying there'. Deviance is referenced through descriptions of behaviour which breaches category-bound expectations of childhood (for example, Sophie is a 10-year-old child and was found wandering around the precinct at 2 am; when she was 8, she was with a group of boys who were smoking). The narration then passes to a social worker who recounts the father's version of events.

Extract 7.2

Part 2: Reporting the father's story

SW: So we wrote to Mrs Byrne and asked her to come into the office . . . she didn't turn up. So we telephoned and asked, and told them we needed to speak to her and we got Mr Byrne who was quite erm irate that we hadn't written to him as well. So I told him we didn't have that information and he came in . . . straight away and we discussed the concerns with Mr Byrne. Mr Byrne initially said that he felt it was just boys talking, the concern about Sophie being shagged was just playground chit chat and he had no concerns about Sophie

TL: He also explained didn't he the 2 am precinct thing

SW: Yeah we talked to him about the 2 am precinct thing and he said that had happened but what he had said was that erm they were unaware that it had happened because she had gone to sleep on the top floor. Sophie came downstairs with Catherine [friend] at 1.45, cos they've got a camera in the

> hall so they can actually see the kids coming downstairs. At 1.45 Catherine
> and Sophie went out the shop to meet two other friends
>
> *TL:* Boys or girls, or do we not know?
>
> *SW:* I don't know, nobody's saying . . . the first they knew about Sophie going
> out was the following morning Mrs Anderson [Catherine's mother] telephoned
> Mrs Byrne and said Sophie, said she's kept hold of Sophie this morning cos
> the police brought Catherine home and Sophie [and they]

Here, the social worker recounts the father's 'normalizing' version of Sophie's behaviour (she's a bit of a handful, but we're not especially worried). In contrast to Kate's account, it is linguistically coded as opinion (he *said*) and reference to him becoming 'quite irate' marks him as potentially irrational. The normalizing parts of the talk are juxtaposed with revelations and intrigue conveying that things do not quite add up: for example, when asked whether the friends were boys or girls, the social worker replies 'I don't know, nobody's saying'. The social worker is not asked whom she has interviewed or to give any further details.

By telling the father's story the social workers are displaying their reasonableness and willingness to see other versions, but this in no way threatens the rhetorical force of the main formulation (Sophie is being abused and this is the proper business of social services because parental accounts do not quite add up).

Extract 7.3

Part 3: Reporting the mother's story

SW: Mrs Byrne got straight on to her GP and said I want Sophie examined, because if Sophie has been touched then I want the ( ) . . . We went out to talk to Mrs Byrne who gave quite a completely different view of things and basically is very worried about Sophie erm mainly around the Catherine Anderson family erm because she says that it's notorious round their way and she doesn't want her daughter mixing with them but it's very difficult because they

TL: =It's quite interesting because the potential perpetrator is a boy who also lives with the Anderson family. There are lots of bits of connections there . . .

TL: Oh right

SW: =and there's a little lad who plays with all these teenage boys

TL: =and he's started exposing himself (joking) (laughter) . . .

SW: Well anyway Mrs Byrne is obviously quite upset that Sophie is mixing with these children.

TL: Didn't she say something about Sophie's had some kind of physical symptom which is . . .

SW: Yeah she said that Sophie's physical care had deteriorated over the last few months, well we went through the whole lot. She still wets the bed at, what is she 10, two or three times a night and because it smells so much she insisted that she had a bath and in fact marched her to the bathroom and stripped her all down and she had all red legs at the top of her legs and everything, which could have been lying in urine, but she said she was worried enough to go and get some cream and it's gone now . . .

Here, it seems that the mother reacts to the initial allegation by becoming concerned for Sophie and requesting that she be examined by the GP. That is, Mrs Bryne is reacting to the suggestion that Sophie is being 'shagged'. Her reaction is a consequence of the investigation not a cause, but it does not appear to be heard as such. The tenor is overwhelmingly of concern and worry for Sophie, with the idea that she is being 'shagged' gradually achieving more a definite status. The boy Mike has now become 'the potential perpetrator'. There are further ascriptions of deviance ('Sophie is mixing with these children'; 'Sophie's had some kind of physical symptom' 'she still wets the bed'; 'she had all red legs at the top of her legs') added along the way. These symptoms are clearly read as evidence of possible sexual activity rather than as, for example, medical problems or a reaction to the recent death of Sophie's grandfather (omitted from this extract). The use of 'gallows' humour (for example, 'and he's started exposing himself') is a routine feature of case talk in meetings amongst many professional groups, and here serves to reference the workers' seasoned familiarity with the such cases.

In the final part of the case the social workers introduce Sophie's account.

Extract 7.4

Part 4: Reporting Sophie's story

TL: Well the suggestions Jenny made, I think Jenny has had a conversation with Mrs Byrne and I haven't got the details, was that maybe for some kind of reassurance, assessing whether there's been any abuse, it might be that one of the options might be asking Dr Palmer [consultant paediatrician] just doing it in a very low-key way. Obviously if Sophie wants an examination there's no harm in asking them to actually examine Sophie. I think that's quite difficult really the apparent soreness has gone and Sophie isn't actually *saying*, well it was a very brief interview

SW: It was a very brief interview with Sophie. Basically Sophie erm wasn't giving any information over at all . . . She was still maintaining that Catherine felt unwell, erm so she took her home and we said that left her on her own to come home and that's very dangerous etc. etc. and she said erm she said oh yeah but she said she didn't meet any friends erm. She says, she was very emotional because she thought we were there to tell her off and erm the usual and erm it was quite obvious erm she did say she can't talk to anyone, she didn't have anyone to talk to. But with regard to the older boys playing with her she's going to be told that they don't collect her from school. But Mrs Byrne maintains that she takes and collects her from school

TL: Which is not what the school says if I remember rightly.

We can see that the social worker has taken the view that Sophie is failing or refusing to produce an account of the abuse and distress which professionals have decided has taken place. The social worker's account is clearly coded to imply that Sophie is reluctant to tell the full story, or has not had the opportunity to do so. The use of the phrases, 'and Sophie isn't actually *saying*, well it was a very brief interview' (repeated by different speakers) and 'she was still maintaining' situates Sophie's version (or lack of it) as a contestable account, not as fact or her subjective experience. At the end of the extract, the mother is reintroduced with the use of a co-narrated contrast structure (Smith 1978), which works to amplify the incongruities in the story, and accomplish a subtle blaming:

> ... But Mrs Byrne maintains that she takes and collects her from school
> TL: =Which is not what the school says if I remember rightly.

Four accounts are invoked in the recitation of this case. The first account, that of the education welfare officer is coded as fact, as are the first-hand, 'eye witness' accounts of the social workers and team leader. However, despite the fact that Sophie, her mother and her father are present in the account through the use of 'reported speech', their stories are coded as disputable and are delivered in such a way that they reinforce the singular professional reading of the case. The father's normalizing story is not pursued as a viable alternative to the 'child at risk' reading. The possibility that Sophie is 'in with a bad crowd' is briefly discussed via the reported speech of the mother. However, Sophie is cast as a passive victim of this and not, for example, as a rather naughty girl who needs a firm hand. Instead, the parents' versions are, in various ways, problematized. The mother's account is treated as more plausible than the father's, although she too is constructed as potentially untrustworthy or negligent (she failed to 'turn up'; she says she collects the children, which the school disputes). The result is that particular versions or 'voices' are silenced in the account (see also Pithouse and Atkinson 1988; Hall *et al.* 1997).

The case-talk has an almost argumentative quality, although the social worker and team leader cannot be cast as opponents. Rather, this 'argument' looks like an example of Antaki's public reasoning: 'more a case of authorizing what one is saying than genuinely reaching an answer unknown at the start of the journey' (Antaki 1994b: 182). Schwitalla (1986) has also noted how social actors can argue in situations where they do not have opposing interests. Whereas Antaki concentrates on the rhetorical effect of this argumentation, Schwitalla argues that it 'constructs and affirms [the] shared knowledge' (1986: 120) of groups. Through narratives such as this, social workers learn how to 'do being' social workers. The legitimacy of the work is endorsed and aspects of occupational identity are reinforced.

Thus, in this one extract there are different layers of meaning. Alongside the local, rhetorical, performative aspect, where the language used constructs this account as a singular factual description of events and shuts down debate about other possible readings, we can see 'imported' notions, derived from the cultural construction of childhood, contemporary notions of risk and ideas about parental responsibilities (for example, that it is inappropriate for a 10-year-old child to walk home from school alone). The processes and layers we can see in social workers' talk are also evident amongst other professional groups.

Example 2: Competing voices of medicine

The following extract is taken from detailed field notes compiled by one of the authors in the course of an ongoing ethnographic study of a paediatric service. The extract shows how, in justifying or authorizing their opinion to each other, professionals may use a range of 'voices' or alternative rationalities.

Extract 7.5

Dr Jones (Consultant Paediatrician) told me about a child Helen, who had been known to the service for some time. In the past, Helen had been very over-weight, and is currently being treated for asthma and eczema. The case formu-lation offered by Dr Jones was that Helen's mother dramatized and exaggerated Helen's symptoms in order to elicit a professional response (it was a case of Munchausen syndrome by proxy, or had features of that phenomenon). Dr Jones reported the mother's account in ironic tone 'apparently she [Helen] *never* sleeps and *never* eats, you know the sort of thing'.

The previous night, Helen had been brought into hospital by ambulance with breathing problems. Apparently Helen's mother called the GP, but before they had arrived, she dialled 999 for an ambulance. Dr Jones' opinion was that the child had not suffered an asthma attack but had been 'wound-up' by her mother. She based this view on the fact that Helen had recovered within 15 minutes of being brought into hospital and that her peak flow was near normal.

Dr Jones received a phone call from the ward while we were discussing the child. The ward reported that Helen had slept well all night and had not woken until 7.30. We went down to the ward to see her . . . Dr Jones had wanted Helen to stay on the ward for a few days so that the mother's account that Helen 'never slept' could be conclusively refuted. However, Helen insisted that she wanted to go home and the plan was changed. We stopped at the nurses' station. A charge nurse and a staff nurse were present. Dr Jones looked at the nursing record for the previous night and read:

    12.00: Helen fast asleep
     2.00: Mother still awake – light on.

Dr Jones looked at me and at the nurses whilst reading aloud, 'mother still awake'. The staff nurse commented, 'you know the curtains at the window, she shut them so they [night staff] couldn't just check she [Helen] was asleep. They had to keep going in. Mum went to the toilet and they had to go in and turn the light off'. The charge nurse added 'how many 8-year-olds do you know who can sleep with a bright light on?' Helen's mother arrived on the ward and I was introduced.

The extract then lists details of a conversation between Helen and Dr Jones about the events of the previous night. The conversation took the form of a debate: about whether Helen's mother should have called an ambulance; what time the GP had actually arrived; when certain medications were administered; whether it had been an asthma attack or the result of Helen 'getting worked up'; whether Helen had slept peacefully or whether she had, as her mother asserted, been restless with itchy feet (due to a rash); and about whether Helen should return to school with the rash.

The interview was skilfully and confidently conducted by Dr Jones as a series of questions and answers which uncovered incongruities in the mother's account. The interview was polite but was interrogative and invest-igative of the mother's actions and opinions rather than of the 'medical' facts of the case. Each party cited 'independent' witnesses for their version of events, although Dr Jones' witnesses were imbued with rather greater credibility (the GP and the nursing staff, as opposed to Helen's older sister). Without this more qualitative, moral inquiry the case formulation could not have been produced. That is, the medical facts alone could only take the paediatrician so far in deciding about treatment and disposal.

Although the exchange between the mother and the paediatrician was in no way aggressive it was in essence an argument and there was no real resolution. The extract continues as follows:

Extract 7.6

We left the bedroom and returned to the nurses' station where Dr Jones gave an account of Helen's mother's version of events as follows: 'She says the GP didn't arrive until 8.30, but I was with her (the GP) from 7 pm!' The charge nurse reiterated the story of the previous night with the clear implication that Helen's mother was intent on disturbing her child's sleep, and had it not been for the action of the nurses, this would indeed have been the outcome. Dr Jones said, 'She (mother) just winds her up until she's on the ceiling, before bedtime they all run round until they are completely high' (laughter).

In this case, observations by staff over time have led to a clear and shared view that Helen's mother is not to be trusted, that she is a bit odd and that she exaggerates and exacerbates the child's (otherwise fairly minor) medical problems. Ambiguous behaviours (shutting the curtains could have been to preserve privacy, sitting up with a sick child is not an uncommon parental re-sponse, some 8-year-old children do sleep with the light on) are reported *and heard* as clear evidence of Helen's mother's oddness. Hence, they reinforce the reading of the case which predates this particular set of observations.

The professional version is supported by clinical evidence of the child's condition on arrival to hospital and her rapid response to treatment, but this does not on its own lead to the conclusion that mother is deviant, as opposed to anxious, or even dedicated and vigilant. Rather, the reading of the case is reproduced and solidified by the collaborative, ironic and slightly comic narration of Dr Jones and the nurses who are able to elicit and mobilize facts in such a way that they support the 'mother as trouble' version. Of course, this is very much an informal exchange. These professionals would not have spoken in this humorous and ironic way in a formal meeting. Nevertheless, through such communications professionals often decide what to look for in a case and these observations then lead to more 'worked up' formulations of fact. The case is an evolving narrative containing many 'voices of medicine' (Atkinson 1995). The paediatrician is a detective (conducting careful question/answer sequences to get at 'the truth' and spotting incongruities in the mother's account), a scientist (using detailed clinical knowledge of asthma and of the pharmacology of the drugs the child had been given), a 'moral judge' (judging that the mother was, in some way, putting her own needs before the child's), and is also drawing upon personal and professional intuition (experience of other cases which have been similarly categorized). These 'voices' are treated by the participants as having equal validity and all work to solidify the story and signal professional competence.

Again, we can see how professional talk both draws upon and reproduces wider knowledges or Discourses. The ascription of a deviant identity to the mother in this case depends on the situated collaborative work of a number of professionals, but it is also affected by the 'discovery' or naming of Munchausen syndrome by proxy (see, for example, Meadow 1980, 1985), which has led to the reclassification of a range of parental behaviours into one, albeit complex, syndrome. The literature on the syndrome generates its own set of expectable behaviours (clinical features) which, in turn, increase the chances of professionals looking for and finding these behaviours in the cases they encounter. In both Sophie's and Helen's cases, we can see strong narratives of the child as a passive victim of parental negligence or dramatic excess. This is a feature of professional talk across many child HW settings (see, for example, King and Piper 1995; Marks 1995; White 1997a, 1998b), and it is often in sharp contrast to parental versions of the child as naughty or unmanageable.

Example 3: Medical vs social selves – negotiating the institutional context

Let us move away from child HW and examine professional talk in another setting. In her study of 'geriatric assessment', Joanna Latimer provides a detailed extract of a transcript of professional discussions about Bernard Gibbon, a 76-year-old man. Latimer notes that professional practice in the geriatric service she studied was characterized by sorting patients into particular categories of identity. In Chapter 1, we used an example of a 'social admission', Jessie, whose problems were constituted as a natural consequence of old age and physical decline, and of her own refusal to accept community based services (Extract 1.1). Jessie was a person out of place, a bed-blocker. Latimer argues that the extension of medical surveillance into the psycho-social aspects of a person's identity (Armstrong 1995, and in the context of nursing, May 1992a,b) presents professionals in geriatrics with a particular problem. Once social and psychological elements are identified and uncovered, it becomes much more difficult to achieve the fast throughput of patients demanded of an acute medical ward in the 'new' National Health Service. Thus, Latimer argues, complex interactive work goes into the construction of patient identities which facilitate movement and disposal.

At the beginning of Latimer's observation of the case of Bernard Gibbon, he is clearly identified as a person with medical problems (arterial disease). He has a wife who is unable to see, but who is supported by community services and requires no additional support from Mr Gibbon. The consultant notes: 'So they just co-exist – with community support' (Latimer 1997a: 149), which reconstructs Mr and Mrs Gibbon's relationship as almost coincidental (they share the same geographical space) and irrelevant (but just exist alongside each other). Such an arrangement presents no impediment to Mr Gibbon's discharge.

However, after ten days on the ward, Mr Gibbon is reported by nurses as 'difficult to mobilize' and reluctant to get up and about. He is becoming redefined as a potential 'social problem'. The following extract is taken from a multidisciplinary meeting held at that time. At the meeting are a senior registrar (SR), occupational and physiotherapists, staff nurses, social worker (SW), resident (Res, junior doctor) and a medical student.

SR: Bernard Gibbon, an arteriopath. Collapsed with horrendous hypotension [low blood pressure].

Res: He has proxysmal AF [atrial fibrillation, a heart arrhythmia] on ECG [electro-cardiogram], so he's started on digoxin [a drug which regulates the heart beat]. He feels tired – I can't find any reason for it – his Us and Es [urea and electrolytes] are normal, he's not constipated, no UTI [urinary tract infection], his spit is negative [these constitute a repertoire of medically competent explanations for the lethargy]. I cannot think why he's so tired except that he's lying in bed all the time. We keep trying to get him up but . . .

SR: Is he depressed?

Res: No! He's really cheerful. Whenever I speak to him it's 'Aye doctor, yes doctor' [robustly] then . . . [Resident throws his head back and snores loudly]! [Everyone laughs. Senior registrar smiles but does not laugh]

SW: He's a bit like you then [the resident has been asleep earlier in the meeting]! [Everyone laughs].

Res: And I'm not constipated either [Laughs].

SR: [he's stopped laughing] Has anybody asked him about that? [serious].

Res: No

SR: I got the impression things are pretty hefty at home – with his wife and all.

Res: She's in and out – she's psychotic I think.

SR: She goes to the day hospital doesn't she?

Res: Yes – but there's some psychiatric history.

SR: She may be demented

Res: No – she's a very dependent personality – that's it. Also she's a cancer phobic.

SR: Right, OK, he's really a medical problem – the home help five days a week is more for his wife than him.

(Adapted from Latimer 1997a: 150)

This extract differs from the previous examples. The professional formulation is much more contested and we can see some of the 'working up' of a version taking place. For example, there is evidence of persuasion being used by the resident to resist the implicit censure of registrar's questions about Mr Gibbon's possible depression, which the resident had omitted from his long list of possible hypotheses to explain Mr Gibbon's tiredness. The registrar makes explicit reference to Mr Gibbon's 'hefty' home situation. With minimal further work from the resident, this version is dropped, and the registrar's concluding comment appears to reconstruct Mr Gibbon as a 'medical problem'. However, this exchange has, for the moment, destabilized Mr Gibbon's securely 'medical' identity and has raised the possibility that he may not be able to go home.

Some days later, a chest X-ray reveals that Mr Gibbon has been suffering from undiagnosed pneumonia. This, in effect, returns Mr Gibbon to the category 'medical' and his 'hefty' home situation is not explored further. He is moved to a side ward, given antibiotics and reassured that he will soon be able to return home and resume looking after his wife. Mr Gibbon's version of events is buried under an evolving professional account which is supported by the artefacts of medical science (X-rays, diagnostics, medication). Latimer herself had spoken to Mr Gibbon and supplies for us (her version of) his version:

For him his life at home was 'hell'. His wife had been made partially blind by a stroke. She had to 'feel her way' to get around . . . He said he could no longer get out of the house: could no longer walk any distance because his breath was so short . . . Further he could not sleep at night . . . He stated that what really got him down was that his wife never stopped complaining and going on to him . . . Sometimes he said he had to go into another room 'to stop something from happening' . . . During his interview with me he broke down and cried when talking about going home

(Latimer 1997a: 151–2)

By ascribing Mr Gibbon to the singular category 'medical', the professionals are able to bracket all these aspects of the person's identity, but again, as in the earlier examples, this is not simply a local phenomenon, a spontaneous reading of a complex situation. Rather, Latimer argues, it is a situated practice, the product of the need to manage identities in such a way that work gets done and patients move on. She notes:

> rather than critique the practitioners concerned for being ignorant or prejudiced, the study has examined what they are accomplishing through these communicative effects, namely the potential to shift identities and keep the appearance of the flow, the movement through the beds, the 'consultant episodes' which have since become one of the measures of efficiency and performance in the health services . . .
>
> (Latimer 1997a: 156)

Latimer's work shows how the presenting of the medical facts of the case can be interpreted and reinterpreted in inter-professional talk, and we suggest that it is rare for decisions to be made without recourse to some other institutional imperative. In Bernard Gibbon's case, Latimer argues, the imperative to achieve a throughput of patients and the status of the ward as an 'acute' unit led to the bracketing of social aspects of Mr Gibbon's identity. In short, the facts were assembled as they were because of a judgement about the amount of *time* Mr Gibbon had spent or may be anticipated to spend on the ward.

The impact of time on decision making is an underexplored area in practice literature, yet there is persuasive evidence that, in making sense of cases together, temporal considerations are highly significant to professionals (see, for example, Zerubavel 1979, 1981; Latimer 1997b; White 1998a). In Roth's (1963) work on tuberculosis sanitoria, we can see a further example of how, despite their solidity and relative certainty, medical tests such as X-rays can be read in different ways. Roth notes:

> When a medical resident presented a patient as having been in the hospital for two years, a consultant promptly announced: 'That's a long time; I think we should try to get her out of here'. One of the nurses pointed out that the resident had made a slight mistake on the matter of the length of hospitalization. The patient had been first admitted about two years ago, but had been discharged after about a year, and had spent half a year on the outside, and had then been readmitted. Her second admission had involved slightly less than six months' stay in the hospital. The consultant replied: 'I'd hate her to go too soon this time'. This doctor then argued in favor of holding the patient for at least another conference three months later. All this time the physician was looking at exactly the same set of X-rays and was considering the same information concerning bacteriological tests and other diagnostic procedures . . .
>
> (Roth 1963 cited in Miller 1997: 77)

Thus, whilst medical science provides more-or-less reliable data which can inform decisions, these decisions are nevertheless made by professionals talking to each other and drawing on other, rather less solid and more contestable, knowledges and meanings, such as what constitutes 'too long' or 'too soon'.

Competing knowledges: professional dominance as action

We have said that inter-professional talk is often characterized by movement towards an agreement on a particular version of a case which is, for some reason, robust and fits with dominant ideas (local or societal). This may have implied that multidisciplinary work takes place on a level playingfield and that all professional voices are equal. You will know that this is not the case. It is important to note that not all ideas carry the same currency, and some professional groups have access to more (rhetorically) potent sources than others. This is often what we mean when we talk of professional hierarchies. For example, it is something of a truism that, in many HW settings, doctors form the dominant group. It is treated often as an inevitable 'given' hierarchical arrangement in which doctors somehow 'gain' and others are exploited and 'lose'.

We may expand this understanding by seeing medical dominance as a product of doctors' monopoly of esoteric technical knowledge and onerous responsibilities (Etzioni 1969; Freidson 1970). For example, only doctors can prescribe medication, and often only they are mandated to carry the ultimate clinical responsibility for the case. It is clear that there are 'hierarchies' of knowledge with some facts and ideas carrying more weight than others. This has been explored by Anne Rogers (1993), who looked at the relationships between duty psychiatrists and police officers who had detained people whom they believed to have a mental disorder and had been found in a public place posing a danger to themselves or others (section 136 of the Mental Health Act 1983). She found that the psychiatrists' powers of gatekeeping over beds and their monopoly claims to the diagnostic criteria of biological psychiatry allowed them to resist referrals from the police and to make specific demands of police officers, such as requiring them to wait whilst the psychiatrist conducted their assessment in order that the officer could remove the patient from the premises if they were not considered to have a treatable mental disorder.

However, these factors alone do not tell the whole story. In the previous chapter, we argued that all institutionalized ideas must be reproduced in real encounters and that all can be resisted in various ways. This is also the case with professional hierarchies. Indeed, in Rogers' study, whilst the detained person remained in the police station, on police territory, officers were able to use strategies, such as asking the police surgeon to act as mediator, to resist 'psychiatric dominance' and to get psychiatrists to respond.

By examining inter-professional encounters in more detail, we can get a clearer picture of some of these complexities affecting multidisciplinary work. For example, in a study of life and death decision making on a neonatal unit, Anspach (1987) shows that, despite the protracted contact between nursing staff and the neonates and their parents, their 'social' observations of qualitative aspects of 'well being' were not granted the same legitimacy as the 'technical' devices used by the physicians. This sometimes caused conflict, but Anspach observed that these disputes were usually resolved by all parties treating the technical cues as more reliable. As Miller notes in a commentary on Anspach's work:

> This tendency might be understood by considering the social positions of physicians and nurses in these settings: the physicians occupied a more central decision making role than the nurses. It is also related to the nurses' orientation to technological cues as always relevant to the meetings. That is their arguments acknowledged the preference for technological cues in this setting . . . even as they asked for other factors to be taken into account.
>
> (Miller 1997: 78)

That is, professional dominance is generally maintained not only by those who are 'dominant' but also by the practices of others. However, professional dominance can lead to 'silencing' of particular versions, and it is important for practitioners to reflect on the workings of these kinds of processes in their own organizations.

In this chapter so far, we have illustrated the need to make ourselves aware as professionals of the interplay of spoken words and institutional contexts in the production of client identities in inter-professional talk. We must be clear that we are not making any judgements about the veracity of the professional constructions of the cases we have discussed. All the cases are constructed on the basis of past professional observation – in Helen's case (Example 2) over some years – and we have no reason to believe that the 'silenced' versions are 'better'. However, it is also clear that, through their talk, professionals are making knowledge.

Of course, it is often necessary for professionals to 'solidify' a version, for example, in order to prepare a court case, to protect a child, or to access resources. However, by analysing transcripts of their own talk as part of regular self-audit, professionals can be made more aware of the embedded alternative readings, so that they may judge for themselves whether those readings are or were worth pursuing.

Talking about each other: constructing and contesting professional identities

The examples above relate to 'knowledge making' about people who have been referred to, or are receiving services from HW agencies. However, professional identities and institutionalized practices are also maintained in professionals' talk about each other. Stories that professionals tell about each other set up expectations and maintain disciplinary boundaries. They are also affected by the specific legal mandates held by the groups. For example, in Rogers' (1993) study referred to above, the police required of the psychiatrists not a simple 'see and assess' service but a specific disposal (hospitalization), whilst the psychiatrists were operating with a criterion of 'treatability' and with an eye to their bed situation. It is plain that these imperatives are in conflict. We need to find ways to think about the situated practices, and the competing and sometimes incommensurable institutional mandates of other professional groups if we are to develop an understanding of multidisciplinary work.

Both the police and the psychiatrists in Rogers' study told negative stories about each other. For example, the police officers commented:

'People keep coming back to us – the success rate can't be high. No one I've met has said "I used to be a nutter, but I'm all right now".'

(Rogers 1993: 38)

'They ignore you when you go in, they're just sitting there writing notes, they don't acknowledge your presence. They just talk to the patient, say he's got X or say to the nurse "open a file on him" without asking your opinion. They treat you like you're thick . . .'

(ibid.: 40)

On the police officers, the psychiatrists commented:

'Mental disorder as I see it has definite symptoms – not just behaving strangely in the street – they just slap on a 136. They can recognise if some one is mad, but is he psychiatrically ill? . . . My definition [of mental disorder] is clear cut and specific . . .'

(ibid.: 40)

'I don't think they handle referrals well, it's a combination of them being frightened and exaggerating the violence and craziness . . . They make people more vulnerable and frightened and they use handcuffs unnecessarily . . .'

(ibid.: 41)

We can see here that the police define the psychiatrists as ineffectual and rude and portray themselves as undervalued, front-line troops who have to pick up the pieces of psychiatric failure. On the other hand, the psychiatrists invoke their specialist knowledge and also the more caring, clinical approach which they argue such understanding can facilitate. The police are constructed as ignorant at best and abusive at worst.

Although Rogers does not treat them as such, we see these accounts as examples of 'atrocity stories'. We used this concept earlier in relation to professional/client encounters, but it can equally be used to understand the ways in which professionals talk about each other. As Dingwall notes:

By casting occupation members as hero, atrocity stories maintain the intrinsic worth of the teller and, by implication, his colleague audience. Acquiring an appropriate repertoire of such stories and being able to identify appropriate occasions for telling them are important parts of being recognised as a competent member of an occupation, or, more generally, any social group.

(Dingwall 1977: 376)

The telling of elaborate stories about clients'/patients' antics or mishaps, and often also about the incompetent response of some other agency, are routine occurrences in HW agencies. In Dingwall's study of health visitors in training, he notes that the tutors often told stories about the incompetence or insensitivity of GPs, situating the health visitor as triumphant rescuer. For example:

Caroline: Why is the youngest child at risk?
Rosemary: He's retarded with a neuromuscular disorder
Pat: When was this found out?
Rosemary: The health visitor was worried quite early on, but the GP pooh-poohed it until after the developmental assessment

(Dingwall 1997: 381)

As Dingwall notes, in using the phrase 'pooh-poohed', the health visitor situates the GP as 'culpably wrong' and the health visitor as 'demonstrably right'. Thus reinforcing for the health visitor trainees the view that 'doctors should accord a more equal role to health visitors and not dismiss their opinions lightly' (Dingwall 1997: 381). This kind of storytelling is one way of accomplishing being a 'professional' and legitimating one's role alongside similar occupations. For example, as we noted in Chapter 6, invoking risk and child protection and pointing to the tardiness or inadequacy of other professions in its recognition is a common social work 'atrocity story', providing a 'monopoly expertise' story and differentiating them from a range of child health professionals (White 1999a).

In this section we have tried to show how professional identities do not simply exist, but need to be 'done'. Once an individual has learnt through storytelling that a competent health visitor, police officer, social worker or nurse thinks a certain way then they are likely to reproduce these forms of thought as 'preferred' readings of cases, as we saw in the examples earlier in the chapter. That is to say, the atrocity stories told by occupational groups provide the blueprint for a 'prototypical [professional] causal *gestalt*' (Bull and Shaw 1992: 640) upon which professionals can draw in the face of the contradictory testimonies presented to them.

The dynamic process of identity performance, then, maintains and transforms organizational or occupational cultures, which, in turn affect knowledge making about cases. These processes are generally routinized and taken for granted, and thus are largely immune from debate and discussion.

As Bourdieu notes: 'It is because subjects do not, strictly speaking, know what they are doing that what they do has more meaning than they know' (Bourdieu 1977: 79). If, as professionals, we are to 'know what we do', we must make use of materials like transcripts of our own talk which can create distance for us and allow us to develop the kind of reflexivity that opens up to scrutiny what we take for granted in our practice.

Summary

This chapter has explored the ways in which conversations taking place far away from the meetings between professionals and their clients can have a real impact on the ways in which practitioners categorize and make sense of cases. This talk can be looked at in various ways: as a local accomplishment, as a vehicle for the reproduction of bigger Discourses, and as a medium for production and maintainance of occupational cultures and identities.

Implications for practice

We have argued that inter-professional talk about cases works to construct and maintain particular client/patient identities. These identities become more fixed and durable over time and with multiple and collective recitations of the case. The identities ascribed will affect which versions are treated as true and will usually lead to some silencing of particular voices. The identities ascribed to individuals impact directly on case 'disposals', as we can see in the case of Bernard Gibbon (Example 3). This is, therefore, a very real practice issue.

Professional talk will also make use of, or 'invoke', certain dominant ideas which may be cherished aspects of professional ideology. We have given the examples of child-centredness in childcare social work and certain notions of efficiency and expertise in medicine. These and other institutional influences need to be understood by professionals if they are properly to debate the nature of their judgements.

There is a strong policy impetus towards multidisciplinary work and we are all encouraged to embrace this as the way forward in many kinds of settings. However, little has been done to help practitioners to think about how their own identity is 'done' in practice: where it comes from and how it is maintained. Similarly, there has been little attention to the competing imperatives of different groups and how these impact upon their feelings about allied professions. It is important for practitioners to reflect on the ways in which they talk about themselves and others, and to think about the impact that these stories have on their occupational cultures and preferred ways of seeing.

We have stressed that we are not making any judgements about the adequacy or veracity of the professional constructions of the cases discussed, or about professionals' views of each other. We are not saying that the silenced versions are better and that the professionals are, therefore, operating oppressively. Rather we have tried to show that, through their talking together, professionals are again making knowledge. It is your job, with your own work, to make the evaluative judgements about the stories you have told.

We have also added to the discussion in Chapter 6 and tried to encourage you again to adopt a critical perspective on the dominant structural reading of professional power (for example, doctors are dominant because they possess more power). We suggest here that you concentrate on how dominance is 'done' and that you examine what are its effects.

In the exercises below, we hope to enable you to become familiar with the taken-for-granted readings which you make about cases by virtue of your professional background and so open these up to debate and dialogue.

Exercises

EXERCISE 1

Make a short audiotape of a professional meeting or discussion. Aim for no more than 20 minutes of 'real-time' talk, or you will be transcribing forever! Useful opportunities include nursing handover meetings, ward rounds, social work allocation meetings or supervision sessions. If you do not have access to such meetings, you can use the extract below in which a social work team leader is describing a case to the team.

> TL: . . . No previous history, basically Joseph, we had a call night duty had a call rather from erm ( ) on Monday night. Joseph had been admitted earlier that day with a condition called ( ) which is where the foreskin appears to have been pulled back and gets stuck and it becomes very swollen and sore. When the referral came through, we were told it was impossible for the child to have done this to himself, or to happen spontaneously. I have subsequently had a number of *other* medical opinions which has been one of the difficulties. The original referral said there were other bruises that Joseph had on his cheek on his frenulum and which is clearly torn, she *said* a pinch mark although it was quite old. His mum is she's quite upset at the mention of NAI [non-accidental injury] but she's cooperative. She has a boyfriend but he doesn't live there. She says she's always present when he's with Joseph. They'll be keeping him in for observation. She's very very woolly about the story, there seems to be lack of clarity about whether it's accidental or

non-accidental ... The surgical registrar was saying it's not impossible but it is unusual and children of that age can pull back their foreskin, but it seems unusual

(Adapted from White 1997a)

Analyse your extract (or the one provided) answering the following questions.

(a) What aspects of the case are constructed as fact? Look for phrases like 'it is', 'he confirmed', 'we know', 'she did', 'he went'.
(b) What aspects of the case are constructed as questionable? Look for phrases like 'we think', 'it is my view that', and for reported speech such as 's/he claimed', 's/he said', 's/he denied'.
(c) Try to generate alternative readings of the case. This will sometimes be easy and at other times quite difficult – some cases are more contested or contestable than others. You may also find it tricky until you have got to grips with what you take for granted.
(d) Can you find instances of moral judgement, or the ascription of deviance to individuals? Look for phrases like 'mother has a drink problem', 'I'm very concerned about the child's behaviour', 'she told me this, but I know that', 'it was very inappropriate'. Do the individuals concerned 'show their working' or is the judgement taken for granted? How much convincing did they have to do before everyone accepted the account as true?

EXERCISE 2

Think about the stories that you and your colleagues share about other professionals and the way they work. You may like to tape a team meeting or similar forum where these issues often come up. What do these stories convey about the contribution you and your colleagues make to HW practice? What is it that you are most frequently rescuing people from, or are providing them with after the failures of everyone else? How do you think these stories feed your own occupational culture and affect your reading of cases?

CHAPTER 8

Analysing written text: documents, records and reports

Texts become crystallized when we treat them as authoritative representations of stable objective realities. Texts might be said to 'encourage' such treatment because they are made up of written words, numbers and visual images that objectify the events, objects or issues that they purport to represent. The words, numbers and images 'freeze' the ongoing events of life, making it impossible for us to return to them from time to time in order to verify our remembrances of, and others' claims about them . . .

(Miller 1997: 72)

We have looked in detail at how knowledge is made in various HW contexts. The previous chapter showed how versions can become solidified in inter-professional talk of various kinds. Developing this theme, the quotation above refers to the capacity for written texts to 'freeze' events. In this chapter, we make a number of claims about the importance of the written documents used in HW practice. We shall argue, like Miller, that written words have the capacity to affect what we do in particular ways, about which we may not always be aware.

Let us start with a very basic question. Why are official documents important? Taking the example of case records, there are at least three ways in which we could begin to answer this question. At the most fundamental level, functioning as a record of work undertaken and to be undertaken and as an *aide-mémoire*, case notes and medical records have obvious uses for HW professionals. In this context, case records are treated as descriptions, as sources of information about patients' or clients' conditions, circumstances or activities.

Second, records are often evaluated to see whether they are sufficiently detailed or up to date, or are examined for evidence of failure to follow procedure (or to have recorded having done so), or are scrutinized for indications of professional negligence. Records, then, are treated as a medium for organizational and public accountability. The following notice, pinned to the wall in a hospital, demonstrates the point: 'Nurses and doctors please note: if it isn't recorded, it didn't happen'. In this context, records are examined as though they *should*, but may well not, be an accurate record of what actually took place. Treated in this way, records are almost always found wanting.

This second approach to records is ubiquitous in contemporary HW organizations, where they are often examined by managers and by various inspectorates when things 'go wrong', or as part of audit activity. However, a similar orientation to case files as 'bad' records can be found within the critical research tradition, where they may also be examined in order to contrast the professional's viewpoint with 'real' events, or 'real' patient or client experiences. As Hak describes in relation to psychiatric practice:

> According to the critical approach, the original trouble is quite different from the interpretation offered by psychiatry. In its most extreme version, the contention is that in reality there is no trouble at all; psychiatry itself creates the object of study (mental illness) out of nowhere . . . A critical sociologist studies psychiatric records neither to obtain information about the patient's condition nor to understand psychiatric practice. In pointing to the differences between the psychiatric record and the 'reality' for which the record stands, the sociologist merely criticizes psychiatric labelling . . .
>
> (Hak 1992: 138–9)

Over thirty years ago, Garfinkel and Bittner noted this propensity for organizational records to be defined as inadequate or inaccurate:

> Any investigator who has attempted a study with the use of clinic records, almost wherever such records are found, has his litany of troubles to recite. Moreover, hospital and clinic administrators frequently are as knowledgeable and concerned about these 'shortcomings' as are the investigators themselves. The sheer frequency of 'bad' records and the uniform ways in which they are 'bad' was enough in itself to pique our curiosity . . .
>
> (Garfinkel and Bittner 1967: 191)

This brings us to the third approach to records, which is the one we shall be encouraging you to try. You will remember that in Chapter 3 we discussed Garfinkel's policy of 'ethnomethodological indifference'. This is his insistence that we suspend judgement on whether statements are true or false, good or bad, right or wrong, and look instead at how facts and statements have been ordered, described or assembled to do particular work or achieve particular effects. Thus, it should come as no surprise that, instead of concerning ourselves with whether records are accurate accounts of what really happened, Garfinkel suggests we look at how records are constructed, what work they do, and what they tell us about the institutional context for which they were created.

Tony Hak (1992) has used Garfinkel's approach to analyse psychiatric records. He treats these records neither as descriptions of the patient's condition nor as a distortion produced by the pernicious and controlling activity of psychiatrists, but as 'a phenomenon intrinsic to social practice itself' (Hak 1992: 139). That is, he treats them as part of psychiatric practice as a social activity which orders phenomena in particular expected ways. By analysing documents in this way, we too can learn something of the ways in which our occupational groups order 'reality', and thus it is an important component of a reflexive approach to our work. This approach can also be applied to policy documents, procedural guidance, the law and even research agendas to reveal more about the tacit assumptions and cherished notions affecting practice. Some examples are considered later in the chapter.

By advocating this process as a part of reflexive practice, we are not suggesting that it would be of little consequence if HW professionals simply wrote works of fiction: professionals must strive to achieve what Michael Sheppard (1998) has called 'practice validity'. What we dispute is Sheppard's notion that there exist (or can be found or created) sure and certain theories and knowledge which can be applied to complex and unique circumstances and which thereby ensure objectivity and moral neutrality, and lead unproblematically to particular courses of action. We are, in short, advocating a different kind of validity, appropriate for the interpretive activity in which we are all engaged as HW professionals. We are calling for a recognition of, and engagement with, the inevitable fallibility of theory and professional judgement, both of which will always be partial and, therefore, demand disciplined and reflexive application through rigorous enquiry and debate.

Documents as organizational time-travellers: the institutional context

We have argued that, by undertaking periodic analysis of their working documents, practitioners can become more aware of the kinds of ideas they take for granted or use unconsciously in their work, and of the institutional frameworks in which they are located. Following Garfinkel's example, we have not concerned ourselves with whether the records accord with 'reality' (with whether they are 'good' and accurate records of professional activity) but have concentrated instead on what the records can reveal about the 'background expectancies' (taken-for-granted aspects) of HW practice. This requires us to see documents, schedules and procedures in new ways: as things that provide clues about how professionals routinely think about and order cases, and as things which draw upon dominant but contestable ideas to constitute and prefigure this professional activity in certain ways.

It may be argued that such an approach provides only a meaningless and self-indulgent distraction from the very proper activity of monitoring outcomes and ensuring the best possible 'evidence-based' service delivery. However, the idea that we should simply get on with the concrete, pragmatic task of form-filling in the name of improved services and measurable outcomes, and ignore the assumptions embedded in these forms, 'reflects a wariness and impatience with critical inquiry' (Garrett 1999: 28). Without this critical engagement we cannot meaningfully claim to be practising reflexivity. One cannot be reflexive about what is taken for granted.

We want, then, to encourage you to see documents as time-travellers, transferring ideas and formulations from one space (for example an office, organization, court, parliament or government department) or time (for example last week when you last saw the patient/client, two years ago when the last referral/admission happened, ten years ago when the legislation was drafted) into another. Procedures, legislation, policy and practice guidance order professional activity across different times and spaces by prescribing or proscribing certain actions. For example, assessment schedules and checklists structure the encounter between professional and service user. They lead the professional to explore aspects of the person's experience which have been deemed relevant by their own profession, by legislation or by policy makers. That is to say, the schedules predate the meeting between the professional and the service user and predispose that meeting to follow a particular course. These schedules tell us a great deal about what is considered the proper activity for occupational groups in the present climate, and by examining them for their fundamental assumptions and organizing features we may open up new possibilities for different courses of action, or we may, as practitioners, resurrect old ones prematurely discarded.

The records compiled by professionals have a similar potency. They are, of course, inanimate, yet, as time-travellers, they can also 'act'. The reader of case records revisits the past, as depicted in the records, in order to plan future interventions. Thus, what is written about the past can affect action in the present and future. As we have said, they can also tell us a great deal about the kinds of issues that discrete professional groups consider relevant to their practice. Thus, rather than telling us only about the case, the examination of individual case files can tell us about institutional contexts.

The rest of this chapter considers examples of various kinds of written document. The discussion is divided into two sections. The first considers documents which are intended to prescribe or proscribe professional activity (for example checklists, policies, procedures, classification systems) and explores the 'moral context of form completion' (Gubrium *et al.* 1989: 197), that is the ways in which HW professionals actually use these ordering frameworks. The second considers examples taken from case notes compiled by professionals after their encounters with service users.

Prescribing and proscribing professional activity: form-filling

Under the regime created by neoliberalism, the new managerialism, and now New Labour's 'modernization' initiative, procedural guidance, schedules and checklists have proliferated and flourished in HW services. As discussed in Chapter 1, this has been fuelled by increasing public suspicion and scepticism about professional ethics and competence. Health and welfare professionals now spend a good deal more of their time filling out forms. These forms are designed to ensure that professionals attend to those aspects of their work currently deemed most relevant and important. These aspects will differ from occupation to occupation. However, forms of all kinds embody certain shared presuppositions. On the basis of ethnographic work in a variety of HW settings, these presuppositions have been analysed by Gubrium *et al.* (1989) who call them the **descriptive demands** of forms. By this they mean the sorts of description that are required of HW professionals and which are considered acceptable in the particular organization.

Before considering these descriptive demands, let us first look at the ways in which forms incorporate knowledge from other arenas, usually social or natural science. We shall show that *completed* forms have simplification and amplification effects, but this process of 'paring down' knowledge takes place in the drafting of the form itself. That is to say, forms tend to transform 'formal' knowledge in particular kinds of ways. Those concerned with the crafting of policy and practice often act to translate 'science' into pragmatically usable tools. Often, when scientific knowledge is translated into user-friendly formats for professional use, it is stripped of its equivocation and qualification. That is, complex ideas are reified (made concrete and immutable) and then are treated as though they were unproblematic. Perhaps the best examples of this phenomenon come from practice in child welfare. Here ideas taken from the various developmental psychologies have become ubiquitous. Burman (1994) has noted the way in which scientific artefacts can be selectively incorporated into assessment tools. She argues that the selective appropriation of Piagetian theory into standardized tests of development and cognitive ability transformed the theory into something altogether more certain, less equivocal and more decontextualized than the detailed observations that informed the theory. Thus, forms and schedules distort and select before they are completed. Furthermore, as we shall show, through their descriptive demands they affect the way in which the recording of new information takes place.

Descriptive demands of forms

Forms usually demand a narrative account of events, presented in sequential order which describes particular aspects of the client's behaviour or experience. They also have particular **stylistic demands**. For example, forms often contain 'mutually exclusive categorizations':

> hospital incident reports typically contain an item asking for information about the 'patient's condition before incident' . . . On one form, the alternatives were: 'normal', 'senile', 'disoriented', 'sedated', and 'other'. The form compelled form-completers to accept the descriptive irrationality of checking both 'normal' and 'senile', even though it was known that, in certain cases, some staff members considered the patient to be senile while other staff members believed the patient to be relatively normal . . .
>
> (Gubrium *et al.* 1989: 199)

Yes/no answers are another example of mutually exclusive categorizations, since they do not allow for the possibility that both answers may apply at different times or in different circumstances. For example, the following extract is taken from a Nottinghamshire Social Services 'children in need' assessment form. The form is designed to help social workers to decide whether a child or family is entitled to services under the Children Act 1989 and, if so, of what type.

Extract 8.1

Preschool/nursery child

1 Does the child receive and respond to the stimulation of their parent/carer according to their age and ability?
   ☐ yes
   ☐ no
2 Does the child explore their environment at home?
   ☐ yes
   ☐ no
3 Are the child's communication skills developing satisfactorily for their age and ability?
   ☐ yes
   ☐ no

(Cited in Stephenson 1998: 151–6)

The social worker is given only a limited amount of space to the right of the boxes to add 'supporting comments and information, including any comments by parents or child/young person' (Stephenson 1998). There are certain underlying assumptions embedded in the form. First, that the social worker is able to make these judgements by making a specified number of visits to the family and observing them. Second, that what they observe is revealing of routine family life and is enduring and consistent, and not, for example, a product of the circumstances of the assessment, or the child or carer's mood. Third, that the statements are either true or untrue. Fourth, that what constitutes 'normal' behaviour or interaction for a child of a particular age is a shared repertoire of knowledge for social workers which is relatively fixed and uncontested. Of course, this assessment schedule may be useful to a social worker, and they may themselves be aware of its limitations, but, once completed, the picture presented in these documents is lent a solidity which the actual encounter between social worker and family probably did not possess. On re-reading this form, subsequent workers must be affected by this solidity.

Solidity is also lent to completed forms by the further 'stylistic demand' that professionals write in a clear, 'diagnostic' manner on forms. For example, if certain diagnostic categories are disputed when professionals talk to each other, this doubt is removed for the purposes of the form. One of the authors is currently undertaking an ethnographic study of paediatrics and child health. During observation of an outpatient clinic a consultant paediatrician was seeing a 7-year-old child referred with encopresis (faecal soiling). The paediatrician had several ideas about why this might be happening which were discussed, before and after the consultation, with the researcher and a medical student who was also present. A range of possible explanations, was considered including whether this was a 'maturational problem', a behavioural problem, or indeed whether it was really a 'problem' at all. In the report to the GP, however, the paediatrician describes the case as follows:

Extract 8.2

the problem does relate to failed potty training. Mark was a potty refuser and would only drop his stool when wearing a nappy . . .

(White, unpublished data)

Here, the paediatrician is not being dishonest but is drawing on shared knowledge between himself and the GP. They share the understanding that the real 'medical' question concerning both of them is whether Mark (name changed) has a physical anomaly which is making him soil (or has a condition such as chronic constipation which they could treat medically), or whether it is a behavioural problem. The paediatrician has decided on the latter and is simply omitting the deliberation and equivocation which saturated the consultation in 'real time' but is considered irrelevant in the context of the report. Forms, then, are designed to be about people referred to the service and not about the professionals themselves, their reasoning or thinking, or any internal disagreements.

This brings us to the final descriptive demand discussed by Gubrium *et al.* (1989). Forms also make **interpretive demands**, which are related closely to their stylistic demands. That is, forms demand of those completing them that they reveal only what is considered appropriate within their area of clinical or professional activity, that they treat it as fixed and enduring until further report is made, and that the information the form requires will always be available given competent professional enquiry. We have seen something of this in the examples above, but let us consider a further example from the social care field. The implementation of the National Health Service and Community Care Act 1990 has radically changed the ways in which services are provided to adults in the community who have social care needs. The 'care management' approach relies on structured assessment schedules which are intended to assess need and inform 'care packages' which are then 'purchased' by the care manager for the service user. Social workers (or care managers) visit people and complete detailed assessment schedules. However, these forms focus almost exclusively on 'health, self-care and functional needs', and not on other aspects of the person's biography (such as bereavement), their friendship networks and informal support. This focus within the form has particular effects:

> When assessors started to identify services which might meet users' needs, they focused on health and social services, together with residential care in the independent sector. The expectation that need would be met by mainstream, professionalized services was, in part, a product of the emphasis on functional ability, but this expectation also contributed to a focus which excluded the personal and individual aspects of users' needs . . .
>
> (Stanley 1999: 426)

We suggest that this focus on functional ability also reveals the tacit agenda of the NHS and Community Care Act 1990, which is barely concealed beneath the rhetoric of consumer choice. The Act is also about rationing statutory health and social care services, not about producing rounded assessments of individual service users. This background expectancy is reflected in the assessment forms and in the data they generate. There is some evidence that some social workers deviate more than others from the prescriptions of the form (Stanley 1999), but these deviations are not shown in the written document.

Thus, written texts tend to gloss over the complexities and deliberations of professionals and to produce a version which is solidified in particular kinds of ways. The simplification effect of the written word is amplified in forms and schedules, which rarely ask professionals to 'show their working' and often predispose them not to do so. Thus, 'the [descriptive] demands mean that form-completers, in some way or other, glossed over the constitutive, interpretive details of their own activity in the form-completion process' (Gubrium *et al.* 1989: 202).

The implications of this 'glossing over' for reflexive practice are self-evident. Whilst forms and schedules are usually presented as objective and neutral, they impose their own interpretive demands on those who are completing them and reading them. They also have effects on subsequent action taken. However, professionals are not 'moral dopes' (Gubrium *et al.* 1989). They accommodate and read forms and undertake form-filling in different ways, making moral judgements as they go. For information on this activity we need to look to ethnographic studies of institutional practices.

Form-filling in practice: the impossibility of perfect order

It is clear that the purpose of forms and schedules is to ensure that professionals attend to and record information deemed most salient to their primary activities as defined at this present moment. They are generally also presented as an aid to professional judgement. However, we have shown that the descriptive demands of forms cause information to be ordered in preferred ways, which can obscure as much of professional activity as they reveal.

There is a further organizational assumption generally made about forms, and that is that they standardize professional activity. They are intended to ensure that everyone does the same thing, at the same time, in the same set of circumstances. In short, prescriptive and proscriptive documents are a form of organizational governance. Like all systems of governance, they assume obedience amongst staff and uniformity in working conditions and practices which organizational theorists (and indeed members of organizations) know seldom, if ever, exists (see, for example, Law 1994; Malpas and Wickham 1995; White 1999b). These attempts at governance assume that HW professionals are passively controlled by the demands of the forms and that they will always use them in the prescribed ways. However, whilst welfare professionals may strive to produce acceptable reports, this process is, as Gubrium *et al.* (1989) argue, necessarily mitigated by the contingencies of everyday organizational life and often by moral considerations. Let us look at some examples.

Many forms are now completed 'on line', and the significance of information technology in HW organizations should not be underestimated. Like forms, databases of various kinds facilitate managerial accountability and appear to provide hard data on admissions, referral rates, presenting problems, interventions or treatments offered, disposal routes and so forth. Yet computers are dreadful pedants, demanding that data are presented in particular ways and refusing to accommodate unusual circumstances. White's (1997a) ethnographic study of childcare social workers working a local authority social services department provides some insight into the ways in which computerized information systems are negotiated by professionals. The computerized 'client information system' in use in the department contains the basic information on referrals received and on the action taken by social workers and team leaders in the routine processing of cases. It is mandatory that major decisions, such as to convene a child protection case conference, admit a child to local authority accommodation, or to change a child's legal status, be entered onto the computer.

Such demands increase the level of 'invisible' surveillance of social workers and team leaders (Newman and Clarke 1994). For example, payments to foster carers are activated automatically by computer after the social worker has entered the relevant information. This means that failure on the part of the social worker to 'move the child' (enter changes onto the computer) will quickly be noticed. Thus, calls from administrators based at headquarters, asking for a particular action to be entered, are a commonplace trigger for office jibes and groans about the 'bloody computer'. A wide range of case categorization codes is recognized by the computer. These are intended to reflect the diverse reasons for referral, allocation and closure of cases. However, team leaders openly acknowledge that, because they are short of time, they use only a fraction of the available categories and tend to have their favourites. These are selected simply because the particular individual happens to remember them and so does not have to look up the relevant code in the manual. Moreover, because there is competition for resources between teams, some team leaders, who believe their team may be seen as less pressured, tend to classify referrals as 'high priority' (such as child protection). Paradoxically, managers of busier teams tend to classify as many cases as possible as low priority so that they can justify decisions not to allocate them to a social worker. That is not to say that any of these team leaders is performing a cynical act of dishonesty, because there are few referrals to contemporary statutory childcare teams which are not compatible with the category 'child protection', broadly conceived. Rather, the actions of the team leaders have local rationality: they make sense within their own time and context.

There are some unintended consequences, however. The information stored in the computer is used in strategy documents by management where it is treated as though it is a true and accurate reflection of activity. Indeed, there is no other way to treat such information, since if its more arbitrary features were explicitly acknowledged it would cease to have any usefulness (rhetorical or otherwise) in the policy arena. Thus the data produced by the local rationality of the team leaders affects allocation of resources both locally and nationally via periodic reports to the Department of Health.

The following example from the work of Gubrium *et al.* (1989) illustrates the role of moral judgement in form completion. In a residential treatment centre for young people in the USA, a behaviour modification system was in operation in which children earned points for good behaviour which could be exchanged for items or for privileges. The following extracts are taken from an exchange between two staff members, Mike and Bob, who are discussing whether to award a child, Robby, a point for 'not being silly' during breakfast.

Extract 8.3a

Mike: You know, Bob [supervisor], I'm not sure it's a good idea to give him his morning points right now. Especially Robby. You know what he's been like since yesterday: zooming one minute and pouting the next. He's really off the wall lately. I'd say we should hold off a while

(Adapted from Gubrium *et al.* 1989: 204)

Bob affirms that Mike should reflect Robby's 'silly' behaviour on the points chart and suggests that the two workers should proceed and fill out the charts, saying 'Let's just get em done okay?' (ibid.: 204–5). Mike then argues that if Robby sees he has been allocated points for the morning, he will know he has earned the chance to go out that night and he will have no incentive to behave himself for the rest of the day:

Extract 8.3b

Mike: You know how he uses the damn system. He'll just sit tight knowing he's got his goddamn points and it's right up here in black and white. I say we should just conveniently forget to fill his in – and all the others too – just for breakfast and job points. That way he can't say he's being picked on and I can see what happens . . .

(ibid.: 205)

Bob agrees and the points are recorded in a notebook and the chart completed later. Bob comments:

Extract 8.3c

Bob: I know what you mean, man. That happens to me now and then. These damn charts can really do you in. Ya use 'em to control the kids but I've seen how the [charts] can really kinda control you sometimes . . . Once you put something down and the kids see it . . . you know how they see it too . . . it's too late. They'll turn the tables on you and yell and scream that 'I got my point' . . .

(ibid.: 205)

What is finally entered onto the chart appears to be a simple recording of the children's behaviour over breakfast, when in fact the decision is taken retrospectively, after a judgement has been made about whether Robby really deserves to go out that night. The forms and charts show no evidence of the work that went into completing them and the moral judgements entailed are ignored.

We have shown that forms make certain stylistic demands. However, form-fillers know what these demands are and make strategic decisions about how to accommodate them. The stylistic demands make entries on forms appear uniform and neutral but complex qualitative judgements or routinized short-cuts are hidden behind the neutral diagnostic discourse. Forms demand of their completers a description, not an argument, a debate or a range of opinion. They demand that completers put aside any doubts they may have about what they describe, the theories and formal knowledge they use to describe it, and whether they have adequate information, and just get on with ticking the box and fixing the description. Once fixed as words or numbers these completed forms become data; they become 'true'. And not only do they affect service users, but they also have the potential to inform research agendas and to drive policy at both national and local levels.

Having discussed documents which prefigure professional work in very structured ways, we now consider the ongoing case records compiled by professionals drawing on their tacit knowledge of 'competent' practice in their own particular field.

Case files: Linguistic strategies, storytelling and retelling

When we examine case files we can often see the same kinds of linguistic strategies for ascribing deviance, moral character and so forth as we have described in previous chapters. In short, records too can do rhetorical work. Moreover, because of the solidifying effects of the written word, records can carry a greater potency, and over a longer period of time than the spoken word. Like institutional talk, case records need to be analysed on a number of levels. They must be examined for what they reveal about the 'practical reasoning' of particular professional groups, and also for their everyday moral character, for example whom do they blame, how and why?

The institutional context: professional texts as transformative

What can case records tell us about the institutional context of professional work? We referred above to the work of Hak (1992) who has used a broadly ethnomethodological approach to study psychiatric records. However, Hak takes issue with Garfinkel's assertion that records can tell us only about the *local* practices of a professional group. Instead, he argues that:

> these records can be studied as a product of a psychiatrist's 'practical theorizing' about a given patient's behaviour [but] a competent reading of – and by implication a competent writing of – psychiatric records cannot be completely defined locally, and the record must bear at least some relation to 'ideal' psychiatric competence, for the simple reason that eventually sanctionable performances by clinic members must be evaluated by outside experts. This means that even a local meaning for present use can be uncovered – at least partially – by using 'ideal' procedures and theories as interpretive tools . . .
>
> (Hak 1992: 142)

That is to say, institutional settings do not straightforwardly determine what sense professionals make of cases, but they might encourage certain interpretive frameworks. The compilation of case records involves the reformulation of original accounts and observations of both others and the original worker in such a way that professional competence, as currently defined, is displayed (cf. Cicourel 1968). Hak compares fragments of transcript of an interview between a patient and a doctor with the subsequent report compiled on the case. Let us first examine an extract of the report.

Extract 8.4

Reason for referral:
    Paranoid state of borderline of drug addict. Repeat visit.
Preliminary diagnosis:
    Borderline state of paranoid coloring and severe protracted disturbance in relationship with her father . . .

. . .

Interview with Pat.
    . . . It is obvious that the client has delusions. She fancies that her sexual past is being disclosed on the radio. And that her father can hear her all the time as well. On the other hand, she frequently hears voices. She seems to hear the voice of her father, even when he is not present. It is not clear to me to what extent these are hallucinations.
    In the presence of her parents she tries to provoke her father. She spews out rather vulgar descriptions of her sex life. Her father reacts with much agitation. Threatens to throw her out of house, to beat her etc., and still he cannot cope with her . . .

                                                            (Hak 1992: 154)

By examining the interview transcript (see below) alongside the report, Hak is able to show the way in which the psychiatrist is making particular choices about what is happening in this family, whilst also reproducing institutional psychiatric classifications. Let us look at an extract from the interview transcript:

Extract 8.5

IE (Pat):   He is bothering me all his life and he has told me that already.
F (Father): I will beat you up. Please get dressed and get the hell out of here . . .
            When I can't hold out with sexual life any longer, I go to the whores.
            I'm not going to use my own kids for that. What she reels off now!
            She has been used to satisfy [my] sexual life

                                                            (Hak 1992: 150)

Here, the father responds to an ambiguous statement made by his daughter by asserting his innocence of any sexual abuse of his children. The psychiatrist is faced with at least two possible interpretations of this. He can take the daughter's apparent distress as evidence of a protracted abusive relationship with her father, or he can interpret the father's reaction as one of frustration with his daughter's disturbed but untrue allegations.

The exchange cited above is reformulated in the report into:

Extract 8.6

She spews out rather vulgar descriptions of her sex life. Her father reacts with much agitation. Threatens to throw her out of house, to beat her etc., and still he cannot cope with her

(Hak 1992: 154)

This reformulation shows several different features. First the very general complaint 'He is bothering me all his life' is transformed into an abstract statement 'She spews out rather vulgar descriptions of her sex life'. This does two jobs. It suggests disclosure of intimate sexual details was taking place regularly throughout the interview. It also grants a moral flavour with the verb 'spew' and the adjective 'vulgar' which suggest excess and render the father's responses understandable in the circumstances. As Hak notes, the reformulation conceals the fact that the doctor has in effect accepted the father's version. However, the doctor's everyday theorizing is warranted by his use of psychiatric diagnostic classification in the first part of his report, and the shared understanding of this form of knowledge is anticipated in his readers (other psychiatrists or mental health professionals). The report begins with a diagnosis and then presents 'findings'. In effect, the end of the report – its conclusion – is placed at the beginning. This is usual in official reports of many kinds. As is noted by Hyden (1997) in an analysis of professional reports compiled as part of the compulsory removal of children from their parents' care and of compulsory admission of a woman to psychiatric hospital: the 'end is the starting point and gives all actions prior to this point their *significance*' (Hyden 1997: 253, original emphasis).

In Hak's example, the reformulations of the utterances of the participants illustrate Miller's point made at the beginning of this chapter:

The words . . . 'freeze' the ongoing events of life, making it impossible for us to return to them from time to time in order to verify . . . others' claims about them . . .

(Miller 1997: 72)

Hak's work illustrates again the coexistence of moral judgement and formal knowledge in professional practice which we encountered in Chapter 7. His methodology allows us to track the transformative features of the professional text. However, it is perfectly possible to examine professional texts without having access to the original encounter. By examining a sample of case records from a particular setting we can learn a great deal about how, for example, that professional group sees and constructs deviance and normality. It will be useful to look in more detail at the ways in which professional accounts, whilst appearing to be neutral descriptions of events, have the character of stories and display moral judgements. How do professional texts 'do' blame and ascribe deviance?

Deviance, risk, blaming and absolution: everyday moral judgement in institutional context

We have said that case records can often accomplish subtle **blamings** and absolutions. As elsewhere in this book, we are using the words 'culpability' and 'blame' to mean attribution of responsibility (cf. Pomerantz 1978). This particular definition is crucial, as professionals frequently offer mitigating statements for their client's 'failure' ('she was brought up in care and suffered dreadful abuse as a child', 'he's a very damaged person', 'he has longstanding mental health problems', 'she's in the early stages of dementia'), which imply that the individual is somehow not to blame, whilst simultaneously ascribing to them a 'deviant' character and preserving the rhetorical force of the blaming (as an attribution of responsibility for causing a particular problem in the present). That is to say, notions of causation and culpability are bound together in HW practice, and this is particularly evident in case files where professionals are trying to produce a competent account and rationale for their view of the case. We have seen this in Hak's example. The following example, taken from White's study of childcare social work, is particularly striking.

Extract 8.7a

[Extract from original referral from the health visitor]
B. [child aged 19 months] has had several breath-holding attacks and has been in hospital twice. Hospital wish him to attend play therapy. Father works long hours. Mother has children 24 hrs a day with no break . . .

(White 1997a: 254)

Here the mother is constructed as victim, the child as difficult, and the father as potentially culpable. However, the initial referral form was completed by the social worker as follows:

Extract 8.7b

Request for financial assistance with 1x session per week childminding fees. Child with medical problems, mum needs respite. B. experiences some problems with breath holding – deliberate and manipulative catching of breath during temper tantrums. This has necessitated 2 hospital admissions because of convulsions. Father works long hours – he clearly sees his role as provider for the family and does not help out much with the children. The health visitor feels that mum is overwhelmed by the difficulties entailed in managing B.'s behaviour and desperately needs some respite . . .

(ibid.: 254)

This passage is interesting for two reasons. With the adjectives 'deliberate and manipulative', B. has become more clearly defined as a problem child.

Furthermore, although the father has conformed to certain normative expectations (breadwinner), he is still subjected to professional censure. Textual devices are employed (describing his lack of availability at home) in order to assign culpability to him. However, as the case progresses things quickly change:

Extract 8.7c

B. is now 20 months old and stronger than ever. Mum finds him very overpowering . . . I felt mum does not help. She is quite anxious and shouts quite a bit . . . I felt a childminder was not going to help B. I felt from what she had been saying, he would feel rejected by her and it is his mother's attention he seeks. I explained that we do not just pay for childminders and asked about a Family Resource Worker [FRW].

(ibid.: 255)

Here there is a clear shift away from a 'service delivery' construction, where the parent's account is accepted, to a 'sceptical professional' position, in which the problem is redefined as mother's fault. The plot thickens; the FRW writes:

Extract 8.7d

Had B for 1½ hrs. He was very good. He fell asleep in the car going home. When mum lay him on the settee he woke and started to cry. Mum tried to comfort him, but he carried on crying and breath-held. Mum was very gentle with him which proved ineffective. I took over from her. I clapped my hands really hard and shouted his name, he caught his breath and was OK.

(ibid.: 255)

Through the reporting of an 'unhappy incident' (Pomerantz 1978), in association with a 'contrast structure' ('Mum was very gentle with him which proved ineffective. I took over from her. I clapped my hands'), a subtle blaming of the mother is accomplished. The child was referred for day foster care so that 'assessment' could continue.

Extract 8.7e

M [day carer] says he is fine with her, yet mum said she had a few breath-holding attacks over the weekend . . .

(ibid.: 255)

This is another particularly clear example of the use of a contrast structure (see Chapter 3) to amplify deviance. The first half of the sentence sets up the expectation, the second references a departure from it. The very material effect of this upon the mother is reported as follows:

Extract 8.7f

Next visit mother began to cry, said she was beginning to hate B., couldn't stand his breath-holding attacks, feels he is doing it to get at her. Mum cannot understand

why B. is good for M. and terrible for her. I have tried to explain that B. is a
bright little boy who needs constructive play and discipline. While he is at M.'s he
gets just that. I suggested a few ways of her changing her attitude towards B.
Dad is just never around. When he is there on a Sunday he can't cope with B.

(ibid.: 256)

In using the expression 'I have tried to explain' the writer implies that the
mother has some difficulty understanding, and with 'I suggested a few ways'
she adopts the role of 'child expert'. Thus, the ascription of blame clearly
shifts in this case, as follows:

child (+ father) → mother → mother + father

We have looked at the linguistic devices at play in the account above, but
can it tell us anything about the institutional context and tacit assumptions
of contemporary childcare social work? As we discussed briefly in Chapter 7, children are currently socially constructed as passive 'potential persons',
who must constantly negotiate the treacherous developmental steps to complete personhood (see, for example, Burman 1994; Stainton Rogers and
Stainton Rogers 1992; Armstrong 1995; King and Piper 1995; Garrett 1999).
Fuelled by a preoccupation with the assessment of risk and dangerousness
in childcare social work (Parton 1991; Howe 1992, 1994a,b; Otway 1996),
and the burgeoning field of developmental psychology, this has led to the
ascent of a 'discourse of parental culpability' (White 1998b). By examining
case files it is possible to detect a preference within social work for 'deviant'
behaviour or development in children to be constructed as an avoidable
consequence of individual parenting styles. This is illustrated in the case
above. That is not say that a quick glance at one or two records will yield
such insights, but by looking at what is taken for granted in records, we
can develop hunches which we can then explore further to increase our
awareness of what we are doing as practitioners.

Summary

This chapter has looked at the different ways in which case records may
be considered to be important. We have encouraged you to examine the
schedules and checklists you may use in your practice in new ways. We have
also shown how the writers of case records use strategies to ascribe blameworthiness and creditworthiness to individuals which are similar to those
displayed in their talk. These strategies underscore the moral nature of professional decision making. Even where they coexist with formal knowledge,
these moral judgements are very clear. However, by lending solidity to
ambiguous and uncertain situations, the written word has particular durability across space and time. It allows certain ideas and formulations to

travel through time. This makes the analysis of documents an indispensable component of a reflexive approach to practice.

We have introduced the following key concepts in this chapter:

- Forms and schedules do not straightforwardly describe a reality. They impose their own descriptive demands. These demands include the use of mutually exclusive categorizations, the use of neutral diagnostic language, the expectation that professionals conceal their deliberations and present their accounts as factual descriptions of the client or patient, their behaviour or circumstances.
- Forms, schedules and databases conceal as much as they reveal.
- The data contained in forms and checklists, precisely because of their solidity, often inform research agendas and policy planning at national and local levels.
- Forms and schedules rely on the assumption of uniform professional application.
- Professionals are not 'moral dopes', and their form-completing activity is affected by contingent situational factors. These factors are concealed in the completed form.
- Case records are transformations of other texts, such as interviews, or accounts of others.
- Case records can be examined for their internal ordering, linguistic strategies and narratives, and also for what they can tell us about the institutional context of professional activity, and about the forms of knowledge taken for granted by that profession at that historical moment.

Implications for practice

Our first point is that we are not adopting the position of the critical researcher who wants to expose error and strives to change practice to achieve a perfect fit between reality and professional description. Rather, our point is that forms, schedules and computer records masquerade as perfect description and are used as such in policy and planning. There is no way that records or forms can ever reproduce material, situated reality. As professionals, we have to order reality and we do so by supporting some versions and burying others. This is something we cannot avoid. However, by reflecting on the process of choice and judgement and thinking about ways in which forms may be redesigned to show more of our 'working' we may develop a different and more critical approach to the data contained within them.

It is also noteworthy that 'freehand' organizational records often contain statements which are clearly qualitative moral judgements, but these same judgements are concealed in prescriptive forms and schedules. We do not think that moral judgements are avoidable, we think they are integral to practice. We are not asking you to do away with them, but are suggesting that you explore them for what they are and hence open them up to debate. Used in this way, records can become an indispensable tool for reflexive practice and can lead to further questions about which aspects of cases are routinely concealed in forms.

Exercises

EXERCISE 1

Select one form which you use habitually in your work or one you can easily obtain, such as a mortgage or benefit application.

(a) What descriptive demands are imposed by the form? In answering this question it may be helpful to think about what frustrates you about the form and how you have to mould your account to fit the form. It may also be useful to find some forms you have completed and to look for examples of descriptive demands: for example, have you adopted neutral diagnostic language, are there examples of mutually exclusive categorizations?

(b) In what ways does the form conceal aspects of the reality it purports to describe?

(c) What effects does the completed form have? By whom is it used, and what does it mean for the service user? Are data from the form aggregated in any way and used in another arena?

EXERCISE 2

Examine five examples of your own recently completed case files, medical notes or nursing records.

(a) Look for the ways in which you have constructed 'fact', that is presented something as a certainty.

(b) Look for examples of the construction of deviance.

(c) Look for examples of blamings (as in the attribution of responsibility) and exonerations. This may not always be in relation to a service user: it may be a reference to another professional, or a statement that exonerates you. Remember, blamings can be done in subtle ways, such as by describing an unhappy incident or using a contrast structure. Who are the heroes/heroines and villains in your version of events?

(d) We have said that it is impossible to return to the scene and check our records of it, and we have also said that it is impossible to produce an infallible account of that scene. However, by practising the creation of different versions of events we can improve our interpretive agility in our next encounter. Think about gathering the information on one of your case examples. What sorts of doubts did you have at the time? From what you remember, what is obscured in your record? What lines of enquiry are left unpursued as a result of your decisions about the heroes/heroines and villains.

EXERCISE 3

Redesign your form from Exercise 1 so that more of what you consider relevant to the case is included.

CHAPTER 9

Making knowledge: the Louise Woodward case

In this chapter, we bring together the elements of a discourse analytic approach and apply them to the Louise Woodward case. We have chosen this case, despite its perhaps harrowing detail, because it was highly publicized in the late 1990s and provoked considerable public response. At the time, most of the public debate centred on 'did Louise really do it or not?'.

Our purpose here is to set aside issues of guilt or innocence and to focus on the complexities of the case, the ambiguity of the evidence and the ways in which the various parties used language in a highly performative way to warrant their claims, to undermine the claims of their opponents, or to present themselves as morally adequate and others as discreditable. The technical detail of the medical information may be unfamiliar to some readers. However, the trial hinged on this detail and explanations for medical terms are given in brackets to assist your understanding. It may help to think about what this experience might have been like for jurors, many of whom presumably were confronted with a completely new vocabulary. In addition, we want to emphasize that our particular focus is on *how* things were said in order to achieve credibility. We begin by providing an overview of the trial, we then explore the way in which the medical facts were constructed and disputed, the problem of judgement, and the construction of the moral character in relation to Louise Woodward and Matthew Eappen's parents. We conclude with the practice implications of our analysis.

The Louise Woodward trial

As judges always tell juries – as *this* judge told *this* jury – evidence is evidence if the jurors believe it; what they choose not to believe is not evidence . . .

(Zobel 1997)

On 4 February 1997, Matthew Eappen aged 8 months was admitted to the emergency room of the Children's Hospital in Boston, Massachusetts. He had lapsed into a coma whilst in the care of Louise Woodward, a 19-year-old au pair from the UK. On examination, he was found to have massive intra-cranial bleeding (bleeding inside the skull) from a subdural haematoma (a blood clot under the dura, the outermost of three membranes between the brain and the skull). He died five days later. Louise Woodward was charged with murder and held in custody without bail. In October 1997 she was tried and convicted of second degree murder, receiving a mandatory sentence of 30 years, with no possibility of parole for 15 years. However, the trial judge, Hiller Zobel, invoked a rarely used power of 'judicial veto', and eleven days later, after reviewing the case, reduced Woodward's conviction to involuntary manslaughter, deeming that the 279 days she had spent in prison to that date should serve as her sentence and that she be set free. The case went to appeal and finally, in March 1998, the US Supreme Court, after extensive deliberations, upheld Zobel's judgement.

The material we have analysed is taken from the Internet, where Zobel elected to deliver his judgement. We have chosen this case because of its immense material significance: Matthew Eappen died. This is not an artefact, a construction or a rhetorical device. The fragility of our bodies is an undeniable product of biology. It cannot be redefined or re-authored. It is irreversible and real. However, Matthew Eappen's death is one of very few indisputable certainties of the case. Indeed, even the irrefutable and tragic fact of his death is lent a different hue by a simple selection between the words 'died' and 'was killed' in various accounts. We have said repeatedly in this book that many of the real and serious issues and events which HW professionals confront cannot be resolved unproblematically by recourse to 'science', 'evidence' or bodies of knowledge. As the above quotation from Judge Zobel illustrates, what serves as evidence is contestable. In this analysis of the case, we show how diverse forms of reasoning informed the judgements. Crucially, it seems that normative judgements about right and wrong, moral worthiness and blameworthiness are central and unavoidable, and that these were applied to the witnesses and the judiciary as well as to the defendant.

The trial of Louise Woodward was played out on the world stage and is an elaborate example of the problem of versions to which we have been referring. The initial legal battle focused on the medical evidence about the trauma to Matthew Eappen's skull and brain, as Judge Zobel notes below.

Extract 9.1

Reduced to its appropriately bare essentials, this case turns on diametrically opposed theories of ultimate causation. Both sides agreed that Matthew Eappen died from massive intra-cranial bleeding. The prosecution's experts attributed the hemorrhage to a combination of extraordinarily violent shaking and overpowering

contact with a hard flat surface, all occurring some time on February 4, 1997;
the defense experts ascribed the hemorrhage to a 're-bleed' in a clot formed
about three weeks earlier following a hitherto undetected injury.

(Zobel 1997)

The prosecution alleged that Matthew Eappen presented with a classic example of a documented and named medical phenomenon, 'shaken baby syndrome' (Dulhaime and Thibault 1987). They supported their case with the assertion that Woodward had told investigating officers at the time of the incident that she may have been 'a little rough' with Matthew. The defence put forward their own case that the initial trauma to the skull had occurred earlier, but showed no symptoms until 4 February. If Louise Woodward did not have sole charge of the children at the time of the initial injury, then the case against her would collapse. The defence disputed that Woodward had been 'rough' with the baby. She argued at trial that she may not have been as gentle as she might have been, with the subtle inference that, had she known about the injury, she would have taken *extra* care.

Alongside this central medical debate, a parallel battle about the moral characters of Louise Woodward and the Eappens was played out in the media and alluded to in the courtroom. In one version, Louise Woodward was portrayed as of dubious moral character, a rather untrustworthy, fun-seeking young woman, in Boston for the high life, who was clearly prone to uncontrolled outbursts of frustration and showed no remorse for Matthew's death. In the other, the Eappen parents, themselves doctors, and particularly Deborah Eappen, Matthew's mother, were portrayed as high achieving professionals who put their career before their children's well-being and worked excessively long hours, leaving in sole charge a young, inexperienced woman whom they had employed 'on the cheap' (Louise was not a qualified nanny, and thus would have attracted a lower rate of pay). We return to this media coverage later in the chapter; first we examine the construction and contestability of the medical facts and the problem of judgement.

Medical facts: the 'missing dura' and other dramas

Contested 'medical facts' were the principal point of argument in the Massachusetts v. Woodward trial in October 1997. The case for the prosecution was that Matthew Eappen sustained the fatal brain injury on the afternoon of 4 February. They alleged that Matthew's head had been struck with a force equivalent to a fall of 15 feet onto concrete, and that he had been shaken violently for about one minute causing his head to 'snap back and forth'. Thus, the injury must have been inflicted by Louise Woodward, the only adult present, since Matthew's 2-year-old brother, Brendan, would not have had the necessary physical capacity for such violence.

The exact 'measurements' of 15 feet and 'one minute' give these arguments the flavour of certainty, as though by looking at the tissue, the pathologists were able to calibrate exactly what had happened. The rhetorical potency of the horrific image so generated was exploited by the prosecution lawyer during his final arguments, when he graphically simulated the alleged violent event by banging his hands on the hard surface in front of the jurors, and shaking an imaginary child.

Against this, the defence asserted that Matthew's symptoms (irritability, crying, poor appetite and excessive drowsiness), reported by Louise Woodward in a telephone conversation with Deborah Eappen before his lapse into a coma, were indicative of raised intra-cranial pressure (pressure inside the skull) from a 're-bleed', which could have been caused by routine handling. The original injury, they contended, could have been sustained during a 'mild impact fall' of two or three feet which remained asymptomatic until the re-bleed. They alleged that the fatal brain swelling was not due to violent trauma, but to anoxia (oxygen deprivation) caused by raised pressure on the brain stem, thus suppressing respiration. To support this version, the defence told the court that paramedics attending the scene had failed in their attempts to intubate Matthew and ventilate his lungs. Furthermore, the defence asserted that the medical examiner, Gerald Feigin, had agreed with their own experts that there were no spinal cord or neck injuries to corroborate the 'shaking' hypothesis.

Both parties supported their case with medical evidence, but this was overlain by various tales of human error and alleged incompetence. In short, the medical facts never did (or could) speak for themselves, but were constructed by the experts and contextualized by other dramas. These concerned, amongst other things, the fate of various parts of the infant's skull and brain tissue following autopsy; the defence team's access to skull photographs; and disputes over whether certain signs and symptoms were the result of the neurosurgery undertaken before Matthew's death, rather than the alleged actions of Louise Woodward.

Let us now examine the most contested medical findings. This is not an exhaustive discussion, but is intended to demonstrate how complex 'the problem of judgement' becomes when what serves as a fact is so unstable. It is also intended to illustrate how the very act of fact-gathering can become imbued with moral significance.

The skull fracture and the missing dura: the moral culpability of the medical examiner

Both the defence and the prosecution were in agreement that, since there was no dispute that the haematoma and the skull fracture were caused at the same time, the age of the fracture was of material significance in establishing Woodward's guilt: it was a 'verdict-determining' issue. Further, it was agreed that the age of the fracture could be established by looking for signs of healing on the fractured edges of the occipital bone (situated at the back of the skull). The autopsy was carried out by the district medical examiner who then discarded the relevant pieces of the skull, apparently in contravention of a tissue preservation order which was in place. The defence pathologists were thus unable directly to examine the fracture site.

The medical examiner was of the opinion that the edges of the fracture appeared to be sharp and without signs of healing. Photographs were taken, but were not presented to the court until the penultimate day of the trial, after the medical experts and Louise Woodward had already given evidence. The defence argued that this precluded the cross-examination of prosecution witnesses about the extent to which the photographs confirmed, or disconfirmed, the medical examiner's view that the edges of the fracture were sharp (indicating a recent fracture), as opposed to lipped (or rounded, indicating a healing fracture). They recalled one witness, Dr Baden, who disputed the medical examiner's view and was of the opinion that the edges were lipped.

For discarding the crucial parts of skull, the medical examiner becomes potentially blameworthy, as either misinformed, stupid or deceitful. This culpability was used by the defence team in the various appeals. Indeed, the defence argued, had the skull been retained, it would have proved conclusively that the fracture was old and there would have been no trial. A safe, and rhetorically potent statement since the action of the medical examiner had rendered it absolutely irrefutable.

Adding further to the ascribed culpability of the medical examiner and his team, as part of the autopsy, the pathologists undertaking the examination of the brain tissue cut two sections from the dura (at the site of the haematoma). Again, at the time, an evidence preservation order was in place, but after taking a small sample from one section, the tissue was discarded.

There was considerable disagreement about the significance of what became known as 'the missing dura'. First, the defence argued that since they should have had an opportunity to examine the intact dura, the tissue had been unlawfully cut. Second, they argued that as the skull and the clot had also been discarded and could not be examined for signs of healing, the dura was of indisputable significance. To support this, their neuropathologist, Dr Leestma, who had examined dura adjacent to the site, testified that she had observed separation of periosteum (a membrane covering bone) from the skull, and the presence of growing bone and osteoblasts (bone-forming cells) all of which were evidence of an old injury. The prosecution, however, argued that it was not clear that there were any missing pieces of dura, or that these were so small as to be insignificant and immaterial to the case.

It is unsurprising that the alleged failure to preserve the sections of dura caused some embarrassment to the pathologists involved. Their attempts to account for this led to inconsistencies in the evidence, which were seized

upon by the defence as is shown in this extract from the Supreme Court
Appeal Brief.

Extract 9.2

Dr De Girolami's flip-flop testimony about missing dura was of critical importance. On September 25th, just prior to trial, Dr De Girolami testified at the
missing tissue hearing that he . . . *personally* made squarish cut-outs 3 by 4
centimeters of both sides of the dura, then *discarded* the left-side square except
for one small strip . . . He also maintained at trial that this whole procedure,
including the disposal of cut but unsectioned dura, was his usual practice . . .
However, having learned at the hearing, to his understandable embarassment,
that he had discarded evidence in violation of an explicit court order, Dr De
Girolami took a completely different position at trial: (1) that he didn't know what
happened when the dura was cut, although he was present; (2) he didn't do the
cutting – Dr Anthony did; and (3) he claimed, based upon his reexamination of
the missing dura, that no dura appeared to be missing or thown away after all.

(Defence Appeal Brief 1998)

In using the frivolous adjective 'flip-flop' to describe the testimony of prosecution witnesses, the defence was able to construct them as rather childlike,
foolish and desperate to cover their tracks. The use of 'a three part list' also
amplifies the rhetorical force of the statement (Heritage and Greatbatch
1986; Hall 1997). The prosecution team itself was not spared, as is shown
in this further statement from the Appeal Brief:

Extract 9.3

the principal way the prosecution sought to evade damage to its own neuro-
pathology case was to capitalize on the *absence* of crucial evidence – missing
clot and right parietal dura – brought about by the improper acts of its own
witnesses.

(Defence Appeal Brief 1998)

What is important here is that, alongside the contested medical facts, a
moral drama is played out in which the defence positions the prosecution
pathologists as incompetent and untrustworthy and the prosecution team
as evasive and deceitful. What appears to be about hard science is actually
about character and moral worth.

This is the result of the meeting of two discourses, medical and legal
(or juridical). Sociological analyses of the law tell us that medicoscientific
discourse allows for disputability and uncertainty, but juridical discourse
demands (near) certainty (beyond reasonable doubt) (Bourdieu 1986;
Teubner 1989; King and Piper 1995). Thus, by exploiting medical uncertainty, the defence team is able to mount a challenge to the prosecution
case, even though, by their own admission, they are unable directly to
refute many of the medical arguments, since the crucial tissue is missing.
The prosecution wants to convince the judge and jury that their version of

the case is certain, which they can do only by discrediting the defence experts. The 'certainties' constructed by this processes, however, are very situated. For example, in a pre-trial hearing specifically about the missing dura (Extract 9.2) the court had accepted that the tissue was indeed missing. However, in the trial, the jury did not appear to believe this to be the case as Zobel notes:

Extract 9.4

Absence of the dura was disputed at trial; the jury were entitled to believe that nothing substantial was gone. In this, the court's previous contrary findings, made in a different context, do not control . . .

(Zobel 1997)

Once the jury had taken the view that 'nothing substantial was missing', the prosecution was able to use this judgement as a warrant for certainty over their own version.

The serum issue

During the trial, the neurosurgeon, Dr Madsen, who had performed Matthew Eappen's brain surgery, testified that, when he made an incision in the dura to remove the haematoma, liquid blood had been released. He said:

Extract 9.5

This appeared to be *clearish* at first and then more red and this was followed by a rapid output of purple blood when the space was decompressed . . .

(Defence Appeal Brief 1998, emphasis added)

The significance of this 'clearish fluid' became a major issue in the trial. There was agreement between prosecution and defence witnesses that this was 'serum', a yellowish fluid, and not cerebrospinal fluid, which is clearer. However, there was disagreement about how this finding should be read. The principal defence expert, Dr Leestma, on being questioned by Barry Scheck the defence lawyer, opined:

Extract 9.6

Q: What significance in your opinion, to a reasonable degree of medical certainty, does it have that serum would have come out of that area, as we're pointing to the dark area on Exhibit 27?

A: The significance is that this is an older subdural hematoma which is partially resolved. There is no blood in that component of it anymore, only straw colored serum-like fluid.

Q: And would you describe for the jury what 'serum' is and how it comes into existence.

A: It's the natural history of a subdural hematoma to eventually be enclosed in a membrane, and the contents within the membrane to gradually disappear.

> Red blood cells gradually disappear, capillaries form and they leak. They leak serum, which is the liquid part of our blood minus the cells. It's a yellow proteinaceous straw-colored fluid. And that is the content of a subdural once the blood has gone away . . .
>
> (Defence Appeal Brief 1998)

However, Dr Madsen for the prosecution did not agree that the serum was unequivocal evidence of an old injury, but argued instead that the fresh blood he had also observed could not be associated with a chronic haematoma.

The jury recognized the significance of the 'serum issue' and asked for transcripts of Dr Madsen's and Dr Leestma's testimony. They were provided with the former, which had already been transcribed, but not the latter because this was lengthy and awaiting transcription. For his failure to insist that the requested portions of Dr Leestma's testimony be transcribed, or to comply with a defence request that a video or audiotape of the testimony be provided instead, Judge Zobel was himself held culpable by the defence in their submissions to the appeals.

Who caused the retinal haemorrhages – Louise Woodward or the neurosurgeon?

The prosecution medical experts asserted that Matthew Eappen had bilateral retinal haemorrhages (bleeding at the back of the eye) at the time of his admission to hospital. This is a diagnostic finding in shaken baby syndrome and, therefore, substantiated the view that Louise Woodward had inflicted the injury to Matthew on the day of his collapse into a coma. However, this opinion relied on the prosecution opthalmologist, Dr Lois Smith, speculating that a routine presurgery funduscope (instrument used to examine the back of the eye) examination by the hospital opthalmologist was incorrect. This examination apparently had not revealed the deep retinal haemorrhages which Dr Smith asserted 'must have been there' at the point of admission. The hospital opthalmologist had made drawings of the funduscope examination which showed the haemorrhages present after, but not before, Matthew's neurosurgery. The defence asserted that these findings indicated that the haemorrhages were a consequence of the neurosurgery. The prosecution case, then, depended on Dr Smith discrediting the observations of the hospital doctor, rather than on undisputed diagnostic facts. It also relied on the jury believing her version rather than the other. It depended upon whether they attributed more credibility to the 'eye witness testimony' of the hospital opthalmologist, or to the professional gravitas of Dr Smith. No neutral evaluative mechanisms were available.

Thus, at the end of this review of the medical evidence, we have found no undisputed 'medical facts'. There are plenty of facts available, or in Hacking's

(1999) terms plenty of 'indifferent kinds'. The haematoma, the skull, the dura and so forth are all objects with no capacity to construct themselves. They cannot answer back. However, all these facts must be interpreted. In turn, the judge and jury must interpret the interpretations. Since they are unlikely to possess the necessary expert knowledge, the jury could not have evaluated the competing hypotheses using anything other than conventional means. In short, they must have found some witnesses more believable than others.

The problem of judgement

The medical facts in this case fail to establish unequivocally anything other than the fact that Matthew Eappen died of the effects of a subdural bleed caused by an injury of contested age. They establish neither Louise Woodward's guilt, nor her innocence. How did the courts deal with this uncertainty? In the initial trial, it seems that the jurors accepted the pro-secution story that the injury was caused on 4 February, and that Louise Woodward, having sole charge of Matthew on that morning must, *ipso facto*, be guilty. However, they may have been influenced by the court's agreement to a defence request that Woodward be tried for murder alone, presumably in the belief that malice and intent could not be established beyond reasonable doubt (a decision for which both Woodward and Judge Zobel were subsequently held morally culpable).

It seems, however, that Zobel was uncomfortable with the verdict and immediately offered to use his powers of judicial veto to review the case in the interests of 'natural justice'. He had a difficult task ahead of him. The defence sought the acquittal of Louise Woodward, and the prosecution affirmation of the jury's verdict. Zobel had a number of major problems to address. First, he had to grapple with the disputability of the medical evid-ence. This was complicated by the defence argument that Zobel had him-self acted in error when he failed to comply with the jury's request to see a transcript of Dr Leestma's verdict-determining testimony on the serum issue. Second, because trial by jury has immense symbolic significance, to interfere with the verdict could provoke severe censure. Zobel knew that he could not afford to imply any fault on the part of the jury for its assessment of the evidence. He needed to change its verdict without implying that the verdict was wrong. Third, if he reduced the charge to manslaughter he faced the accusation that he had allowed Louise Woodward to 'second guess' the judicial system. That is, the defence team had requested that Woodward be tried for murder, with the belief that this would be difficult to prove 'beyond reasonable doubt', and the gamble had not paid off. Zobel himself, as trial judge, could have insisted that the jury consider a manslaughter charge but he had not done so. Clearly, all this placed Zobel in an ethically precarious position. An examination of his judgement is, therefore, of considerable interest.

Zobel's reasoning

Let us look first at the issue of the disputed medical evidence. In his review of the case, Zobel explicitly refers to a possible alternative reading. It is clear from his decision that this corresponds to his own view.

Extract 9.7

Had the manslaughter option been available to the jurors, they might well have selected it, not out of compromise, but because that particular verdict accorded with at least one rational view of the evidence, namely: (1) Matthew did indeed have a pre-existing, resolving (i.e., healing) blood clot; (2) Defendant did handle him 'roughly'; (3) the handling (although perhaps not the roughness) was intentional; (4) the force was, under the circumstances, excessive, and therefore unjustified; (5) the handling did cause re-bleeding; and (6) the re-bleeding caused death . . .

(Zobel 1997)

This is a sophisticated argument in which Zobel is able to reference the believability of this alternative reading (it is 'one *rational* view of the evidence'), but to do so without blaming the jury (because the manslaughter option was not available to them). Moreover, by treating the possibility that Woodward had 'been rough' with the baby as established fact, rather than as a contested assertion, Zobel preserves her culpability for the death, but exonerates her from any intent to kill. He continues as follows:

Extract 9.8

If the jury determined that those were the facts, the combination would amount to an unjustified, intentional, unconsented-to touching (i.e., a battery) which resulted in death. Manslaughter is simply a fatal battery, Commonwealth v. Campbell, 352 Mass. 387, 397 (1967). Defendant's lack of intent to cause death or even injury would have been, legally speaking, irrelevant, as would Defendant's lack of knowledge about Matthew's pre-existing condition. The principle is simple: If you apply force to another person's body, you take the risk that (unknown to you) your blow, which an ordinary person could physically tolerate, may kill the individual you strike. The victim's hidden physical weakness does not exonerate the perpetrator . . .

(Zobel 1997)

In this neat turn, Zobel is able to use his institutional powers of 'judgement' to deliver a hypothetical alternative verdict which renders the disputed medical evidence irrelevant. He simply brackets it out, and by citing this definition of manslaughter and the relevant case law, he invokes instead an institutional, legal rationality. Zobel has dealt with the uncertainty created by the medical evidence not by resolving the disputes, but by recognizing the essential incommensurability of the two versions and moving onto firmer terrain. We should also note the way that he writes out his authorship of this version and presents it as a dispassionate survey of the case (an example of empiricist discourse; see Chapter 2 and Gilbert and Mulkay 1984). In so doing, he renders defence accusations about the transcribed evidence less potent, since they have in effect become irrelevant. Nevertheless, considerable rhetorical work goes into Zobel's statement on the transcription issue.

Extract 9.9

Absence of a contemporaneous transcript of Dr Jan Leestma's testimony – a normal occurrence in the Massachusetts Superior Court, and not to be held against the faithful, dedicated court reporter necessitated either not responding to the jury's request, or interrupting the deliberations of a sequestered jury for the time necessary to transcribe the testimony (which had lasted for parts of two days). The alternative, preparing a transcript of only selected portions, was not possible here, where counsel could not agree on the selections. Even if they had agreed, the delay would have held the jury idle an unacceptably long time. Thus in accordance with the normal practice in Superior Court trials, the transcript was not read. Unless one or both of the parties make arrangements for daily transcripts, none is available . . . The lack of a Leestma transcript was, from the defense standpoint, unfortunate. However, here again, nothing prevented counsel, in final argument, from putting to the jurors his own recollection and urging them to draw the appropriate conclusion.

(Zobel 1997)

Here, by making two separate references, Zobel situates the absence of a transcript as a normal occurrence in the Massachusetts Superior Court. His exonerative comments about the court reporter further construct the judge as a reasonable and honourable person. His assertion that complying with the request would necessitate 'either not responding to the jury's request, or interrupting the deliberations of a sequestered jury' situates it as an impossible task. The reference to the sequestered jury, invokes the sacredness of their deliberations (which should not be interrupted), and mitigates Zobel's refusal to comply with their request. Zobel then effortlessly transfers the blame to 'counsel' who 'could not agree on the selections'. Having noted the 'unfortunate' effect the absence of the transcript may have had on the defence case, he argues: 'nothing prevented counsel, in final argument, from putting to the jurors his own recollection'. This implies that perhaps the defence team did not think the issue sufficiently important to use in their closing summary, or had erred in their decision not to do so.

Zobel has dealt with the contested evidence and has mitigated his own actions in relation to the transcript. However, he may be accused of overriding the sanctified verdict of 'twelve good men and true' and he must do some work on this issue. His first strategy is to underscore the unalienable right of a jury to decide whom and what they believe (as is illustrated in the quotation at the beginning of this chapter). However, he must qualify this, because if it were wholly true, he would have to let the verdict stand. Hence, he invokes the principle of 'natural justice', which as a judge he is mandated to define. The original version of the following extract includes numerous references to case law. These have been omitted for the sake of concision, but obviously boosted the rhetorical force of Zobel's reasoning.

Extract 9.10

The judge does not sit as a second jury . . . or even as a thirteenth juror . . . he should not second-guess the jury . . . Nonetheless, he is entitled to consider testimony that the jury may have disbelieved . . . including such of Defendant's own testimony as he finds credible . . . Because Rule 25(b)(2) is a kind of safety valve, . . . a means of rectifying disproportionate verdicts . . . the test is not whether the evidence could support a verdict of second degree murder, but whether a lesser verdict more comports with justice.

(Zobel 1997)

Here again, Zobel has been able to shift the terms of the debate. He is not disputing the jury's reading of the case, but is considering other matters. Since the jury could not be held responsible for the 'disproportionate' sentence because it is mandatory, they cannot be culpable for the alleged breach of natural justice. This exoneration is given further force with a eulogy at the end of the judgement.

Extract 9.11

One final word. All of us – the prosecution, the defense, the Court, and the public – owe a deep gratitude to the jury here, deliberating jurors and alternates alike, who gave of their time and effort and, in the aftermath, their privacy. Neither they nor anyone else should interpret today's decision as in any way a criticism of them . . .

(Zobel 1997)

Zobel is also aware of the possibility that he may be accused of a callous disregard for the feelings of the Eappen family. Here, Zobel invokes his empathy for the Eappens as a 'father and grandfather' and juxtaposes this with his legal mandate as a public servant to ignore such sentiments. He is thus able to underscore the material tragedy of the death of Matthew Eappen whilst both preserving and reducing Woodward's blameworthiness.

Thus, by rendering it irrelevant, Zobel has dealt with the medical evidence. He has also performed an effective prospective self-exoneration in relation to 'second-guessing' the jury, but he may still be accused of allowing Louise Woodward to have her cake and eat it too. She chose to be tried for murder and then did not like the outcome. She gambled, lost and wanted her money back. Does not Zobel's rule of 'natural justice' dictate that she get her just deserts for playing such a cavalier game of chance? Here, Zobel turns the gambling metaphor on its head and seizes the moral high ground.

Extract 9.12

Should Defendant now be permitted to second-guess herself and her lawyers? If one regards the trial of a criminal case as a high-stakes game of chance where losers must accept their losses, the answer is, Certainly Not. Massachusetts . . . never has and does not now view Justice as a handmaiden to Tyche, the Goddess of Good Fortune. Of course chance plays a part in litigation, as it does in every aspect of life. A court, nonetheless, is not a casino . . .

(Zobel 1997)

The declaration, that the court 'is not a casino' renders unseemly any references which protesters may make to Woodward gambling. Anyone who uses such a metaphor is constructed as morally offensive to the court, with its venerable principles of justice. Zobel and his court will have no truck with what he calls 'justice by plebiscite' (the rule of the mob). The artfulness of the performance is especially noteworthy here: the learned reference to the little-known Tyche and the extreme case formulation 'Massachusetts never has' add to the potency of Zobel's talk. The offensive and defensive rhetoric (Potter 1996) in his judgement is masterly.

Zobel's judgement has been considered and reconsidered in appeal hearings and has proved robust over these spaces and times. That is not to say that it has gone uncontested. The prosecution appeal to the Supreme Court reads like an indictment not so much of Woodward but of Zobel, who is variously accused of 'erroneously' allowing Woodward to ' "gamble" that she would be acquitted if the jury's only other option was to convict her of murder', of failing to make her 'accept her losses', of failing to take proper account of the Eappens' sentiments, and of violating the sacred, constitutional right of the jury to decide upon the facts of the case.

Zobel does not escape completely the censure of the Supreme Court judges, who note particularly the importance of the jury in the US judicial system. However, they construct Zobel's actions as an honourable attempt to correct his own 'error' (of failing to instruct the jury to consider a manslaughter verdict) and conclude:

Extract 9.13

We uphold this judge's reduction in verdict because, from our reading of the transcript and our review of all other reported murder and manslaughter convictions involving the battery of young children, we conclude that the judge acted within his discretion in determining that a conviction of manslaughter was more consonant with justice than a conviction of murder.

Zobels' judgement is elegant and extraordinarily rich. We have barely scratched the surface. It contains multiple rationalities, all invoked for particular rhetorical purposes to support a judgement which Zobel explicitly and self-consciously locates in his own moral conscience. Zobel's morality forms the ultimate warrant for his decision, and this was accepted by the

Supreme Court. Of course, as a judge, he is particularly well situated to 'make knowledge' and is institutionally more able than most HW professionals to invoke his conscience in this way and to use a normative warrant for his opinions. However, this analysis of his judgement provides a clear example to illustrate what we have been trying to say in this book. Even where 'facts' and forensic evidence exist they are often disputable. Decisions are made by invoking a range of rationalities, of which normative judgement is one. It is, therefore, incumbent upon us to look carefully at how we ascribe moral worth and at what are the effects of these attributions.

We have examined the formal trial proceedings and have explored how the courts dealt with the 'problem of judgement'. However, a parallel moral struggle was played out in the world media and, at times, this leaked into the courtroom. It will be useful to explore some of this media coverage as this, too, shows how the facts of the case can be assembled in different ways to ascribe guilt or to exonerate particular parties.

Louise Woodward v. The Eappens: the construction of moral character

From the outset, this case provoked a media extravaganza in which particular moral identities were ascribed to the defendant and to Matthew Eappen's parents. Throughout the trial, the representations of these principal actors as 'wronged' or as 'wrongdoers' proved extremely fickle, with blame shifting frequently from one party to the other. For the most part, these versions were treated as mutually exclusive. For example, reports generally either constructed Louise Woodward as a culpable 'killer' who failed to show remorse, or as a vulnerable young woman, in the wrong place at the wrong time, who was exploited by a powerful Bostonian family. On the other hand, the Eappens were seen either as a tragically bereaved family, whose trust in Louise Woodward had been violated with the worst possible consequences, or as selfish, career-obsessed individuals who were paying the highest price for their wanton disregard of their children's needs.

This was, in part, a consequence of the moral struggles being played out in the courtroom. For example, in claiming that, prior to Matthew's death, they had been concerned about Louise Woodward's supposedly enthusiastic engagement with Boston social life, the Eappens fuelled the 'culpable killer' version. However, they had to face the unintended consequence that they would themselves be deemed blameworthy for failing to act upon their misgivings.

These moral struggles were mirrored in the media. For example, immediately after the trial and Zobel's review of the case, Deborah Eappen gave an interview to *Time Magazine*, entitled 'One mother's story' (Eappen 1997). This was in response to negative media coverage in which the Eappens, and particularly Deborah Eappen, were accused of neglecting their parental duties, with the implication that this made them accomplices to Matthew's death. The negative media coverage made liberal use of the membership category 'mother' with its associated range of category-bound expectations (nurturance, care, commitment, self-sacrifice) and contrasted this with reports about Deborah Eappen's failure to put the children's needs before her own aspirations. In so doing, they invoked the common populist sentiment, 'why did she have children if she didn't want to look after them?' In the interview, Deborah Eappen repeatedly asserts Louise Woodward's guilt and, as in the prosecution appeal that followed, she accuses Judge Zobel of gullibility (he was taken in by Woodward) and culpability (he should not have interfered with the jury's verdict). She also attempts to 'answer' some of the criticism she has been receiving in the press, for example, by describing the various career opportunities she had not pursued because of her primary commitment to the children. Her closing remarks are as follows:

Extract 9.14

I just feel like, how did Louise become the hero and I become the villain? What is the real issue here? It is child abuse and child murder. I strive in a lot of different directions in life, and now suddenly that striving to be good seems to be bad. The only decision I wish I had made differently was [the decision] not to fire Louise. I wish we had.

(Eappen 1997)

Here, Deborah Eappen clearly reinforces the Louise Woodward as murderer version and also strives to resuscitate her own moral character. Note in particular the use of contrast structures (for example 'hero' and 'villain') to press home her point, the use of the ubiquitous extreme case formulation ('the only . . .') and the shift from 'I' to 'we' to incorporate her partner into responsibility for not sacking Louise. However, by implying that there were grounds to 'sack' Woodward, she inadvertently refuels the case against her and her partner. Why did they continue to leave small children for long hours in the care of someone whom they did not trust and had considered sacking?

As for Woodward herself, during her trial she received a fluctuating, but overall moderately sympathetic representation in the press, particularly in the UK. The tables turned dramatically on both sides of the Atlantic after the Supreme Court appeal. The following vitriolic extract from a column by Andrea Peyser in the *New York Post* captures the mood:

Extract 9.15

Looking to beat the pesky murder rap? Anxious to walk free – perchance, as a hero – soon after slicing, shooting or shaking the life out of innocent folk? . . . If you really want to improve your odds of getting sprung from jail, preferably while your victim is still warm, I suggest you follow the lead of Louise Woodward . . . Get yourself a fan club.

(Peyser 1998)

How does the journalist discredit Woodward and the outcome of the trial here? Partly by referring ironically to 'the pesky murder rap', representing it as a minor irritation easily brushed aside, and also by evoking sympathy for the dead child ('the victim still warm') to suggest the speed with which she was freed.

After the trial the UK tabloid press vilified Woodward, using her status as a convicted 'killer' to amplify the rhetorical force of their statements. The BBC website of 18 June 1998 summarizes this coverage as follows:

Extract 9.16

Tabloid editors have torn up their Justice for Louise campaigns and gone for the jugular. 'First Class Child Killer' was the splash headline in *The Mirror*, which highlighted the cost of the first class flight Woodward and her father took back to Britain. *The Sun*, which buried the story on page seven, highlighted the fight by the parents of Matthew Eappen to stop Woodward cashing in on her crime. But the paper's cartoon perhaps summed up the tabloid turnaround . . . Etched on a be-ribboned tree were the words: 'Louise Woodward VIP', and on a grave: 'Matthew Eappen, RIP'.

(BBC 1998)

The stark contrast of the be-ribboned tree and the grave is highly evocative. It underlines the press's preoccupation with Louise's alleged good fortune, epitomized by her first-class travel arrangements. This is very significant. In the pre- and post-trial coverage, the British press had constructed Woodward as an ordinary English girl in trouble abroad. However, by taking a first-class flight, she had breached the rules of 'ordinariness'. She was above her station. She was 'profiting' from Matthew Eappen's death. These shifting moral judgements were not based on new facts, or hitherto undisclosed pieces of evidence. Rather, they were based on moral judgements about behaviours unrelated to the substantive facts at issue.

Sometimes, these moral judgements were made on a 'guilty by association' basis. For example, in her trial Woodward was defended by Barry Scheck, the defence lawyer in the notorious murder trial of O.J. Simpson earlier in the 1990s. This was read by some as evidence of Woodward's guilt. For example, the following quotation is taken from a US *Court TV* website, where members of the public could give their opinions on the first hearing of the case:

Extract 9.17

'I have to be honest in stating that I feel that Barry Scheck being involved with this trial may have affected the jury's decision . . . As soon as I saw him involved with this trial my gut reaction was "She must be guilty if they hired him to represent her, she must be guilty, he got OJ off, they must think they really need a miracle here".' Dawn, New York.

(*Court TV* 1997)

These extracts illustrate the capacity for language to construct and reconstruct moral character, and also show that judgements about guilt and innocence turn, not just on 'facts', but also upon their representation and interpretation. The language of press coverage is more florid than that of the court, but moral judgement still plays a very significant role in the judicial arena.

Summary

In this chapter we have reviewed the complex forms of rhetoric and reasoning in the Louise Woodward case. We have suggested that many of the 'troubles' referred to HW agencies cannot be analysed entirely by recourse to neutral algorithms, but demand the kind of layered judgement-making we have seen in Zobel's statements. These judgements, because of their essential complexity, will always be partial and open to contention. In showing this, we have not wanted to imply that they are inferior, but to underscore their inevitability. We have used the concept of fact 'construction', or 'making and moulding' (cf. Hacking 1999), not to consign HW practice into a descending vortex of moral relativism, but to rediscover the compound forms of reasoning upon which we all depend in our everyday sense-making activities. We are advocating, again, a more 'realistic realism' (Latour 1999: 15), through which practitioners can engage with the very material complexities, uncertainties and contingencies of *real* practice. Let us now consider how the Louise Woodward case is relevant to practice.

Implications for practice

Firstly, clinical decisions should be based on the best available scientific evidence; secondly, the clinical problem – rather than the habits of protocols – should determine the type of evidence to be sought; thirdly the best evidence means using epidemiological and biostatistical ways of thinking; fourthly, conclusions derived from identifying and critically appraising evidence are useful if put into action in managing patients or making health care decisions; and, finally, performance should be evaluated.

(Davidoff *et al.* 1995 cited in Hope 1996: 3)

The quotation above advocates a dispassionate and neutral approach to judgement making. It presupposes the existence of objective knowledge. However, we have seen that the only 'props' available in the Woodward case were highly contestable. Imagine that Matthew Eappen had lived. What sense would the child welfare professionals have made of the case?

Some of the forensic evidence uncovered by examinations before and during neurosurgery would have been available, but it would have remained contestable. Louise Woodward was charged with battery before Matthew Eappen's death and so would have faced criminal charges if he had lived. The central issue would still have been the causation and timing of the blow to the head which caused the haematoma.

In this sense, the Woodward case is similar to many child protection investigations, which are often characterized by competing and incommensurable accounts. Sometimes one account may be shot through with inconsistencies, or doctors may be able to say with a reasonable degree of certainty that a particular explanation does not fit the pattern of injury; but often this is not the case. Practitioners have to act and judge in these uncertain circumstances and they do this by making qualitative judgements about the 'plausibility' of the different versions, as we saw in the case of Helen in Chapter 7 (Example 2). Here 'evidence', in its usual sense, provides no neat prescriptions, and practitioners have to decide what counts as proof or truth, just as the jurors and Zobel did in the Louise Woodward case (significantly coming to different conclusions). This element of HW practice needs to be opened up to discussion. It is not helpful for practitioners to be told that, if only they look hard enough and are sufficiently erudite, they will find neutral bodies of knowledge to help them in all cases. Rather, what is needed is dialogue and debate about the range of evaluative mechanisms upon which we all draw in judging people. We hope that the concepts and methods introduced in this book will help in opening up this dialogue. Saying that we cannot with certainty know everything about a given situation is not the same as saying there is nothing to know. The debate is not about whether things are real – of course they are real – but about what kinds of devices we use to decide between competing versions of the 'truth', or 'reality', or events. The evidence-based practice movement, as it is currently dominantly defined, leaves the business of 'diagnosis' and judgement hopelessly underexplored, yet it is these activities that preoccupy practitioners in their everyday work. This leads practitioners to assert certainty where none exists: for if they do not, they will be deemed to have failed properly to assess the situation. We have tried to eschew evaluation and judgement of practice in this book, but this kind of 'certainty making', however apparently unavoidable in the contemporary climate, must have some undesirable effects.

Exercises

You may like to undertake an extended case study to apply some of the ideas described in this book and illustrated in this chapter. Think of it as another way of approaching 'critical incident' analysis. Use a case in which you had some involvement, or about which you have some knowledge. If you do not have access to relevant material, you may want to use a high-profile legal case, such as the murder trial of Dr Harold Shipman which took place in 1999/2000, or the trial of O.J. Simpson.

(a) Can you map out the various different interpretations of 'the facts', as presented by different parties?

(b) How was moral character ascribed to different actors, including the professional players?

(c) What kinds of accountabilities did you have to consider in dealing with the case? For example, Judge Zobel had to grapple not only with the contested facts but also with the institutional framework of the US legal system, the sacredness of the jury's verdict, the moral judgement of the American people, and the emotions of the Eappen family. If you are a social worker, it may be that you had to consider the department's budget or resources when you were making sense of a case, or the views of a previous worker who had taken a different perspective from your own. If you are a charge nurse or ward sister, you may have had to consider staffing levels and morale on your ward and the condition of other patients before you decided whether to accept a troublesome admission from accident and emergency. How did you frame your responses to take account of all these different accountabilities? Were you candid, or did you use another warrant for your decision?

(d) Can you think of any situation in which you were clear about what you thought, but were faced with competing explanations, viewpoints or diagnoses? Did you own up to your opinions, or did you bow to alternative viewpoints? If you argued your case, what warrants did you use for your opinion? If you did not, why was this?

CHAPTER 10

Practising reflexivity: beyond objectivity and subjectivity

This chapter has broader focus and content than the preceding ones in Part II. In those we have gradually built up the elements of our suggested discourse analytic approach to talk and text in HW. We have explored how service users attempt to convey their moral adequacy in situations where they are trying to gain access to or refuse services. We then looked in Chapter 6 at how practitioners and clinicians establish their professional authority in client/worker encounters and try to control the interaction. Service users also have their agendas and will work to accomplish these and to resist the professional ones. Subsequently we examined collegial discourse and how workers build the case out of the available information by emphasizing certain aspects at the expense of others. In Chapter 8 we argued that documentary records should not be taken to be mirror images of reality but as artful constructions intended to convey a particular reading of events, situations and the moral character of those concerned.

In Chapter 9 we brought together the various strands of this analysis using the case of the murder trial of the au pair Louise Woodward. This brought home that even medical evidence, which we tend to treat as true knowledge generated according to strict scientific principles, can actually be intensely problematic. There was no conclusive proof of how Matthew Eappen died. Different interpretations were put on the evidence by the medical experts and lawyers (and by the public) and these were highly contentious. We suggested that this uncomfortable process of making sense of complex and confusing situations and events is intrinsic to much of HW professional practice. A different approach, which acknowledges this, is therefore fruitful. We have proposed one such approach.

We have now completed our exposition of this discourse analytic approach. We have tried to make the approach accessible and encouraged you to try it for yourself by making available the relevant concepts and tools. Something that might hold you back is uncertainty about where it might take you in relation to your practice. Does our approach undermine the usual way that you treat HW practice? Can you adopt it and continue to practise in your customary way? What does it change and how much does it change things? In this remaining chapter we want to consider these issues and provide some answers. In brief, our position is that, yes, it does change things, but it does not mean that you should discard the knowledge and skills you currently use and start again. It is central to our argument that a discourse analytic approach enables us to examine HW practice more systematically and thoroughly than other forms of realism currently on offer to HW practitioners, namely evidence-based practice and reflective practice. In short, it offers the possibility of *practising reflexivity*. The remainder of the chapter is devoted to exploring this claim. It examines the strengths and weaknesses of evidence-based and reflective approaches before re-examining what we mean by reflexivity (a term first used in Chapter 2) and what is distinctive and helpful about practising reflexively. In effect, we are looping back to issues that we set out in Part I about the current state of professional practice, the problems with (naive) forms of realism and our contention that there is a need to move beyond these unrealistic forms of realism.

Is evidence-based practice the answer to the crisis in the professions?

Crisis may perhaps be overstating it, nonetheless HW professions and their personnel are undergoing fundamental and unprecedented change. New legislation has been introduced which has altered the structures and organizational practices of statutory bodies as well as changed their relationship with the voluntary, non-profit and private sectors. A new vocabulary has been brought into being (for example purchase/provider, performance indicators) and new mantras and buzzwords pervade HW talk and text (such as economy, efficiency and effectiveness). These changes are ongoing, indeed the current New Labour government has signalled its determination to 'modernize' local government and health services (Department of Health 1998a, b,c). Central to this agenda is the intention to bring greater rationality to service planning and delivery, and evidence-based practice (hereafter EBP) is regarded as a key element of this, having recently received official sanction by central government. The National Institute for Clinical Excellence (NICE) has been established and a similar organization is planned for social care, the Social Care Institute for Excellence (SCIE).

The promise of EBP

Since the 1980s, as concern about the effects of HW provision on recipients and on the public purse deepened, there has been a preoccupation in the UK and North America with 'what works?' State intervention was criticized by many commentators for allegedly increasing dependency and placing an unreasonably costly burden on national budgets. This has led to a strong preoccupation with measuring the outcomes of HW provision and assessing its effectiveness, efficiency and economy. In the UK this has encouraged managerialist control of service delivery in order to plan service delivery and to establish targets and intended outcomes against which to measure performance. Schools in England and Wales have been subject to league tables for some time; HW agencies will now be subject to a similar process in order that national comparisons can be made about performance in relation to designated criteria.

Evidence-based practice is increasingly regarded as a central element of this drive for efficiency and effectiveness, particularly in health care, but there are increasing signs of the adoption of the terminology in social work also (Shaw 1999; Trinder 2000). So what exactly is EBP? The standard definition in relation to medicine, which has been applied to health care generally, is provided by Sackett *et al.* (see also Rosenberg and Donald 1995; Gray 1997):

> Evidence-based medicine is the conscientious, explicit and judicious use of best current evidence in making decisions about the care of individual patients. The practice of evidence-based medicine means integrating individual clinical expertise with the best available external clinical evidence from systematic research.
>
> (Sackett *et al.* 1997: 2)

The common theme in such definitions is that decision making should be informed by sound evidence derived from rigorous research. It is argued that a more stringent approach is needed to avoid 'doing more harm than good' or making interventions that are 'of no known benefit'. Two concerns have been strongly expressed about the inadequacies of existing health care: one is the adherence to 'ritual', that is the tendency to rely on established methods even though their efficacy has been questioned (for example, using grommets to treat glue ear in children; see Appleby *et al.* 1995). The second and related problem is the failure to make available to patients newer, more effective treatments such as clot-busting drugs for heart attacks (Department of Health 1998a). A concern for patients is also said to lie at the heart of EBP. Consumers, it is argued, have a right to be involved in decisions about health care and should be treated with respect. Indeed, in 1996, the Standing Advisory Group on Consumer Involvement in the NHS Research and Development Programme was established.

You might like to pause to think for a moment about the extent to which your agency is taking up issues of clinical effectiveness and governance, and EBP and implementing them. How do staff view these developments? What do they see as the main benefits and disadvantages of this approach? Proponents of EBP assert that it is essential to incorporate EBP into HW policy making and practice. Muir Gray, for example, argues that:

in the 21st century, the healthcare decision maker, that is, anyone who makes decisions about groups of patients or populations, will have to practise evidence-based decision-making. Every decision will have to be based on a systematic appraisal of the best evidence available. To accomplish this, the best available evidence relating to a particular decision will have to be found...

(Gray 1997: 1)

In short, EBP introduces rational planning into the HW process. If planners and decision makers are wondering how to allocate resources such as expensive, newly developed drug treatments or highly specialized operations, then they need evidence about whether such treatments will be of benefit to patients generally and who exactly will benefit so that resources can be targeted where they will be effective. Recently, for example, a debate has been initiated about the efficacy of the national breast cancer screening programme for women. EBP can also be applied at the level of individual cases. A social worker may draw on research evidence about the effects of long-term residential care on young people in the public care system to argue in favour of placing a child in foster care or for adoption, or they may draw on the research evidence about risk in child abuse to argue in favour of the child being removed from an abusing parent. Decisions at all levels within HW organizations are seen to be made on the basis of a careful appraisal of general findings about what works or does not work and what is of proven benefit, rather than via an arbitrary process of acting on intuition or relying on (outmoded) custom and practice. In order to achieve consistent standards of service provision across local and health authorities, it is important that decisions are grounded in properly formulated evidence. In essence, this is technical rationality for the twenty-first century.

Technical rationality and EBP

The term 'technical rationality' was used by Donald Schön (1983, 1987) to describe the dominant form of professional knowledge which he regarded as possessing four essential properties: 'It is specialised, firmly bounded, scientific and standardised' (Schön 1983: 23). The inheritance from Enlightenment thinking (see Chapter 2) is clear. Schön (1983) argues that there are three linked components to professional knowledge within the technical/rational model: first, an underlying discipline or science; second, an applied science from which diagnostic procedures and problem solutions are derived; third, a skills and attitudinal component concerned with service provision to clients and which draws on the first and second.

Thus, within HW, researchers generate knowledge which is taken up by policy makers and translated into guidelines and procedures for practice. These are passed onto practitioners for them to incorporate into their practice. There may be some differences between disciplines here. Clinical knowledge for medical practice may be generated by practising clinicians through their own research and clinical trials as well as by full-time researchers. Within social work, knowledge is usually produced by academics researching into practice, rather than social work practitioners. Nonetheless the model of 'pure' research which is then turned into applied knowledge and taken up by practitioners generally pertains.

Since the aim is to produce 'really useful' knowledge for organizations and practitioners, and not simply knowledge for its own sake or because some researcher(s) find it interesting to study, the purpose and procedures for conducting evidence-based research are also strictly defined. The recent NHS Research and Development Strategy has laid down the criteria for the production of knowledge. The criteria emphasize that research must be conducted according to a clear protocol, subject to peer review, carefully managed and should result in data that are 'open to critical examination and accessible to all who could benefit from them' (Gray 1997: 69). The whole tenor of this is to emphasize the carefully controlled production of 'new' and highly relevant knowledge which has credence within the research community, is publicly available and can be subject to critical scrutiny by experts, decision makers and consumers.

Strengths and weaknesses of EBP

The main strength of EBP is surely its appeal to rationality. If, for example, someone has heart disease, it would be helpful for them to know which drugs might be most effective and whether surgery might prolong life. It would also be comforting to know that there was some rational application of this evidence so that need and likely benefit determined resource allocation rather than some more arbitrary criterion such as ability to pay, age, or postcode. Managers might feel that it could help in the determination of resource allocation.

However, there are some problems with the approach. Shaw has identified a fundamental one in the way the term EBP is taken for granted: 'What do we mean by "evidence"? What do we mean by "practice"? How is one "based" on the other? Far too much is assumed. But of course one does not describe a Holy Grail – one simply searches' (Shaw 1999: 3). The status of 'evidence' is also problematic. Chapter 2 discussed at length the problem with realist (or objectivist) approaches to knowledge: the presumption that we can somehow encase the mind in glass in order to protect it from any contaminating interaction with the phenomena being studied (the mind-in-a-vat as Bruno Latour (1999) so memorably calls it) and that out of this process of detachment we get pure, unbiased knowledge. This is a key problem with EBP: it assumes that such a detached process is possible and necessary for the production of knowledge.

Indeed, it is striking that, despite the plethora of claims that we now live in a postmodern world how distinctly 'modern' are the current preoccupations of politicians and policy makers (Smith and White 1997). There is little sign among them that knowledge is conceived of as local, provisional and in a constant state of flux and transition as postmodernism would have it. Instead we have very 'modern' truth claims being advocated and an 'unexamined technicalism' (Palumbo 1987: 31). Much of the literature on EBP seems to consist of defining briefly what it is before providing bibliographies of relevant research data, details of computer databases of information such as MEDLINE and guidance about how to access these and evaluate information (see, for example, Booth 1997; Ridsdale 1998). As we noted elsewhere, this technicalism means that problems with such research are explained methodologically (flaws in the research design/process), in psychological terms (the characteristics of the researcher) or sociologically (problems in the context for the research and its implementation). 'Good research' need not be questioned as long as it can be demonstrated that it has been produced according to the canons of science (hence the need for careful procedures including peer review to demonstrate the lack of bias). Only when it is flawed or biased in some way does the process of its production require explanation. An issue raised by this is how science is conceived of by HW practitioners. We would contend that, in general, rather unrealistic suppositions are made about scientific knowledge.

Is science 'scientific'? Some lessons from the sociology of scientific knowledge

A difficulty for HW practitioners is the sheer range of available material relating to professional practice. The pragmatic response is usually to concentrate on *propositional* knowledge (Eraut 1994), that is on substantive knowledge relating to a particular area of work. The other focus is likely to be on *process* knowledge, or know-how (Eraut 1994), that is material intended to promote skill development *vis-à-vis* communication skills, methods of intervention and so forth. Otherwise the response is likely to be one where formal knowledge is eschewed in favour of a more practical, 'just getting on and doing' approach which is often accorded with what are seen as the day-to-day realities of the work. Certainly within social work it has been argued that there can be a tendency towards anti-intellectualism and the dismissal of 'theory' (Thompson 1995).

The great volume of propositional and process knowledge available to practitioners is highly daunting and may result in information overload. This has important effects in relation to students, practitioners and academics in that knowledge derived from the social sciences tends to be drawn on to provide substantive information about health, poverty, welfare, illness and so forth. Little attention is paid to ongoing debates within the social sciences about how knowledge is made (epistemological issues), in particular how scientific knowledge and research data are regarded. Research knowledge tends simply to be accepted as the truth, that is a mirror of reality, derided as biased and erroneous for the reasons suggested above, or dismissed as irrelevant. And yet there are important things that we can learn from the sociology of scientific knowledge (SSK) about the ways in which scientific research is conducted. If we can show that scientific facts are made rather than discovered or revealed then this has important consequences for how we treat not just science but social science data and 'practice wisdom' too.

Sociologists of scientific knowledge (for example Knorr-Cetina and Mulkay 1983b; Gilbert and Mulkay 1984; Latour 1999) remind us that scientific knowledge is made rather than revealed. It is not just research regarded as problematic that can be analysed, but the production of *all* such research. Just as throughout this book we have subjected the talk and text of HW professionals to scrutiny, it is also possible to conduct these processes with science to examine how scientists construct knowledge, how they produce convincing arguments for a particular version of the facts and persuade colleagues and peers of their moral adequacy, in this case their authoritative position as a scientist. Let us look at some examples drawn from the seminal work of Gilbert and Mulkay (1984) about scientists' discourse. Extract 10.1 is taken from a research paper in biochemistry. Extracts 10.2 and 10.3 reproduce two extracts of scientists talking about how they write and why they write in the way they do. It does not matter if you do not understand the technical detail: the point is to compare the differences in the way the text and talk are constructed.

Extract 10.1

[A particular strain of yeast] **was grown** in continuous culture under conditions of glycerol limitation (Conran and Spender) or sulphate limitation (Hill and Spender). A variant of this yeast that does not require copper and has a cyanide insensitive terminal oxidase (Jason and Spender) **was grown** in continuous culture in a copper extracted medium . . . Harvested and washed cells (Conran and Spender) **were converted** into protoplasts and mitochondria **isolated** as described by Castle. Protein **was determined by** the method of Sheridan. Measurements of respiration-driven proton translocation **were made** with the apparatus described by Mason and Spender in 1.0 ml of anaerobic 0.6 M-mannitol . . . Polarographic measurements of P/O ratios **were performed** as described by Shoesmith, by using the experimental conditions of Spender . . .

(Gilbert and Mulkay 1984: 51–2, emphasis added)

It sounds impressive, doesn't it? The references to previous research and following the methods described by Sheridan and Shoesmith clearly mark this out as a piece of rigorous scientific research able to stand up to peer scrutiny. To a lay person it sounds real and authentic. In the next extract we can see what a scientist says about the method used in response to an interviewer's question about why certain methods and chemicals are used.

Extract 10.2

The convention is that you normally use what you used last time round. You don't want to change. Let's look at an example. We want to suspend mitochondria in water until they swell and burst. So they need support. Why did we use 0.6 ml? 0.6 ml is about right. Why did we use mannitol and not sucrose or something else? Well, because somebody in Japan 10 years ago had published the first paper on mitochondria and he used mannitol. I don't know why they used mannitol . . . We saw no reason to change from the original recipe. And 'recipe' is the right word. It's like cooking. [Spender, 18]

(Gilbert and Mulkay 1984: 54)

This gives us a rather different 'take' on the scientific process. It strips away much of the mystique and the rather high-flown ideas that lay people tend to have about science and laboratories. Instead it presents a mundane practice that is likened to the everyday activity of cooking. Instead of rigorous attention to conventional techniques we are given an image of scientists relying on custom and practice and being rather 'unrigorous' in their conduct of experiments, using materials without thinking about why they do so. Science too can become routinized and mundane. You may be able to see some parallels here with your own practice. There are many things in your daily practice that you will have come to take for granted. Often it is only when someone new comes to the team that these practices are questioned and you have to look at them afresh.

Finally, let us look at the conventions which are applied to the writing of scientific papers. Scientists employ a specific impersonal style which uses the passive voice (this is the polar opposite to the examples of active voicing we have come across in talk). In doing so they write out their own involvement. If agency is introduced, 'we' is used in preference to 'I' because it sounds more authoritative and 'can spread the blame if it's wrong' (Gilbert and Mulkay 1984: 59). Gilbert and Mulkay make the following comment on this convention about report writing:

Methods sections . . . appear to be formally constructed as if all the actions of researchers relevant to their results can be expressed as impersonal rules; as if the individual characteristics of researchers have no bearing on the production of results; as if the application of these rules to particular actions is unproblematic; and, as if, therefore, the reproduction of equivalent observations can be easily obtained by any competent scientist through compliance with the rules.

(Gilbert and Mulkay 1984: 52)

In interview talk with Gilbert and Mulkay, scientists debunked this empiricist discourse and opted for a much more contingent form which makes 'an appeal to personal motives and thoughts, insights and biases, social settings and commitments' (Edwards 1997: 58). In doing so they acknowledged the rules of the empiricist game and indicated the ways in which personal and social circumstances influenced their research activities. Here is one such example:

Extract 10.3

One is a myth that we [that is scientists] inflict on the public, that science is rational and logical. It's appalling really, its [sic] taught all the way in school, the notion that you make all these observations in a Darwinian sense. That's just rubbish, this 'detached observation'. What do you *see*? Well what *do* you see? God knows you see everything. And, in fact, you see what you want to see, for the most part. Or you see the choices between one or two alternatives. That doesn't get admitted into the scientific literature. In fact, we write history all the time, a sort of hindsight. The order in which experiments are done. All manner of nonsense. So the personal side gets taken out of this sort of paper ...

(Gilbert and Mulkay 1984: 59)

This scientist makes the important points that accounts in scientific papers are written after the event and are 'history'. They are in effect a sanitized version of the research process which produces a logical and ordered account of something that was much more messy and disjointed. This is exactly the same process of history making that is engaged in by HW practitioners when they write case files, records and reports (see Chapter 8). As noted in Chapter 2, SSK studies suggest that 'scientific' research is not dissimilar to non-scientific activity, that is it is also messy and complex, and we should be extremely cautious about assuming otherwise. You might like to look at an evidence-based research report or research synopsis (for example in journals such as *Evidence-based Mental Health*, *Evidence-based Nursing* and *Journal of Clinical Effectiveness*) and examine the way in which an empiricist discourse is used to add weight and certainty to the findings. You will find the same devices are used to achieve scientific authenticity and to eradicate traces of personal or social influences on the research process and its outcomes.

To end this discussion we should make several points. One is that Gilbert and Mulkay (1984) do not set out to argue that we should disbelieve the empiricist repertoire of scientists and believe the contingent one. Their argument is that both are forms of talk, neither mirrors 'what really happens' in science. Both are worked-up descriptions and are used in different circumstances: the empiricist repertoire in the formal arena of disseminating findings, the contingent repertoire in the more informal accounting that takes place in everyday institutional talk or the quasi-conversational medium of the interview. The task, therefore, is to analyse the way in which the descriptions are produced and the effects they have in practice, not to decide which is 'more real' in the objectivist sense. The second point to underline is that this empiricist repertoire is just that, a form of discourse which produces an idealized scientist who is a seemingly detached, disengaged observer who can be substituted by any other observer to produce a 'view from anywhere'. It follows that experience and involvement are regarded as introducing not meaningful understanding but dangerous bias. Moreover, EBP assumes compatibility between 'top-down' scientific evidence and 'bottom-up' consumer perspectives without exploring satisfactorily how these two can be brought together. Our final point here is that we need more than propositional and process knowledge to work in HW. Microsociologies, SSK and discursive psychology have a lot to teach us about not taking HW knowledge for granted but looking at how it is made in particular local situations.

Is EBP of use to practitioners?

If we are arguing that the knowledge produced by the technical/rational approach and advocated by the EBP movement does not consist of neutral and detached observations of the real world, does this mean that it is worthless and should be disregarded? Most definitely not. We are suggesting that evidence-based knowledge should not be regarded as engraved in stone and simply accepted as the truth (or discredited as biased and erroneous). A danger of EBP is that it puts practitioners in the role of technicians whose skills lie in applying knowledge created elsewhere rather than in considering its relevance and utility in specific practice situations. Moreover, EBP may well underestimate the difficulties that practitioners may have in applying 'theory' to 'practice'. You will be able to think of examples in your own work where you have thought 'well, that's alright in theory, but in practice . . .'. On the other hand, think for a moment about the sorts of 'theory-based' knowledge that you do use in practice. What do you use? How is it helpful? For example, as a mental health worker you may consider that drug treatments do assist in treating certain conditions and that the benefits to patients outweigh the possible side-effects. As a health visitor or childcare social worker you are likely to believe that you need a body of knowledge about child development in order to be able to assess whether children are developing satisfactorily and to make judgements about the need for intervention.

It is undeniable that evidence-based knowledge can assist in the decision making process and sometimes evidence of this kind will prove adequate. In apparently straightforward situations, for example where a child has sustained a simple fracture and there is no indication that it is anything other than an accident, we will accept that an X-ray can provide the information needed in order to set the bone and mend the injury. However, in more complex situations, for example where practitioners have reason to believe that an injury is caused by child abuse, then the X-ray can only tell us so much. It will still be needed in order to mend the injury and it may throw some light on how the injury might (not) have occurred but it cannot tell us who did what to whom. And these are the very things that practitioners will need to 'know' in these more messy, ambiguous situations. As we saw in Extract 6.3 and throughout Chapter 7, practitioners will also need to work up a version of what happened based on the available information. This should not fly in the face of the medical evidence and other available information, but equally it can only be a representation of what is most likely to have happened. Moreover, as highlighted in the Woodward case in the previous chapter, medical evidence is not necessarily clear and unambiguous. At times, there will be disagreements amongst medical experts about the nature of the evidence and the form that treatment should take. Labelling something as 'science' does not remove ambiguity and complexity, as our discussion of SSK indicates.

We want to return to the issue of what lessons are to be learned here about how we approach EBP. First we want to look at another way of looking at HW practice which has become prevalent in recent years, namely the reflective practice approach. We can then compare this with the EBP approach and with our own perspective which is perhaps better characterized by the term 'practising reflexivity'.

Reflective practice: from objectivity to subjectivity

Technical rationality, or objectivism, is an important strand within HW generally and fits closely with a managerialist agenda and the search for efficiency, effectiveness and economy, as noted in Chapter 1. It is an approach that is primarily concerned with content issues about knowledge (what professionals know or ought to know), policy and procedures, and the measurement of outcomes (was this intervention effective and the best, most efficient use of resources?). It accords little or no attention to the *process* issues of practice and the minutiae of day-to-day practice.

Within medicine, technical rationality continues to be the dominant paradigm. In social work and nursing (as well as education) the concept of reflective practice has gained considerable purchase as a counterweight to the technical/rational approach. Within social work education and training, it might be argued that these two approaches exist side by side: qualifying social workers are expected not only to use research findings in their practice but also to be 'reflective practitioners' (CCETSW 1995).

The work of Donald Schön has been a key influence in this area so we begin our examination of reflective practice by outlining his concept of reflective practice. We then explore how reflective practice is conceived in social work and nursing education and practice before subjecting the concept to a critical appraisal.

Schön's starting point is an indictment of technical/rational approaches to professional activity. His oft-quoted metaphor is a topographical one:

there is a high, hard ground overlooking a swamp. On the high ground, manageable problems lend themselves to solution through the application of research-based theory and technique. In the swampy lowland, messy confusing problems defy technical solution.

(Schön 1987: 3)

Schön suggests that there is an implicit hierarchy within a technical/rational model with the production of pure knowledge ('general principles') assumed to take precedence over the more 'lowly' task of applying it to practice ('concrete problem-solving'). He further suggests that this should be inverted: the important problems are those of the 'swampy lowlands', whereas the problems of the high ground are 'relatively unimportant' (Schön 1987: 3). Moreover, Schön argues that this depiction of the application of theory to practice does not fit the realities of professional endeavour. Central to his argument is the thesis that professional practice is characterized by 'uncertainty, uniqueness and value conflict' and that the problems that arise for practitioners are not amenable to solution by positivist-inspired technical/rational approaches. For Schön, 'technical rationality is inadequate both as a prescription for, and as a description of, professional practice' (Eraut 1994: 143).

In its place, Schön conceives of professional activity as a combination of knowing-in-action and reflection-in-action followed by reflection-on-action. Schön describes the first of these as 'spontaneous, skilful performance [which] we are characteristically unable to make explicit' (1987: 25). He cites riding a bicycle and the instant analysis of a balance sheet as classic examples. Reflection-in-action occurs within these 'spontaneous, routinized responses' (1987: 28), usually when something surprising happens which disrupts our implicit knowing, prompting us to reflect, to question our knowing and to experiment to solve the puzzle. The third concept, reflection-on-action, is given less attention in Schön's work but can be defined as referring to 'the process of making sense of an action after it has occurred and possibly learning something from the experience which extends one's knowledge base' (Eraut 1994: 146).

Whilst there are certain problems with Schön's work (see Eraut (1994) for a brief but thoughtful consideration of some of the issues), its influence is undeniable and the notion of professional practice as artistry and of the need for reflective practice have gained widespread support. Two linked but distinctive strands seem to have emerged: one focuses on the artistry of professional practice (knowing- and reflecting-in-action), whilst the other focuses on developing reflection-on-action.

Professional practice as artistry

A focus on the artistic and intuitive aspects of nursing practice is usually connected with the work of Patricia Benner and associates (Benner 1984;

Benner and Wrubel 1989; Benner *et al.* 1996). This approach plays down the technical/rational aspects of nursing knowledge ('knowing that') in favour of a concentration on the 'knowing how' (for example, how to talk to seriously ill or injured patients and their relatives) and 'knowing the patient': aspects of nursing practice in a more 'holistic' approach to patient care. This sort of knowing is described as 'tacit' (Polanyi 1967) or embedded in action (Schön 1987). This ability to practise intuitively is acquired over time as practitioners proceed from a novice stage, characterized by dependency on taught rules or plans, through stages of increasing competence and proficiency to an expert stage where they have an intuitive grasp of the right things to do and can function without (overtly) relying on rules and procedural guidance (Benner 1984).

This highest stage of skill development is akin to the concept of 'unconscious competence' where we know intuitively how to do something without being able to put our knowledge into words. In HW there are many aspects of the work which to the novice are unfamiliar and troubling. Student social workers may get anxious about making home visits because they are not sure what to say or what response to expect from service users. Experienced social workers take such things for granted because they reach a stage where they 'just know' what to say and do in initial meetings with clients. They will have acquired an enormous range of (now tacit) knowledge in relation to their practice. In effect, some aspects of professional practice become mundane and routine, but, according to Benner, this does not mean that such practice is not highly skilful. Benner *et al.* give the following example of expert practice by a 'critical care' nurse dealing with a patient who was haemorrhaging and had stopped breathing.

Extract 10.4

So we didn't even call the code. We just called the doc[tor] stat [emergency] and we got him up there . . . I looked at his heart rate and I said: 'O.K. he is bradying down. Someone want to give me some atropine?' I just started calling out the drugs that I needed to get for this guy, so we just started to push these drugs in. In the meantime, I said, 'can we have some more blood?' I was just barking out this stuff [the things that were needed and had to be done]. I can't even tell you the sequence. I was saying, 'WE need this.' I needed to anticipate what was going to happen and I could do this because I had been through this a week before with this guy and knew what we had done [and what had worked]. The anesthesiologist came in and did a good intubation. He asks: 'What kinds of [IV] lines do we have?' I said, 'We have a triple lumen and we have blood. All [IV] ports are taken. We need another kind of line. He's got no veins left. He goes, 'O.K., fine, give me a cut-down tray . . .

(Benner *et al.* 1996: 142–3, bracketed inserts in original)

The authors describe the nurse's actions as 'fluid and knowing' because they are based partly on a previous first-hand experience of a successful resuscitation. They talk of nurses in this situation being deeply involved in the situation and closely attuned to it: 'with expertise comes fluid, almost seamless performance. Organisation, priority setting, and task completion do not show up as focal points in [the nurses'] narrative accounts' (Benner *et al.* 1996: 143). We should note, however, how much technical knowledge may be embedded in this 'intuitive' approach. Another area of competence lies in expert nurses' comfort with an emotional involvement with patients and families. They 'know' what the latter are thinking and feeling, what they are going through and what they want to hear, and can do the right thing to provide support in times of distress.

Having pursued our argument through the various chapters you will be able to read the nurse's account in Extract 10.4 as other than a literal description of what really happened, which is how it is presented. It is a post hoc description by the nurse, not a contemporaneous transcript. It is the only version available to us and it can be read as an account of the nurse as heroine (or hero). If you compare it with the empiricist discourse in Extract 10.1, the differences are marked. The nurse displays commitment and strong engagement. She consistently uses active voicing and reported speech to bring home the drama of the situation and her unconscious actions in response. She is the main protagonist, and although there are clearly other staff there, the anaesthesiologist is the only other person who is allowed a voice. The expert nurse is the person exercising authority and in control.

Within the nursing literature, Benner's approach is clearly influential. However, her tendency to disregard reflection-in-action and to present intuition as 'unknowing' and somehow 'unknowable' has evoked some criticism. For example, Gary Rolfe cites the following example as indicative of the dangers of this tacit form of knowing: 'When I say to a doctor "the patient is psychotic", I don't know always how to legitimize the statement. But I am never wrong. Because I know psychosis inside out. And I feel that, and I know it, and I trust it' (Benner 1984 cited in Rolfe 1998: 51).

This is a good illustration of the difficulties that intuitive practice may produce. We have probably all felt at some time or other that 'we can't explain it, we just know', and sometimes we will have been right. But we do get into difficulties with 'just knowing' especially when 'we are never wrong'. This inaccessibility of our judgements is very problematic since we cannot share the basis for them with other people. We also need to recognize that concepts such as 'psychotic' are worked up through a particular interpretation of the available evidence. Psychosis is a contestable and contested category and, whilst other professionals may accept its application to a patient, the patient in question may strongly refute it. If we are to have dialogue with other professionals and with clients then we need to be able to articulate the basis for our judgements. Indeed, in certain situations 'just knowing' simply will not do. As a childcare social worker you cannot go to court in care proceedings and simply assert that parents have abused their child, 'you just know'. It is incumbent upon you to demonstrate how you know.

Developing reflection-on-action

The other strand in the literature on reflective practice focuses on the development of reflection-on-action, in particular practitioners' development of skills in reflecting on and evaluating their practice. There are several benefits that are claimed for this approach. First it is said to facilitate personal and professional growth by offering the practitioner a way to mature in their professional thinking and to come to a fuller understanding of their role and tasks and how values, attitudes and beliefs impinge upon their practice. Reflection is said also to allow greater knowledge about oneself and one's practice, and the context for practice. It can thus act as a counterbalance to the tendencies to take things for granted and to become immersed in familiar routines. It is also claimed that reflection may assist practitioners 'to look with eyes other than my own' (L'Aiguille 1994: 87), thereby understanding the patient's perspective and the meaning they attribute to HW intervention, as well as other professionals' standpoints.

Moreover, reflection is said to assist skill development. By reviewing their actions, practitioners can work out how to improve their performance to the benefit of patients. In contrast to the Benner approach we can see that the emphasis here is upon 'conscious competence' where the practitioner has a clear understanding of their knowledge and skills, and the contribution they are making to patient care. Furthermore it is argued that reflection aids the development of good practice by enabling the worker to get in touch with their own feelings about what they are doing, or about the people they are working with so that they may harness these productively in their practice. L'Aiguille (1994) also suggests that it may help practitioners to make sense of personal experiences and how these can be used beneficially in practice. In all, it is suggested that reflection enables the practitioner to acquire a broader vision of the professional task, offering opportunities for creativity and innovation in practice.

We will come back to these claims for reflective practice, but let us first examine two examples of the genre taken from the nursing literature. In Extract 10.5 a nurse, Nesta, is reflecting on her care of Peter, a patient who had been acutely ill with renal failure and whose condition was now improving which meant that other patients on the ward were being given greater priority.

Extract 10.5

What would I have done differently? Two aspects of nursing have always remained constant: the need to care and the need to communicate. Peter, my patient, was often lonely in a crowded ward. He suffered from the loss of casual chat, which can often cause a major and distressing deprivation. The failure to communicate causes more suffering than any other problem except when relieving pain. We were all guilty of paternalism by interfering with Peter's liberty which affected his welfare, needs, happiness and interests. The need to talk to Peter and explain things was my firm responsibility and the failure to do so did him harm. I believe I was guilty of causing Peter harm in this way by sometimes bowing to pressure from his relatives and partner. If I were to do anything different it would have to be to remember I am accountable and responsible for my patient; I must always put them first. In being involved in the situation, by being aware of the components of the situation and then by examining my responses, I believe I have become increasingly more effective in my work by the knowledge gained through reflective practice.

(Graham 1998: 130–1)

It is immediately apparent that this form of writing eschews objectivism in favour of subjectivism. Acknowledging errors or omissions in one's practice is seen as a means to producing better future practice. Let us look at our second example before we comment further. This extract is by June, an experienced palliative care nurse who has been asked by a ward sister to talk to a patient, Molly. The latter is described as a young mother who is terminally ill and has recently had chemotherapy but has expressed a desire to return home.

Extract 10.6

I went into Molly's room and started to ask her why she wanted to go home. She just said that was all she wanted. I asked her if she had thought how her mother would cope. She withdrew from communications, the eye to eye contact was gone. She shrank down into her bed and completely avoided any contact with me. I sat very quietly and looking at this tiny emaciated girl blending into the whiteness of the pillow . . . I was overwhelmed with sadness at my total inability to have communicated and helped her. I felt the tears (run) and I must have muttered 'Oh Molly, this must be really awful for you, how on earth can I help you?'. Her tiny hand came from under the covers and her hand clasped mine as she gave me eye to eye contact and started to cry. We cried together for five minutes and then we sat in silence for five minutes. Then Molly communicated with me like she has never done before.

She told me how frightened she was of dying and leaving her family, especially her children and the two men who mean most to her – her ex-husband and the man she was living with now. We discussed where she would best feel supported as regards her fears and she admitted that the hospital ward was best. We then discussed personalizing her room and that we would be able to do that. She went very tired and I left her.

(Duke and Copp 1994: 104)

It is not our intention to suggest that Extract 10.6 concerns a piece of problematic practice, but we do want to raise some concerns with this form of writing. Duke and Copp (1994) intend us to read it as an example of a nurse who is able to integrate the personal and professional and to express openly her feelings with a patient. In addition they assert that it gives evidence of the nurse allowing a two-way caring process, that is allowing the patient to give care as well as receive it. We want to suggest that it is open to a rather different reading. First, it does seem that the 'hidden agenda' of nursing staff is to dissuade Molly from going home 'in her own best interests'; and by the end of the interaction Molly's agreement has been achieved. This seems like mission accomplished for the nursing staff (who may well have knowledge that we are not privy to which causes them to discount the return home). However, it is arguable that Molly, given her situation, should be given a more open opportunity to express her views and have them listened to. By raising an immediate obstacle to Molly's going home (how her mother will cope), it could be said that Molly is effectively asked to place the needs of others above her own. Viewed in this light, being asked to care for other people and do what is right for them may not be such a positive thing for Molly.

What this 'touchy-feely' kind of writing can achieve is to place the practitioner centre-stage. It is what they were thinking and feeling which is of primary interest, chiefly because one of the major premises of this kind of work is that, by critically evaluating one's practice, better practice will emerge. At one level, that seems perfectly acceptable. If we do not reconsider how we have undertaken our practice, how can we expect to acknowledge what did not go well and how we might seek to make improvements? It seems important to recognize that practitioners are not simply technicians but people who bring into their work issues from elsewhere and are strongly affected by the situations they encounter. In addition, the highly charged emotions of patients and clients will be extremely difficult to deal with sensitively. By introducing subjectivity, reflective writing brings us much closer to practice than objectivist accounts. However, we also need to recognize that such accounts are not what 'really happened'. They are narrative accounts written up later and from one particular perspective. Often they are written for a third party, such as a practice teacher or mentor and to a particular format. They may be intended to demonstrate the writer's competence as a reflective practitioner as much as to develop specific areas of practice. In Extract 10.5, for example, we can read the references to paternalism as the nurse's demonstration that she can link theoretical knowledge about nursing ethics to practice. In other words, these documents have a local context which is not acknowledged in the literature. They are situated accounts produced under certain conditions and for a particular audience, and this has important effects. We need to 'read' these accounts, not simply accept them as 'the truth' (see Chapter 8).

A second point is that the claims of reflective writing to facilitate understanding of the patient/client are not entirely convincing. Indeed it is arguable that reflective accounts occlude the patient's perspective and substitutes the practitioner's version. In Extract 10.6 we get the nurse's account of Molly, not Molly's own version. As we have seen in our earlier explorations of client/practitioner encounters, we cannot assume that the agendas and concerns of clients and professionals coincide. Nor can we assume that our reading of the patient would be the same as that of the practitioner writing the account.

One of the benefits of analysing transcripts of talk is that the analysis can give a more detailed outline of the interaction from which to make a reading. It also allows readers, other than the author, better access to the material from which to author their own reading. If Extract 10.6 had been written up as a piece of talk we would probably read it and feel reassured that June handled the situation well and enabled Molly to make a difficult choice, but one that she could feel comfortable with. Without more direct access to patient talk, though, we are not so sure that June did not simply take over, controlling the interaction in a beneficent way but one which ultimately does not give due consideration to the patient's autonomy and at the same time placing a considerable burden upon the patient to put the needs of her mother and family above her own wishes and needs. (For a discussion of these ethical concepts in relation to nursing see Yeo and Moorhouse 1996.)

In broader terms, these practitioner reflective accounts can be seen as particular kinds of narrative which function to demonstrate the moral adequacy of the narrator. As Riessman notes: 'Human agency and imagination determine what gets included and excluded in narrativization, how events are plotted, and what they are supposed to mean. Individuals construct past events and actions in personal narratives to claim identities and construct lives' (1993: 2; see also Hall 1997). Reflective practice accounts seem designed to render the practitioner an 'appropriate and sympathy-worthy' worker (cf. Loseke 1992; Spencer 1994), albeit by invoking different criteria to EBP, based on caring and self-awareness.

Practising reflexivity

We have argued that evidence-based and reflective practice have their place in HW practice, but that they are not sufficient. Our argument is that we need to go further and practise reflexively, but this begs the questions what is reflexivity and how is it an improvement on evidence-based and reflective practice?

What is reflexivity?

Reflexivity is a curiously elusive term. It is widely used in the social sciences, but often in passing and without clear definition. It is used in different ways which makes its meaning quite difficult to fix. Indeed, some characterizations of it render it interchangeable with reflection. Its origins lie in the Latin word *reflectere* which means to bend back. So, a reflexive analysis:

> interrogates the process by which interpretation has been fabricated: reflexivity requires any effort to describe or represent to consider how that process of description was achieved, what claims to 'presence' were made, what authority was used to claim knowledge.

> (Fox 1999: 220)

This may help us to mark a distinction between reflection and reflexivity. In our view, reflection is the process of thinking about our practice at the time (reflection-in-action) or after the event (reflection-on-action). For example, as a practitioner you will be 'thinking on your feet' as you go about your daily work and responding to whatever comes up. Given the nature of the work and its people orientation, it can never be entirely predictable. You will constantly be called on to work out what to do next to defuse conflict, to manage deep distress, to convey bad news, to ask awkward and difficult questions and so forth. You will also be subjecting your work to reflection after the event, working out what went well or badly, whether you said and did the appropriate thing at the appropriate time, how you might do things differently next time. You will thus be acknowledging your impact on the situation for good or ill. The primary focus of reflection is on process issues and how the worker handled their practice. Its focus on knowledge is primarily confined to the application of 'theory to practice'.

Reflexivity includes these forms of reflection but takes things further. Specifically, it problematizes issues that reflection takes for granted. Reflection tends to accept the client/worker relationship and concerns itself with how to improve it. It also takes propositional and process knowledge at face value. For example, it assumes that through reflection the worker can become more adept at applying child development and attachment theory to childcare practice or that workers can apply intervention theories more effectively. Reflexivity suggests that we interrogate these previously taken-for-granted assumptions (Ixer 1999).

The 'bending back' of reflexivity is not simply the individualized action of separate practitioners in the manner suggested by reflective practice. Rather it is the collective action of an academic discipline or occupational group. In the case of HW practitioners, it implies that they subject their own knowledge claims and practices to analysis. In other words, knowledge is not simply a resource to deploy in practice. It is a topic worthy of scrutiny. We need to question the Discourses within which social workers, nurses, doctors and others work, and indeed compare them. How does attachment theory shape our thinking about childhood, children's 'needs' and the roles of mothers and fathers? How does biological psychiatry shape our thinking about mental illness and its treatment? We also need to think about how the client/practitioner relationship and the concept of needs are constituted within HW practice. Authors such as Fraser (1989) and Rojek *et al.* (1988) argue that concepts of need are socially constructed, as the latter indicate:

> discourse analysis reverses the accepted priority of need in humanist social work . . . [which] portrays the social worker as the servant of needs which spread out from the client . . . Among the most prominent are the needs for compassion, respect, dignity, and trust. Social work, the humanists say, is about fulfilling these needs through the provision of care with responsibility. Yet, from the perspective of discourse analysis, this puts the cart before the horse. Compassion, respect, dignity etc., do not arise spontaneously from the client. Rather they are constructed through discourse and the client is required to fit in with them.
>
> (Rojek *et al.* 1988: 131)

This in turn can lead us to unpick some of the concepts that are regarded as unproblematic and inherently positive within HW. Empowerment and autonomy are two obvious candidates here. It is not a question of applying these principles better in practice, as reflective practice suggests, but exploring *how* they are deployed in practice and to what end. We are also led into a more fine-grained analysis of power relations between HW practitioners and clients. On the one hand, we do not assume that power exists as an entity which is brought into all such encounters (or that social factors such as race, class or gender offer straightforward causal explanations of events and situations). Alternatively, we do not deny that power relations exist. This is a tendency with reflective practice (and with EBP, which assumes the neutrality of technical expertise) where it is implicitly assumed that there is a harmony of goals and perspectives between worker and client and that workers may speak for clients. This means that we are subjecting to scrutiny both the Discourse and the discourses which both shape our practice and are constituted within it.

Knowledge does not have fixed, stable meanings. It is made rather than revealed. Embedded within the conception of reflexivity is the notion that, as Hall argues, 'By considering the constructedness of social reality we accept the constructedness of all claims, including our own' (1997: 240). This also applies to our own writing. We cannot escape the constraints of language and within this text we have employed particular devices in order to convince you of the 'truth' of our approach. Usually these have been of the standard academic variety and you may have noticed that we have used empiricist discourse to make claims in such a way that their 'constructedness' is disguised. In order to make this knowledge making process more obvious some authors have chosen to write using alternative forms. Hall (1997), for example, has included dialogues between himself and various interested parties (a social worker, a researcher and so forth) to emphasize that his is but one (contestable) version and to introduce other voices into the text (although it is arguable that he retains control over these alternative voices). We have adopted a more conventional style; however, our conventional approach does not make it immune to the type of scrutiny suggested in Chapter 8. Nor do we forget that, although authored by us, you will make your own reading of this text and produce other versions of it.

Reflexivity and uncertainty

One of the principal objections to practising reflexively is the uncertainty it is said to produce. It can seem much more straightforward to work with the certainties of evidence-based research and the technical problems of applying it to practice; or so it may seem. However, the fit between 'objective theory' and 'practice' may not be so easy to manage in daily work routines where formal propositional knowledge may seem to have little bearing on how to manage the client/worker relationship. Herein lies the appeal of reflective practice because it switches focus from the application of technical knowledge to managing the (often painful and difficult) minutiae of day-to-day practice. It offers the comfort of dealing with 'the real issues' and focusing on the subjective elements of practice. However, whilst reflective practice opens up the possibility of a more uncertain, ambiguous and complex world, it tends to close much of this down again by obscuring clients' perspectives and freezing practitioners' confessional accounts as true representations of what happened.

Our overriding message is that unexamined forms of realism, whether objectivist or subjectivist, are problematic foundations on which to build professional practice. Moreover, the debate between the 'high ground' of research and the 'swampy lowlands' of practice (Schön 1983, 1987) is misplaced. There is no high ground; rather there are swampy lowlands in (scientific and social science) research as there are in practice. Difficulty, ambiguity and complexity characterize the making of technical/rational knowledge just as they do HW work. We cannot eliminate uncertainty simply by denying its existence. It is something which has to be confronted in all professional work. We have therefore to work out better ways to deal with it, and the refinement of objectivist, technical rationality in the form of evidence-based practice or an individualized focus on practitioners' thought, feelings and actions are insufficient.

We need to produce better understandings of HW practice in an overarching sense (Discourse) and at a micro level (discourse). Other writers, notably Foucauldians, have produced analyses which examine Discourse (see, for example, Armstrong 1983; Rojek *et al.* 1988; Rose 1989; Petersen and Brunton 1997; Chambon *et al.* 1999). Our suggestion is that microanalyses of talk and text can further contribute to this process of sense making. Do such analyses inhibit the capacity to practise? We would argue not. In relation to charges of political quietism, Herrnstein Smith contends that:

Those . . . persuaded . . . of the political necessity of objectivism, commonly cannot imagine themselves – or by extension – anyone else making judgments,
taking sides, or working actively for political causes without objectivist convictions and justifications. Consequently they resist – indeed cannot grasp – the
idea that the reason other people reject objectivism is not only that its claims
seem, to them, conceptually problematic, but that such claims are, for them,
otherwise ('practically' or 'politically') unnecessary. Contrary to the charge of
quietism, non-objectivists need not and characteristically do not refuse to *judge*.
Nor, also contrary to that charge, must they or do they characteristically refuse
to *act*. Nor must they be, or are they characteristically, incapable of acting
effectively. Nor are they incapable of *justifying* – in the sense of explaining,
defending, and promoting – their judgements and actions to other people . . .

(Smith 1994: 291)

A similar argument can be applied to HW practice. We are not asking you
to abandon action, but we are asking you to approach your practice differently. Our suggestion is that practising reflexively is essential for good practice and that it entails analysing how practitioners make knowledge in their
daily work routines. In adopting this approach it was our intention to raise
questions and issues which may well have unsettled your previous ways
of thinking. We have endeavoured to provide analytical tools for you to use
in making sense of how you produce knowledge of clients and situations in
your day-to-day practice. Since we cannot escape these processes of knowledge making, it is important to understand them better.

Glossary

A glossary is 'a collection of glosses; a list with explanations of abstruse, antiquated, dialectal, or technical terms; a partial dictionary (*Oxford English Dictionary*). There is something paradoxical about providing a glossary of social constructionist terms given its central argument that meanings are not fixed and stable. Terms are variously glossed (explained) and meanings are more situated and provisional than a glossary would suggest (Lemert 1997). However, we have supplied provisional explanations here with the aim of assisting your understanding of social constructionism.

accounts and accounting practices: these are versions of events produced by participants in encounters. The concept of accounts is derived from **ethnomethodology**, which argues that all social action involves both an act (or an utterance) and a subsequent (or prospective) account of that act. Accounts of events, also usually embody some kind of account or justification for the action taken. The justification offered will depend on the context in which the talk is taking place. Thus, what people say cannot be taken as an unproblematic reflection of what really happened.

active voicing: term used by Wooffitt (1992) to describe how people deploy the present tense and reported speech to recount previously occurring events and situations. This serves to add immediacy, to strengthen the factual status of claims and to fend off any sceptical response.

authorization procedures: strategies by which speakers or writers seek to establish the authenticity of their version of events.

blamings: used here to refer to attributions of responsibility for causing particular problems; it does not necessarily imply malicious intent.

category-bound activities: *see* **membership categorization devices** and **category entitlement**

category entitlement: 'the idea that certain categories of people, in certain contexts, are treated as knowledgeable' (Potter 1996: 133; see also Sacks 1992a). Entitlement may derive from membership of a category (witness, doctor, lawyer and so forth) but it may be contested; people work to assert their category entitlement in their talk and to ward off challenges (see discussion of 'K is mentally ill' (Smith 1978) in Chapter 3).

claim stake: *see* **dilemma of stake**

closed questions: these questions usually limit the options for reply to 'yes' or 'no', for example 'are you feeling upset about that?'. They are not necessarily intended to lead the respondent but have the effect of cutting off the latter's opportunity to describe the situation or event in their own words.

co-narration: derived from the work of Eder (1988), co-narration refers to the practice of telling a story together. It is argued that this builds group cohesion and collective identity.

contrast structures: derived from the work of Dorothy Smith (1978), these are two-part sequences in talk or text, in which the first part of a statement sets up expectations, and the second signals deviation from these 'norms'. Contrast structures are a powerful way of marking deviance in talk.

conversation analysis: grew from **ethnomethodology**'s focus on the detail of what people actually do. Using detailed transcripts, conversation analysis focuses on the sequential features of talk, that is the turns people take, the pauses in the talk, the way new topics are introduced and so forth.

correspondence theory of truth: the belief that truth mirrors reality. Language is regarded as a neutral medium for the conveyance of facts about the real world.

definitional privilege: derived from the work of Dorothy Smith (1978), this refers broadly to the storyteller's use of their power to define what is true and untrue, normal or deviant.

descriptive demands: derived from the work of Gubrium *et al.* (1989) these are the specific demands imposed on those filling in or reading forms by the forms themselves. Forms many require particular types of description (**descriptive demands**), or impose a certain style (**stylistic demands**), or may be interpreted in a particular and specific way (**interpretive demands**).

dilemma of stake: refers to the issue that being involve in a situation is a good warrant for a claim to knowledge but it may also lay a person open to the charge of bias. Speakers may work to inoculate themselves from claims of bias (see discussion of 'K is mentally ill' (Smith 1978) in Chapter 3) or to claim stake where this is easier to sustain (for example Burchill's World's Worst Mother, *q.v.* Chapter 4).

discourse: this may refer to language used within organizations or in encounters with service users, as this is displayed in talk or written texts such as case notes. It may also refer to ways of thinking, or 'knowledges' or 'discourses' about particular phenomena, such as sex, race, the family or mental health, and how these reflect particular historical, political or moral positions.

discursive psychology: a branch of psychology concerned to remedy the neglect in traditional psychology of the subtleties of language use, and particularly its ambiguity and contestability. Discursive psychology draws on insights from **ethnomethodology, discourse, conversation** analysis, **rhetoric** and **narrative** analysis and is particularly concerned with the capacity of language to 'perform' things in the world and the ways in which individuals experience and think about their social world.

empiricist repertoire or discourse: a term developed by Gilbert and Mulkay (1984) to refer to the way that scientists (and by extension other people) write or talk in order to present their work as neutral and objective. The devices used within empiricist discourse are: the use of grammatical impersonality ('it was found that . . .'); data primacy (the facts exist out there waiting for scientists to discover them); and universal procedural rules ('this research was conducted according to standard scientific methods').

Enlightenment: European intellectual movement of the late seventeenth and eighteenth century which challenged a traditional, religious world-view and emphasized freedom of the individual, rational thought, the pursuit of universal truth and science as the model of reason and progress.

epistemology: (from the Greek *epistëmë* 'knowledge') concerned with how we 'know' the world. It refers to 'the claims or assumptions made about the ways in which it is possible to gain knowledge of this reality, whatever it is understood to be; claims about how what exists may be known (Blaikie 1993: 6–7).

ethnomethodology: derived from the work of Harold Garfinkel this refers simply to 'folk' (ethno) 'methods' (ways of doing things). Ethnomethodology studies the complex forms of shared knowledge, upon which we all draw in making sense of and acting in everyday encounters with others.

everyday talk: talk which occurs in everyday encounters between people; contrasted with **institutional talk.**

evidence-based practice: a term which came to prominence in the 1990s which asserts that health and welfare decisions should be based on 'the best available scientific evidence' (Davidoff *et al.* 1995; see Chapter 10 for discussion).

externalizing device: used by Woolgar (1988a) to refer to a range of descriptive and explanatory devices which serve to place facts 'out there' as objects to be discovered. *See also* **empiricist discourse.**

extreme case formulation: a device which invokes the maximal ('best value') or minimal ('the worst mother in the world') attributes of a person, thing, event or situation; used to defend against complaint, to 'blame' someone else or to invoke rightness or wrongness (Pomerantz 1986).

incommensurability: a term derived from philosophy and social theory to refer to competing ideas which are not measurable by the same standard. This means that these viewpoints can never be reconciled in order to obtain a consensus view: we have to choose between the different versions.

indifferent kinds: these are ideas we have about objects which have no capacity to answer back. Usually these will be part of the physical world, such as metals, gravity, blood or bone. They can act upon us in various ways but they do so without consciousness; for example, if a microbe makes us ill, it interacts with our bodies but it does not know that it is doing so – it is indifferent (contrast with **interactive kinds**).

institutional talk: talk which occurs between professionals and clients/patients/ service users, or between workers within and across workplaces, disciplines and agencies. Contrasted with **everyday talk** although they share many features.

interactive kinds: derives from the work of Ian Hacking (1999) and refers to understandings, usually about people, which can in some way loop back into our ideas about ourselves and influence the way we think and feel. Examples would include the concepts we have about childhood, or being female, or about mental health and illness. Contrast with **indifferent kinds.**

interpretive demands: *see* **descriptive demands**

leading questions: these are associated with the courtroom in particular but are used widely to push the respondent to answer in a particular way, often with the intention of undermining their moral adequacy, for example, 'you went to the bar to pick someone up, didn't you?' might be asked of a complainant in a rape trial to suggest that they are promiscuous and, by implication, not an innocent victim.

membership categorization devices: devices used in talk and text to assign individuals to social categories such as woman, mother, father, child, nurse. These categorizations are linked to certain expectable behaviours or **category-bound activities**, which may be breached. For example, if the category-bound expectations of a person in the category 'mother' are that she will be nurturing and caring, a description of behaviour deviating from this expectation will mark deviance.

narrative: usually defined as a particular kind of recapitulation which presents events as the antecedents or consequences of each other. These kinds of consequential accounts attribute cause and effect in particular ways. Narratives can be analysed for their structural features, their characterizations and for their effects. Professional work depends to a large extent on storytelling and narrative.

objectivism: the stance that there is a reality independent of human beings whose nature can be known and that the aim of research is to produce accounts that correspond to that reality which are not contaminated by personal influences and social processes. *See also* **realism.**

ontology: (from Greek *ont-* 'being') the study of the nature of things which exist in the world: it refers to 'the claims or assumptions that a particular approach to social enquiry makes about the nature of social reality – claims about what exists, what it looks like, what units make it up and how these units interact with each other' (Blaikie 1993: 6).

open questions: questions posed in such a way as to leave open the response, for example 'how are you feeling at the present time?'.

perspective display series: a device used in everyday and institutional talk to find out the other person's view and to prepare them for a contrary perspective (for example asking parents what they think is the problem as preparation for giving them bad news about their child's development (Maynard 1991).

positivism: perspective strongly linked to the **Enlightenment** which espouses the ideals of pure objectivity and value-neutrality. Knowers are assumed, through the exercise of autonomous reason, to transcend particularity and contingency ('a view from somewhere') to achieve a 'view from anywhere'. It is associated with a belief in a natural scientific method: 'sensory observation in ideal observation conditions is the privileged source of knowledge offering the best promise of certainty' (Code 1995: 24–5). Knowledge thus generated can be applied rationally to control the natural and social worlds and to achieve progress.

realism: the assertion that there is a reality independent of human beings whose nature can be known. The task of research is to produce accounts that provide literal descriptions of that reality. There is also a subjectivist version of realism which argues that we get more accurate information about the world by studying people's thoughts and feelings or day-to-day activities. *See also* **objectivism.**

reflective practice: an approach to practice which rejects objectivism and technical, procedural approaches. It embraces subjectivism and individual experience, focusing on the practitioner's processes of intuitive artistry, reflection-in-action and reflection after the event (reflection-on-action).

reflexivity: an elusive term which is often used interchangeably with reflection. In this book we use it not only to encompass reflection but also to incorporate other features. For us the 'bending back' of reflexivity is not simply the individualized action of separate practitioners in the manner suggested by reflective practice, rather it is the collective action of an academic discipline or occupational group. In the case of HW practitioners it implies that they subject their own knowledge claims and practices to analysis. In other words, knowledge is not simply a resource to deploy in practice, it is also a topic worthy of scrutiny.

relativism: a stance which denies that there is any single universal standard for judging the truth of different descriptions of reality. Truth is provisional and situated. We cannot achieve a 'view from anywhere' or from 'nowhere' (Nagel 1986); we always arrive at a 'view from somewhere'. We can, however, make judgements and take decisions on the basis of the versions of the truth that we construct (see Brown 1994; Smith 1994). *See also* **social constructionism**.

rhetoric: powerful and potent words and phrases deployed in talk and text. Rhetoric is not a contrast to factual reporting; rather, it mobilizes facts in certain ways to achieve particular effects.

social constructionism: an epistemological stance which states that we cannot set ourselves apart from the world in order to study it and produce objective facts. In the act of describing the world we are also constructing it, by choosing one way of describing it we are inevitably closing down other descriptions. Language is therefore of central importance in constituting the things it describes. Meanings and understandings are not stable and fixed, but fluid and provisional, situated in the local practices of **everyday talk** and text. They are also historically and culturally contingent.

stake, claim: *see* **dilemma of stake**

stake inoculation: *see* **dilemma of stake**

standardized relational pairs: membership categories which often occur in pairs, such as mother/child, and which set up expected sets of relationships between the parts of the pair.

stylistic demands: *see* **descriptive demands**

tacit knowledge: a term first used by Michael Polanyi (1967) to indicate the way in which we become so skilful at performing certain actions in both our personal and professional lives that we do not seem to have to think about them and probably cannot describe to anyone else the processes involved. In effect we 'just know' how to do something, for example, ride a bicycle or drive a car. Donald Schön (1987: 25) uses the term 'knowing-in-action' to refer to this 'spontaneous, skillful [sic] execution of performance'.

turn-type pre-allocation: describes the situation in certain formal arenas (courts and official ceremonies are the prime examples) where there are strict conventions about who may speak, when and what they might say.

Transcription conventions

The following transcription symbols are commonly used in conversation analysis.

[or ⌈	overlapping talk
//	onset of overlapping talk
( )	inaudible, and hence untranscribed, passage
(talk)	uncertainty about the transcription
[. . .]	omitted talk or talk which cannot be heard
((laughs))	contextual information not transcribed as actual sounds heard
(0.8)	pauses timed in tenths of second
(.)	audible, but very short pause
talk	italics indicates emphasis
talk	underlining indicates emphasis
TALK	upper case indicates loudness in comparison to surrounding talk
tal-	abrupt end to utterance
> <	noticeable speeding up of talk
< >	noticeable slowing of tempo of talk
=	latching of utterances
-	a hyphen marks a sudden end to an utterance
::	colons mark a prolonged syllable or sound
.h	laughter (or, without full stop, an outbreath)
'h	intake of breath (the number of h's indicates the length of the breath)

Suggested further reading

Social constructionism or relativism

There is no easy beginner text that we can recommend. If you are coming new to this material, it may help to start by looking at a textbook which sets out the main perspectives within the social sciences, with specific sections on symbolic interactionism, ethnomethodology, Foucault and the postmodern turn. For example:

May, T. (1996) *Situating Social Theory*. Buckingham: Open University Press.

Textbooks on social constructionism

Gergen, K. (1999) *An Invitation to Social Construction*. London: Sage.
Jaworski, A. and Coupland, N. (eds) (1999) *The Discourse Reader*. London: Routledge.
Potter, J. (1996) *Representing Reality: Discourse, Rhetoric and Social Construction*. London: Sage.
Sarbin, T. and Kitsuse, J.I. (eds) (1994) *Constructing the Social*. London: Sage.
Shotter, J. (1993) *Conversational Realities: Constructing Life through Language*. London: Sage.

Microsociologies and discursive psychology

Silverman, D. (1993) *Interpreting Qualitative Data: Methods for Analysing Talk, Text and Interaction*. London: Sage. Silverman is a leading British exponent of conversation analysis and this book provides a useful survey of methods for analysing talk, text and interaction. It includes lots of examples and exercises for practice.
Silverman, D. (ed.) (1997) *Qualitative Research: Theory, Method, Practice*. London: Sage. This is an edited collection of papers that supplements *Interpreting Qualitative Data* (above). It contains contribution by leading exponents of microsociologies and discourse analysis.

Studies of talk and text in health and welfare

We have tried to refer to as wide a range of literature as possible although doctors and courtrooms have been most intensively studied. The following collected works contain classic papers on institutional talk and text; the more specific examples relate to different aspects of HW practice.

Collected works

Boden, D. and Zimmerman, D.H. (eds) (1991) *Talk and Social Structure: Studies in Ethnomethodology and Conversation Analysis*. Cambridge: Polity Press.
Drew, P. and Heritage, J. (eds) (1992) *Talk at Work: Interaction in Institutional Settings*. Cambridge: Cambridge University Press.

Social workers

Baldock, J. and Prior, D. (1981) Social workers talking to clients: a study of verbal behaviour, *British Journal of Social Work*, 11: 19–38.
Hall, C. (1997) *Social Work as Narrative: Story Telling and Persuasion in Professional Texts*. Aldershot: Ashgate.

Doctors

Atkinson, P. (1995) *Medical Talk and Medical Work*. London: Sage.
Silverman, D. (1987) *Communication and Medical Practice*. London: Sage.

Nurses

Published examples of nurses' talk to patients, doctors and each other are rare, unlike interview talk about doing nursing. However, see:

Latimer, J. (1997) Figuring identities: older people, medicine and time, in A. Jamieson, S. Harper and C. Victor (eds) *Critical Approaches to Ageing and Later Life*. Buckingham: Open University Press.
Latimer, J. (1997) Giving patients a future: the constituting of classes in an acute medical unit, *Sociology of Health and Illness*, 19(2): 23–53.

Health visitors

Heritage, J. and Sefi, S. (1992) Dilemmas of advice: aspects of the delivery and reception of advice in interactions between Health Visitors and first-time mothers, in P. Drew and J. Heritage (eds) *Talk at Work: Interaction in Institutional Settings*. Cambridge: Cambridge University Press.

Family therapy

Buttny, R. and Jensen, A.D. (1995) Telling problems in an initial family therapy session: the hierarchical organisation of problem-talk, in G.H. Morris and

R.J. Chenail (eds) *The Talk of the Clinic: Explorations of Medical and Therapeutic Discourse*. Hillsdale, NJ: Lawrence Erlbaum.
Gubrium, J.F. (1992) *Out of Control: Family Therapy and Domestic Disorder*, Newbury Park, CA: Sage.

Counselling

Miller, G. and Silverman, D. (1995) Troubles talk and counselling discourse: a comparative study, *Sociological Quarterly*, 36(4): 725–47.
Peräkylä, A. (1995) *AIDS Counselling: Institutional Interaction and Clinical Practice*. Cambridge: Cambridge University Press.
Silverman, D. (1997) *Discourses of Counselling: HIV Counselling as Social Interaction*. London: Sage.

Mental health

Mehan, H. (1990) Oracular reasoning in a psychiatric exam: the resolution of conflict in language, in A.D. Grimshaw (ed.) *Conflict Talk: Sociolinguistic Investigations of Arguments in Conversations*. Cambridge: Cambridge University Press.

References

Ainsworth, M.D., Blehar, M.C., Waters, E. and Wall, S. (1978) *Patterns of Attachment: Assessed in the Strange Situation and at Home*. Hillsdale, NJ: Lawrence Erlbaum.

Anspach, R.R. (1987) Prognostic conflict in life and death decisions, *Journal of Health and Social Behaviour*, 28: 215–31.

Antaki, C. (1994a) *Explaining and Arguing: The Social Organization of Accounts*. London: Sage.

Antaki, C. (1994b) Common sense reasoning: arriving at conclusions or travelling towards them?, in J. Seigfreid (ed.) *The Status of Commonsense in Psychology*. Norwood, NJ: Ablex.

Antaki, C. and Widdicombe, S. (1998) Identity as an achievement and as a tool, in C. Antaki and S. Widdicombe (eds) *Identities in Talk*. London: Sage.

Appleby, J., Walshe, K. and Ham, C. (1995) *Acting on the Evidence: A Review of Clinical Effectiveness. Sources of Information, Dissemination and Implementation*. Health Services Management Centre, University of Birmingham: National Association of Health Authorities and Trusts.

Armstrong, D. (1983) *The Political Anatomy of the Body*. Cambridge: Cambridge University Press.

Armstrong, D. (1995) The rise of surveillance medicine, *Sociology of Health and Illness*, 17(3): 393–404.

Atkinson, J.M. and Drew, P. (1979) *Order in Court: The Organization of Verbal Interaction in Judicial Settings*. London: Macmillan.

Atkinson, P. (1995) *Medical Talk and Medical Work*. London: Sage.

Atkinson, P. and Heath, C. (eds) (1981) *Medical Work: Realities and Routines*. Aldershot: Gower.

Baker, C. (1997) Membership categorization and interview accounts, in D. Silverman (ed.) *Qualitative Research: Theory, Method and Practice*. London: Sage.

Baldock, J. and Prior, D. (1981) Social workers talking to clients: a study of verbal behaviour, *British Journal of Social Work*, 11: 19–38.

Baly, M. (1984) *Professional Responsibility*, 2nd edn. Chichester: John Wiley.

Baruch, G. (1981) Moral tales: parents' stories of encounters with the health professions, *Sociology of Health and Illness*, 3(3): 274–96.

Baruch, D. (1982) Moral tales: interviewing parents of congenitally ill children. Unpublished PhD thesis, University of London.

BBC (1998) at http://news.bbc.co.uk/hi/english/special_report/1998/woodward/ newsid-115000/115048 (accessed November 1999).

Bell, M.M. and Gardiner, M. (eds) (1998) *Bakhtin and the Human Sciences*. London: Sage.

Benner, P. (1984) *From Novice to Expert: Excellence and Power in Clinical Nursing Practice*. Menlo Park, CA: Addison-Wesley.

Benner, P. and Wrubel, J. (1989) *The Primacy of Caring: Stress and Coping in Health and Illness*. Menlo Park, CA: Addison-Wesley.

Benner, P., Tanner, C.A. and Chesla, C.A. (1996) *Expertise in Nursing Practice: Caring, Clinical Judgement, and Ethics*. New York: Springer.

Bernstein, R.J. (1983) *Beyond Objectivism and Relativism: Science Hermeneutics and Praxis*. Philadelphia, PA: University of Pennsylvania Press.

Billig, M. (1987) *Arguing and Thinking: A Rhetorical Approach to Social Psychology*. Cambridge: Cambridge University Press.

Billig, M., Condor, S., Edwards, D. *et al.* (1988) *Ideological Dilemmas: A Social Psychology of Everyday Thinking*. London: Sage.

Blaikie, N. (1993) *Approaches to Social Enquiry*. Cambridge: Polity Press.

Bloor, M. (1976) Bishop Berkeley and the adeno-tonsillectomy enigma, *Sociology*, 10: 43–61.

Booth, A. (1997) *Scharr Guide to Evidence-based Practice*. Sheffield: University of Sheffield Health and Related Research.

Bourdieu, P. (1977) *Outline of a Theory of Practice*. Cambridge: Cambridge University Press.

Bourdieu, P. (1986) The force of law: towards a sociology of the juridical field, *Hastings Law Journal*, 38: 814–53.

Brown, R.H. (1994) Reconstructing social theory after the postmodern critique, in H.W. Simons and M. Billig (eds) *After Postmodernism: Reconstructing Ideology Critique*. London: Sage.

Bull, R. and Shaw, I. (1992) Constructing causal accounts in social work, *Sociology*, 26(4): 635–49.

Burman, E. (1994) *Deconstructing Developmental Psychology*. London: Routledge.

Burr, V. (1995) *An Introduction to Social Constructionism*. London: Routledge.

Burton, L. (1975) *The Family Life of Sick Children*. London: Routledge & Kegan Paul.

Buttny, R. (1993) *Social Accountability in Communication*. London: Sage.

CCETSW (Central Council for Education and Training in Social Work) (1995) *Assuring Quality in the Diploma in Social Work – 1: Rules and Requirements for the DipSW*. London: CCETSW.

Chambon, A.S., Irving, A. and Epstein, L. (1999) *Reading Foucault for Social Work*. New York: Columbia University Press.

Cicourel, A. (1968) *The Social Organization of Juvenile Justice*. New York: John Wiley.

Clarke, J. (1991) *New Times and Old Enemies: Essays on Cultural Studies and America*. London: Hutchinson.

Code, L. (1995) *Rhetorical Spaces: Essays on Gendered Locations*. London: Routledge.

Corby, B. (1987) *Working with Child Abuse: Social Work Practice and the Child Abuse System*. Milton Keynes: Open University Press.

Corby, B. (1994) Sociology, social work and child protection, in M. Davies (ed.) *The Sociology of Social Work*. London: Routledge.

Court TV (1997) at http://www.courttv.com/trials/woodward/comments/html (accessed November 1999).

Cuff, E. (1993) *Problems of Versions in Everyday Situations*. Lanham, MD: University Press of America.

Dale, P., Davies, M., Morrison, T. and Waters J. (1986) *Dangerous Families: Assessment and Treatment of Child Abuse*. London: Tavistock.

Davidoff, F., Haynes, B., Sackett, D. and Smith, R. (1995) Evidence-based medicine: a new journal to help doctors to identify the information they need, *British Medical Journal*, 310: 1085–6.

Davis, K. (1988) *Power under the Microscope: Towards a Grounded theory of Gender Relations in Medical Encounters*. Dordrecht: Foris.

Davis, K. (1991) Critical sociology and gender relations, in K. Davis, M. Leijenaaar and J. Oldersma (eds) *The Gender of Power*. London: Sage.

Defence Appeal Brief (1998) http://www.louise.force.9.co.uk/march/defence_appeal_doc.htm (accessed November 1999).

Department of Health (1988a) *Protecting Children: A Guide for Social Workers undertaking a Comprehensive Assessment*. London: HMSO.

Department of Health (1988b) *Report of the Inquiry into Child Abuse in Cleveland 1987*, Cm 412. London: HMSO.

Department of Health (1995) *Child Protection: Messages from Research*. London: HMSO.

Department of Health (1998a) *A First Class Service*. London: The Stationery Office.

Department of Health (1998b) *Modernising Social Services – Promoting Independence, Improving Protection, Raising Standards*. London: The Stationery Office.

Department of Health (1998c) *The New NHS, Modern and Dependable: A National Framework for Assessing Performance*. London: The Stationery Office.

Department of Health (1999) *Framework for the Assessment of Children in Need and their Families: Consultation Draft*. London: Department of Health.

Department of Health, Department for Education and Employment and Home Office (2000) *Framework for the Assessment of Children in Need and their Families*. London: The Stationery Office.

Dingwall, R. (1977) 'Atrocity stories' and professional relationships, *Sociology of Work and Occupations*, 4(4): 371–96.

Dingwall, R. (1989) Some problems about predicting child abuse and neglect, in O. Stevenson (ed.) *Child Abuse: Professional Practice and Public Policy*. London: Harvester Wheatsheaf.

Drew, P. (1992) Contested evidence in a courtroom cross-examination: the case of a trial for rape, in P. Drew and J. Heritage (eds) *Talk at Work: Interaction in Institutional Settings*. Cambridge: Cambridge University Press.

Drew, P. and Sorjonen, M-L. (1997) Institutional Dialogue, in T.A. van Dijk (ed.) *Discourse as Social Interaction*, Discourse Studies: A Multidisciplinary Introduction, Vol. 2. London: Sage.

Duke, S. and Copp, G. (1994) The Personal Side of Reflection, in A. Palmer, S. Burns and C. Bulman (eds) *Reflective Practice in Nursing*. Oxford: Blackwell Science.

Dulhaime, A.C. and Thibault, L.E. (1987) The shaken baby syndrome: a clinical, pathological and biomechanical study, *Journal of Neurosurgery*, 44: 409–15.

Eappen, D. (1997) One mother's story, interview, *Time Magazine*, 27 November, Vol. 150, No. 2. Also available at http://www.pathfinder.com/time/ma . . . /971124/ nation.one_mothers_s.html (accessed November 1999).

Eder, D. (1988) Building cohesion through collaborative narration, *Social Psychology Quarterly*, 5(3): 225–35.

Edwards, D. (1995) Two to tango: script formulations, dispositions, and rhetorical symmetry in relationship troubles talk, *Research on Language and Social Interaction*, 28(4): 319–50.

Edwards, D. (1997) *Discourse and Cognition*. London, Sage.

Edwards, D. and Mercer, N.M. (1987) *Common Knowledge: The Development of Understanding in the Classroom*. London: Routledge.

Edwards, D. and Potter, J. (1992) *Discursive Psychology*. London: Sage.

Edwards, D., Ashmore, M. and Potter, J. (1995) Death and furniture: the rhetoric, politics and theology of bottom line arguments against relativism, *History of the Human Sciences*, 8(2): 25–49.

Eraut, M. (1994) *Developing Professional Knowledge and Competence*. London: Falmer Press.

Etzioni, A. (1969) *The Semi-professions and their Organisation: Teachers, Nurses and Social Workers*. New York: Free Press.

Fish, S. (1995) Rhetoric, in F. Lentricchia and T. McLaughlin (eds) *Critical Terms for Literary Study*, 2nd edn. Chicago: Chicago University Press.

Fisher, S. and Todd, A. (eds) (1983) *The Social Organization of Doctor–Patient Communication*. Washington, DC: Center for Applied Linguistics.

Fitton, F. and Acheson, H.W.K. (1979) *The Doctor/Patient Relationship: A Study in General Practice*. London: HMSO.

Foucault, M. (1973) *The Birth of the Clinic: An Archaeology of Medical Perception*. New York: Vintage Books.

Foucault, M. (1976) *Mental Illness and Psychology*. New York: Harper Colophon.

Foucault, M. (1980) *Power/Knowledge: Selected Interviews and Other Writings 1972–1977*, C. Gordon (ed.). Hemel Hempstead: Harvester Wheatsheaf.

Fox, N. (1999) *Beyond Health: Postmodernism and Embodiment*. London: Free Association Books.

Frankel, R. (1990) Talking in interviews: a dispreference for patient-initiated questions in physician–patient encounters, in G. Psathas (ed.) *Interaction Competence*. Washington, DC: University of America Press.

Fraser, N. (1989) *Unruly Practices: Power, Discourse and Gender in Contemporary Society*. Cambridge: Polity Press.

Freidson, E. (1970) *The Profession of Medicine*. New York: Dodd, Mead.

Garfinkel, H. (1967) *Studies in Ethnomethodology*. Cambridge: Polity Press.

Garfinkel, H. and Bittner, E. (1967) Good organizational reasons for 'bad' clinic records, in H. Garfinkel *Studies in Ethnomethodology*. Cambridge: Polity Press.

Garfinkel, H. and Sacks, H. (1970) On formal structures of practical actions, in J.C. McKinney and Tirakian, E.A. (eds) *Theoretical Sociology*. New York: Appleton Century Crofts.

Garrett, P.M. (1999) Mapping child care social work in the final years of the twentieth century: a critical response to the 'Looking After Children' system, *British Journal of Social Work*, 29(1): 27–47.

Gergen, K.J. (1994) *Realities and Relationships: Soundings in Social Construction.* Cambridge, MA: Harvard University Press.

Gilbert, G.N. and Mulkay, M.J. (1984) *Opening Pandora's Box: A Sociological Analysis of Scientists' Discourse.* Cambridge: Cambridge University Press.

Goffman, E. (1959) *The Presentation of Self in Everyday Life.* Harmondsworth: Penguin.

Goffman, E. (1972) *Interaction Ritual: Essays on Face-to-face Behaviour.* Harmondsworth: Penguin.

Goldman, A.I. (1999) *Knowledge in a Social World.* Oxford: Clarendon Press.

Graham, I. (1998) Understanding the nature of nursing through reflection: a case study approach, in C. Johns and D. Freshwater (eds) (1998) *Transforming Nursing Through Reflective Practice.* Oxford: Blackwell Science.

Gray, J.A.M. (1997) *Evidence-based Healthcare: How to Make Health Policy and Management Decisions.* Edinburgh: Churchill Livingstone.

Greatbatch, D. and Dingwall, R. (1998) Talk and identity in divorce mediation, in C. Antaki and S. Widdicombe (eds) *Identities in Talk.* London: Sage.

Gubrium, J.F., Buckholdt, D.R. and Lynott, R.J. (1989) The descriptive tyranny of forms, *Perspectives on Social Problems,* 1: 195–214.

Hacking, I. (1999) *The Social Construction of What?* London: Harvard University Press.

Hak, A. (1992) Psychiatric records as transformations of other texts, in G. Watson and R.M. Seiler (eds) *The Text in Context: Contributions to Ethnomethodology.* London: Sage.

Hall, C. (1997) *Social Work as Narrative: Storytelling and Persuasion in Professional Texts.* Aldershot: Ashgate.

Hall, C., Sarangi, S. and Slembrouck, S. (1997) Moral construction and social work discourse, in B-L. Gunnarsson, P. Linell and B. Nordberg (eds) *The Construction of Professional Discourse.* Harlow: Addison Wesley Longman.

Hamilton, P. (1992) The Enlightenment and the birth of social science, in S. Hall and B. Gieben (eds) *Formations of Modernity.* Cambridge: Polity Press.

Hammersley, M. (1992) *What's Wrong with Ethnography? Methodological Explorations.* London: Routledge.

Hearn, J. (1998) Men will be men: the ambiguity of men's support for men who have been violent to women, in J. Popay, J. Hearn and J. Edwards (eds) *Men, Gender Divisions and Welfare.* London: Routledge.

Heritage, J.C. (1984) *Garfinkel and Ethnomethodology.* Cambridge: Cambridge University Press.

Heritage, J. (1997) Conversation analysis and institutional talk: analysing data, in D. Silverman (ed.) *Qualitative Research: Theory, Method, Practice.* London: Sage.

Heritage, J. and Greatbatch, D. (1986) Generating applause: a study of rhetoric and response at party political conferences, *American Sociological Review,* 92: 110–57.

Heritage, J. and Sefi, S. (1992) Dilemmas of advice: aspects of the delivery and reception of advice in interactions between health visitors and first-time mothers, in P. Drew and J. Heritage (eds) *Talk at Work: Interaction in Institutional Settings.* Cambridge: Cambridge University Press.

Hester, S. (1992) Recognizing references to deviance in referral talk, in G. Watson and R.M. Seiler (eds) *The Text in Context: Contributions to Ethnomethodology.* London: Sage.

Holmes, J. (1993) *John Bowlby and Attachment Theory*. London: Routledge.

Hope, T. (1996) *Evidence-based Patient Choice*. London: King's Fund.

Howe, D. (1995) *Attachment Theory for Social Work Practice*. London: Macmillan.

Howe, D. (1992) Child abuse and the bureaucratisation of social work, *The Sociological Review*, 40(3): 491–518.

Howe, D. (1994a) Modernity, postmodernity and social work, *British Journal of Social Work*, 24(3): 513–32.

Howe, D. (1994b) Knowledge, power and the shape of social work practice, in M. Davies (ed.) *The Sociology of Social Work*. London: Routledge.

Hughes, D. (1982) Control in a medical consultation: organizing talk in a situation where participants have differential competence, *Sociology*, 10(3): 359–76.

Hutchby, I. and Wooffitt, R. (1998) *Conversation Analysis: Principles, Practices and Applications*. Cambridge: Polity Press.

Hyden, L.C. (1997) The institutional narrative as drama, in B-L. Gunnarsson, P. Linell and B. Nordberg *The Construction of Professional Discourse*. Harlow: Addison Wesley Longman.

Hyden, M. and McCarthy, I. C. (1994) Women battering and father–daughter incest disclosure: discourses of denial and acknowledgement, *Discourse and Society*, 5(4): 543–65.

Ixer, G. (1999) There is no such thing as reflection, *British Journal of Social Work*, 29(4): 513–28.

Jayyusi, L. (1984) *Categorization and the Moral Order*. London: Routledge & Kegan Paul.

Jayyusi, L. (1991) Values and Moral Judgement, in G. Button (ed.) *Ethnomethodology and the Human Sciences*. Cambridge: Cambridge University Press.

Johnson, T.J. (1972) *Professions and Power*. Basingstoke: Macmillan.

King, M. and Piper, C. (1995) *How the Law Thinks about Children*. Aldershot: Arena.

Knorr-Cetina, K. and Mulkay, M. (1983a) Introduction: emerging principles in the social study of science, in K. Knorr-Cetina and M. Mulkay (eds) *Science Observed: Perspectives on the Social Study of Science*. Beverley Hills, CA: Sage.

Knorr-Cetina, K. and Mulkay, M. (eds) (1983b) *Science Observed: Perspectives on the Social Study of Science*. Beverley Hills, CA: Sage.

Kuhn, T. (1962) *The Structure of Scientific Revolutions*. Chicago: Chicago University Press.

Kvale, S. (1996) *InterViews: An Introduction to Qualitative Research Interviewing*. Thousand Hills, CA: Sage.

Labov, W. (1972) The transformation of experience in narrative syntax, in W. Labov (ed.) *Language in the Inner City*. Philadelphia, PA: University of Pennsylvania Press.

L'Aiguille, Y. (1994) Pushing back the boundaries of personal experience, in A. Palmer, S. Burns and C. Bulman (eds) *Reflective Practice in Nursing: The Growth of the Reflective Practitioner*. Oxford: Blackwell Science.

Lannamann, J.W. (1989) Communication theory applied to relational change: a case study in Milan systems family therapy, *Journal of Applied Communication Research*, 17: 71–91.

Latimer, J. (1997a) Figuring identities: older people, medicine and time, in A. Jamieson, S. Harper and C. Victor (eds) *Critical Approaches to Ageing and Later Life*. Buckingham: Open University Press.

Latimer, J. (1997b) Giving patients a future: the constituting of classes in an acute medical unit, *Sociology of Health and Illness*, 19(2): 23–53.

Latour, B. (1988) The politics of explanation: an alternative, in S. Woolgar (ed.) *New Frontiers in the Sociology of Knowledge*. London: Sage.

Latour, B. (1999) *Pandora's Hope: Essays on the Reality of Science Studies*. London: Harvard University Press.

Latour, B. and Woolgar, S. (1986) *Laboratory Life: The Construction of Scientific Facts*, 2nd edn. Princeton, NJ: Princeton University Press.

Law, J. (1994) *Organizing Modernity*. Oxford: Blackwell.

Lemert, C. (1997) *Postmodernism Is Not What You Think*. Oxford: Blackwell.

Leuder, I. and Antaki, C. (1996) Discourse participation, reported speech and research practices in social psychology, *Theory and Psychology*, 6(1): 5–29.

Levi, J. and Walker, A.G. (eds) (1990) *Language in the Judicial Process*. New York: Plenum.

Levinson, S.C. (1992) Activity types and language, in P. Drew and J. Heritage (eds) *Talk at Work: Interaction in Institutional Settings*. Cambridge: Cambridge University Press.

Lloyd, M. and Taylor, C. (1995) From Hollis to the Orange Book: developing a holistic model of social work assessment in the 1990s, *British Journal of Social Work*, 25(6): 691–710.

Logan, J. (1996) *Post-adoption Arrangements for Openness and Contact – An Evaluation of an Information Exchange Scheme. The Report of a Study Commissioned by the Leverhulme Trust to Evaluate the Information Exchange Scheme in Operation at Chester Diocesan Adoption Services*. Manchester: Department of Social Policy and Social Work, University of Manchester.

London Borough of Brent (1985) *A Child in Trust. Report of the Panel of Inquiry Investigating the Circumstances Surrounding the Death of Jasmine Beckford*. The London Boroughs.

London Borough of Greenwich (1987) *A Child in Mind: Protection of Children in a Responsible Society. Report of the Commission of Inquiry into the Circumstances Surrounding the Death of Kimberley Carlisle*. The London Boroughs.

Loseke, D. (1992) *The Battered Woman and Shelters*. Albany, NY: State University of New York Press.

Lyotard, J.F. (1984) *The Post-modern Condition: A Report on Knowledge*. Manchester: Manchester University Press.

McHoul, A. (1978) The organization of turns in formal talk in the classroom, *Language in Society*, 7: 183–213.

McHoul, A. (1994) Towards a critical ethnomethodology, *Theory, Culture and Society*, 11: 105–26.

McKinlay, A. and Dunnett, A. (1998) How gun-owners accomplish being deadly average, in C. Antaki and S. Widdicombe (eds) *Identities in Talk*. London: Sage.

Malpas, J. and Wickham, G. (1995) Governance and failure: on the limits of sociology, *Australia and New Zealand Journal of Sociology*, 31(3): 37–49.

Marks, D. (1995) Gendered 'care' and the structuring of group relations: child–professional–parent–researcher, in E. Burman, P. Alldred, C. Bewley, *et al.* (eds) *Challenging Women: Psychology's Exclusions, Feminist Possibilities*. Buckingham: Open University Press.

May, C. (1992a) Individual care: power and subjectivity in therapeutic relationships, *Sociology*, 26: 589–602.

May, C. (1992b) Nursing work, nurses' knowledge and the subjectification of the patient, *Sociology of Health and Illness*, 14: 472–87.

May, T. (1996) *Situating Social Theory*. Buckingham: Open University Press.

Maynard, D. (1984) *Inside Plea Bargaining: The Language of Negotiation*. New York: Plenum.

Maynard, D.W. (1991) Interaction and asymmetry in clinical discourse, *American Journal of Sociology*, 97: 448–95.

Meadow, R. (1980) Factitious epilepsy, *Lancet*, 1: 25.

Meadow, R. (1985) Management of Munchausen syndrome by proxy, *Archives of Disease in Childhood*, 60: 385.

Megill, A. (1994) Introduction: four senses of objectivity, in A. Megill (ed.) *Rethinking Objectivity*. London: Duke University Press.

Mehan, H. (1985) The structure of classroom discourse, in T.A. van Dijk (ed.) *Handbook of Discourse Analysis*, Vol. 3. New York: Academic Press.

Mehan, H. (1990) Oracular reasoning in a psychiatric exam: the resultion of conflict in language, in A.D. Grimshaw (ed.) *Conflict Talk: Sociolinguistic Investigations of Arguments in Conversation*. Cambridge: Cambridge University Press.

Milgram, S. (1974) *Obedience to Authority*. New York: Harper & Row.

Miller, G. (1994) Toward ethnographies of institutional discourse: proposal and suggestions, *Journal of Contemporary Ethnography*, 23(3): 280–306.

Miller, G. (1997) Contextualizing texts: studying organizational texts, in G. Miller and R. Dingwall (eds) *Context and Method in Qualitative Research*. London: Sage.

Miller, P. and Rose, N. (1988) The Tavistock Programme: the government of subjectivity and social life, *Sociology*, 22(2): 171–92.

Miller, P. and Rose, N. (1994) On therapeutic authority: psychoanalytic expertise under advanced liberalism, *History of the Human Sciences*, 7(3): 29–64.

Mishler, E. (1984) *The Discourse of Medicine: Dialectics of Medical Interviews*. Norwood, NJ: Ablex.

Mishler, E.G. (1986) *Research Interviewing: Context and Narrative*. Cambridge, MA: Harvard University Press.

Munro, E. (1998) Improving social workers' knowledge base in child protection work, *British Journal of Social Work*, 28, 89–105.

Nagel, T. (1986) *The View from Nowhere*. New York: Oxford University Press.

Newman, J. and Clarke, J. (1994) Going about our business? The managerialization of public services, in J. Clarke, A. Cochrane and E. McLaughlin (eds) *Managing Social Policy*. London: Sage.

O'Brien, M. (1993) Social research and sociology, in N. Gilbert (ed.) *Researching Social Life*. London: Sage.

Otway, O. (1996) 'Social work with children and families: from child welfare to child protection', in N. Parton (ed.) *Social Theory, Social Change and Social Welfare*. London: Routledge.

Palumbo, D. (1987) Politics and evaluation, in D. Palumbo (ed.) *The Politics of Program Evaluation*. Newbury Park, CA: Sage.

Parsons, T. (1967) *Sociological Theory and Modern Society*. New York: Free Press.

Parton, N. (1998) Risk, advanced liberalism and child welfare: the need to rediscover uncertainty and ambiguity, *British Journal of Social Work*, 28(1): 5–28.

Parton, N. (1991) *Governing the Family: Child Care, Child Protection and the State*. Basingstoke: Macmillan.

Parton, N. (1994a) Problematics of government: (post) modernity and social work, *British Journal of Social Work*, 24(1): 9–32.

Parton, N. (1994b) The nature of social work under conditions of (post)modernity, *Social Work and Social Sciences Review*, 5(2): 93–112.

Parton, N. (1996) Social work, risk and 'the blaming system', in N. Parton (ed.) *Social Theory, Social Change and Social Work*. London: Routledge.

Paterson, F.M.S. (1989) *Out of Place: Public Policy and the Emergence of Truancy*. London: Falmer Press.

Penman, R. (1990) Facework and politeness: multiple goals in courtroom discourse, in K. Tracy and N. Coupland (eds) *Multiple Goals in Discourse*. Philadelphia, PA: Multilingual Matters.

Peräkylä, A. (1995) *AIDS Counselling: Institutional Interaction and Clinical Practice*. Cambridge: Cambridge University Press.

Petersen, A. and Brunton, R. (eds) (1997) *Foucault, Health and Medicine*. London: Routledge.

Peyser, A. (1998) *New York Post*. Also available at http://new.bbcs.co.uk/hi/english/special_report/1998/woodward/newsid_114000/114929.stm (accessed November 1999).

Pithouse, A. (1987) *Social Work: The Social Organisation of an Invisible Trade*. Aldershot: Avebury Gower.

Pithouse, A. and Atkinson, P. (1988) Telling the case: occupational narrative in a social work office, in N. Coupland (ed.) *Styles of Discourse*. Beckenham: Croom Helm.

Polanyi, M. (1967) *The Tacit Dimension*. New York: Doubleday.

Pollner, M. (1974) Mundane reasoning, *Philosophy of the Social Sciences*, 4: 35–54.

Pollner, M. (1987) *Mundane Reason*. Cambridge: Cambridge University Press.

Pomerantz, A.M. (1978) Attributions of responsibility: blamings, *Sociology*, 12: 115–21.

Pomerantz, A.M. (1986) Extreme case formulations: a new way of legitimating claims, *Human Studies*, 9: 219–30.

Potter, J. (1996) *Representing Reality: Discourse, Rhetoric and Social Construction*. London: Sage.

Potter, J. (1997) Discourse analysis as a way of analysing naturally occurring talk, in D. Silverman (ed.) *Qualitative Research: Theory, Method, Practice*. London: Sage.

Potter, J. and Wetherell, M. (1994) Analysing discourse, in A. Bryman and R.G. Burgess, *Analysing Qualitative Data*. London: Routledge.

Potter, J. and Wetherell, M. (1995) Discourse analysis, in J.A. Smith, R. Harré and L. van Langenhove (eds) *Rethinking Methods in Psychology*. London: Sage.

Rawlings, B. (1981) The production of facts in a therapeutic community, in P. Atkinson and C. Heath (eds) *Medical Work: Realities and Routines*. Farnborough: Gower.

Reissman, C.K. (1993) *Narrative Analysis*. Newbury Park, CA: Sage.

Ridsdale, L. (ed.) (1998) *Evidence-based Practice in Primary Care*. Edinburgh: Churchill Livingstone.

Rogers, A. (1993) Police and psychiatrists: a case of professional dominance? *Social Policy and Administration*, 27(1): 33–44.

Rojek, C., Peacock, G. and Collins, S. (1988) *Social Work and Received Ideas*. London: Routledge.

Rolfe, G. (1998) *Expanding Nursing Knowledge: Understanding and Researching Your Own Practice*. Oxford: Butterworth Heinemann.

Rorty, R. (1979) *Philosophy and the Mirror of Nature*. Princeton: Princeton University Press.

Rorty, R. (1980) Pragmatism, relativism and irrationalism, *Proceedings and Addresses of the American Philosophical Association*, 53: 719–38.

Rorty, R. (1982) *The Consequences of Pragmatism*. Minneapolis, MN: University of Minnesota Press.

Rose, N. (1985) *The Psychological Complex: Psychology, Politics and Society in England 1869–1939*. London: Routledge & Kegan Paul.

Rose, N. (1989) *Governing the Soul: The Shaping of the Private Self*. London: Routledge.

Rose, N. (1998) *Inventing Our Selves: Psychology, Power and Personhood*. Cambridge: Cambridge University Press.

Rosenberg, W. and Donald, A. (1995) Evidence-based medicine: an approach to clinical problem-solving, *British Medical Journal*, 310: 1122–6.

Roth, J.A. (1963) *Timetables*. Indianapolis, IN: Bobbs-Merrill.

Sackett, D.L., Richardson, S., Rosenberg, W. and Haynes, R.B. (1997) *Evidence-based Medicine: How to Practise and Teach EBM*. Edinburgh: Churchill Livingstone.

Sacks, H. (1967) The search for help: no one to turn to, in E. Schneidman (ed.) *Essays in Self Destruction*. New York: Aronson.

Sacks, H. (1972a) An initial investigation of the usability of conversational data for doing sociology, in D. Sudnow (ed.) *Studies in Social Interaction*. New York: Free Press.

Sacks, H. (1972b) On the analyzability of stories by children, in J. Gumpertz and D. Hymes (eds) *Directions in Sociolinguistics: The Ethnography of Communication*. New York: Holt, Rinehart & Winston.

Sacks, H. (1984) On doing being ordinary, in J.M. Atkinson and B. Heritage (eds) *Structures of Social Action: Studies in Conversation Analysis*. Cambridge: Cambridge University Press.

Sacks, H. (1992a) *Lectures on Conversation*, Vol. 1, G. Jefferson (ed.). Oxford: Blackwell.

Sacks, H. (1992b) *Lectures on Conversation*, Vol. 2, G. Jefferson (ed.). Oxford: Blackwell.

Sacks, H., Schegloff, E.A. and Jefferson, G. (1974) A simplest systematics for the organization of turn taking in conversation, *Language*, 50: 696–735.

Schegloff, E.A. (1972) Notes on a conversational practice: formulating place, in D. Sudnow (ed.) *Studies in Social Interaction*. New York: Free Press.

Schön, D.A. (1983) *The Reflective Practitioner*. New York: Free Press.

Schön, D.A. (1987) *Educating the Reflective Practitioner: Towards a New Design for Teaching and Learning in the Professions*. San Francisco, CA: Jossey-Bass.

Schwitalla, J. (1986) Common argumentation and group identity, in F.H. van Emerson, R. Grootendorst, J.A. Blair and C.A. Willard (eds) *Argumentation: Perspectives and Approaches. Proceedings of the Conference on Argumentation, 1986*. Dordrecht, Netherlands: Foris Publications.

Searle, J. (1969) *Speech Acts*. Cambridge: Cambridge University Press.

Semin, G.R. and Gergen, K.J. (eds) (1990) *Everyday Understanding: Social and Scientific Implications*. London: Sage.

Sharrock, W. and Button, G. (1991) The social actor: social action in real time, in G. Button (ed.) *Ethnomethodology and the Human Sciences*. Cambridge: Cambridge University Press.

Shaw, I. (1999) *Qualitative Evaluation*. London: Sage.

Sheppard, M. (1995) Social work, social science and practice wisdom, *British Journal of Social Work*, 25(3): 265–93.

Sheppard, M. (1998) Practice validity, reflexivity and knowledge, *British Journal of Social Work*, 28(5): 763–81.

Shotter, J. (1989) The unique nature of normal circumstances: contrasts and illusions, in R. Maier (ed.) *Norms in Argumentation. Proceedings of the Conference on Norms, 1988*. Dordrecht, Netherlands: Foris Publications.

Shotter, J. (1993) *Conversational Realities: Constructing Life through Language*. London: Sage.

Sibeon, R. (1994) The construction of a contemporary sociology of social work, in M. Davies (ed.) *The Sociology of Social Work*. London: Routledge.

Silverman, D. (1985) *Qualitative Methodology and Sociology*. Aldershot: Gower.

Silverman, D. (1987) *Communication and Medical Practice*. London: Sage.

Silverman, D. (1993) *Interpreting Qualitative Data: Methods for Analysing Talk, Text and Interaction*. London: Sage.

Silverman, D. (1997a) *Discourses of Counselling: HIV Counselling as Social Interaction*. London: Sage.

Silverman, D. (ed.) (1997b) *Qualitative Research: Theory, Method and Practice*. London: Sage.

Silverman, D. and Jones, J. (1976) *Organizational Work: The Language of Grading / the Grading of Language*. London: Collier Macmillan.

Sinclair, J.M. and Coulthard, M. (1975) *Towards an Analysis of Discourse: The English Used by Teachers and Pupils*. Oxford: Oxford University Press.

Smith, B. Herrnstein (1994) The unquiet judge: activism without objectivism in law and politics, in A. Megill (ed.) *Rethinking Objectivity*. London: Duke University Press.

Smith, C. and White, S. (1997) Parton, Howe and postmodernity: a critical comment on mistaken identity, *British Journal of Social Work*, 27(2): 275–95.

Smith, D.E. (1978) K is mentally ill: the anatomy of a factual account, *Sociology*, 12: 23–53.

Spencer, J.W. (1994) Homeless in River City: client work in human services encounters, *Perspectives on Social Problems*, 6: 29–45.

Spender, D. (1980) *Man Made Language*. London: Routledge & Kegan Paul.

Stainton Rogers, R. and Stainton Rogers, W. (1992) *Stories of Childhood: Shifting Agendas of Child Concern*. Hemel Hempstead: Harvester Wheatsheaf.

Stancombe, J. and White, S. (1998) Psychotherapy without foundations: hermeneutics, discourse and the end of certainty, *Theory and Psychology*, 8(5): 579–99.

Stanley, N. (1999) User–practitioner transactions in the new culture of community care, *British Journal of Social Work*, 29(3): 417–36.

Stenson, K. (1993) Social work discourse and the social work interview, *Economy and Society*, 22(1): 42–76.

Stephenson, O. (1998) *Neglected Children: Issues and Dilemmas*. Oxford: Blackwell Science.

Stimson, G. and Webb, B. (1975) *Going to See the Doctor*. London: Routledge.

Stubbs, M. (1976) *Language, Schools and Classrooms*. London: Methuen.

Tannen, D. (1990) *You Just Don't Understand: Women and Men in Conversation*. New York: William Morrow.

Taylor, C. (1999) Deconstructing developmental psychology: opportunity or threat for social work? Paper presented to the BASW/University of Central Lancashire Conference: Social Work – Making a Difference, Southport, 22–25 March 1999.

Teubner, G. (1989) How the law thinks: towards a constructivist epistemology of law, *Law and Society Review*, 23(5): 727–56.

Thompson, N. (1995) *Theory and Practice in Health and Social Welfare*. Buckingham: Open University Press.

Thornton, P. (1992) Psychiatric diagnosis as sign and symbol: nomenclature as an organizing and legitimating strategy, *Perspectives in Social Problems*, 4: 155–76.

Travers, M. (1994) The phenomenon of the radical lawyer, *Sociology*, 28(1): 245–58.

Trinder, L. (2000) Reading the trends: postmodern feminism and the 'doing' of research, in B. Fawcett, B. Featherstone, J. Fook and A. Rossiter (eds) *Practice and Research in Social Work: Postmodern Feminist Perspectives*. London: Routledge.

Ussher, J. (1991) *Women's Madness: Misogyny or Mental Illness?* Hemel Hempstead: Harvester Wheatsheaf.

Varley, M. and White, S. (1995) Accounting for self-harm: holding the balance, *Journal of Social Work Practice*, 9(2): 141–54.

Walker, T. (1988) Whose discourse? in S. Woolgar (ed.) *New Frontiers in the Sociology of Knowledge*. London: Sage.

Watson, D.R. (1992) The understanding of language use in everyday life: is there a common ground? in G. Watson and R. Seiler (eds) *The Text in Context: Contributions to Ethnomethodology*. London: Sage.

West, C. (1979) Against our will: male interruptions of females in cross-sex talk, *Annals of the New York Academy of Science*, 327: 81–97.

West, C. (1996) Ethnography and orthography: a modest methodological proposal, *Journal of Contemporary Ethnography*, 25(3): 327–52.

White, S. (1996) Regulating mental health and motherhood in contemporary welfare services: anxious attachments or attachment anxiety, *Critical Social Policy*, 16(1): 67–93.

White, S. (1997a) Performing Social Work: An Ethnographic Study of Talk and Text in a Metropolitan Social Services Department. Unpublished PhD thesis, University of Salford.

White, S. (1997b) Beyond retroduction? Hermeneutics, reflexivity and social work practice, *British Journal of Social Work*, 27(6): 739–53.

White, S. (1998a) Time, temporality and child welfare: notes on the materiality and malleability of time(s), *Time and Society*, 7(1): 55–74.

White, S. (1998b) Interdiscursivity and child welfare: the ascent and durability of psycholegalism, *Sociological Review*, 46(2): 264–92.

White, S. (1999a) Examining the artfulness of risk talk, in A. Jokinen, K. Juhila and T. Poso (eds) *Constructing Social Work Practices*. Aldershot: Ashgate.

White, S. (1999b) Performing rationality: the limits of management in a social Services Department, in M. Dent and M. O'Neill (eds) *Dilemmas for European Health, Education and Social Services*. Stafford: Staffordshire University Press.

Widdicombe, S. and Wooffitt, R. (1995) *The Language of Youth Subcultures: Social Identity in Action*. Hemel Hempstead: Harvester Wheatsheaf.

Wodak, R. (1997) Gender in discourse, in T.A. van Dijk (ed.) *Discourse as Social Interaction*, Discourse Studies: A Multidisciplinary Introduction, Vol. 2. London: Sage.

Wooffitt, R. (1991) 'I was just doing X . . . when Y': some inferential properties of a device in accounts of paranormal experiences, *Text*, 11: 267–88.

Wooffitt, R. (1992) *Telling Tales of the Unexpected: The Organization of Factual Discourse*. Hemel Hempstead: Harvester Wheatsheaf.

Woolgar, S. (1980) Discovery: logic and sequence in scientific text, in K. Knorr, R. Krohn and R. Whitley (eds) *The Social Process of Scientific Investigation*. Dordrecht, Netherlands: Reidel.

Woolgar, S. (1988a) Reflexivity is the ethnographer of the text, in S. Woolgar (ed.) *New Frontiers in the Sociology of Knowledge*. London: Sage.

Woolgar, S. (1988b) *Science: The Very Idea*. Chichester: Ellis Horwood.

Yeo, M. and Moorhouse, A. (eds) (1996) *Concepts and Cases in Nursing Ethics*, 2nd edn. Peterborough, Ontario: Broadview Press.

Zerubavel, E. (1979) *Patterns of Time in Hospital Life*. Chicago: University of Chicago Press.

Zerubavel, E. (1981) *Hidden Rhythms: Schedules and Calendars in Social Life*. Chicago: University of Chicago Press.

Zimmerman, D. and Boden, D. (1991) Structure-in-action: an introduction, in D. Boden and D. Zimmerman (eds) *Talk and Social Structure: Studies in Ethnomethodology and Conversation Analysis*. Cambridge: Polity Press.

Zobel, H. (1997) http://courttv.com.trials/woodward/week6.html#nov10 (accessed November 1999).

Index